SEXUALITIES IN WORLD

As LGBTQ claims acquire global relevance, how do sexual politics impact the study of International Relations (IR)? This book argues that LGBTQ perspectives are not only an inherent part of world politics but can also influence IR theory making.

LGBTQ politics have simultaneously gained international prominence in the past decade, achieving significant policy change, and have provoked cultural resistance and policy pushbacks. *Sexualities in World Politics* responds to the call for more empirically motivated but also critical scholarship on this important subject. Gathering scholars from different political venues, geographical regions, and subfields of IR—from area studies to development and political sociology, the book offers comparative case-studies from regional, cultural and theoretical peripheries to identify ways of rethinking IR. Outlining and analysing previously unrecognized perspectives in an accessible manner, the book asks what contribution LGBTQ politics can provide for conceiving the political subject, as well as the international structure in which activism is embedded.

Seeking to mainstream sexuality debates in the fields of international relations and politics, it will be essential reading for students and scholars of gender politics, cultural studies and international relations theory.

Manuela Lavinas Picq is Professor of International Relations at Universidad San Francisco de Quito, Ecuador.

Markus Thiel is Associate Professor at Florida International University, USA.

INTERVENTIONS
Edited by: Jenny Edkins, Aberystwyth University and
Nick Vaughan-Williams, University of Warwick

The series provides a forum for innovative and interdisciplinary work that engages with alternative critical, post-structural, feminist, postcolonial, psychoanalytic and cultural approaches to international relations and global politics. In our first 5 years we have published 60 volumes.

We aim to advance understanding of the key areas in which scholars working within broad critical post-structural traditions have chosen to make their interventions, and to present innovative analyses of important topics. Titles in the series engage with critical thinkers in philosophy, sociology, politics and other disciplines and provide situated historical, empirical and textual studies in international politics.

We are very happy to discuss your ideas at any stage of the project: just contact us for advice or proposal guidelines. Proposals should be submitted directly to the Series Editors:

- Jenny Edkins (jennyedkins@hotmail.com) and
- Nick Vaughan-Williams (N.Vaughan-Williams@Warwick.ac.uk).

'As Michel Foucault has famously stated, "knowledge is not made for understanding; it is made for cutting". In this spirit The Edkins–Vaughan-Williams Interventions series solicits cutting-edge, critical works that challenge mainstream understandings in international relations. It is the best place to contribute post disciplinary works that think rather than merely recognize and affirm the world recycled in IR's traditional geopolitical imaginary.'

Michael J. Shapiro, University of Hawai'i at Manoa, USA

Critical Theorists and International Relations
Edited by Jenny Edkins and Nick Vaughan-Williams

Ethics as Foreign Policy
Britain, the EU and the other
Dan Bulley

Universality, Ethics and International Relations
A grammatical reading
Véronique Pin-Fat

The Time of the City
Politics, philosophy, and genre
Michael J. Shapiro

Governing Sustainable Development
Partnership, protest and power at the world summit
Carl Death

Insuring Security
Biopolitics, security and risk
Luis Lobo-Guerrero

SEXUALITIES IN WORLD POLITICS

How LGBTQ claims shape International Relations

Edited by
Manuela Lavinas Picq and Markus Thiel

Routledge
Taylor & Francis Group

LONDON AND NEW YORK

First published 2015
by Routledge
2 Park Square, Milton Park, Abingdon, Oxon OX14 4RN

And by Routledge
711 Third Avenue, New York, NY 10017

Routledge is an imprint of the Taylor & Francis Group, an informa business

British Library Cataloguing in Publication Data
A catalogue record for this book is available from the British Library

Library of Congress Cataloging in Publication Data
Sexualities in World Politics : how LGBTQ claims shape
international relations / edited by Manuela Lavinas Picq
and Markus Thiel.
pages cm. -- (Interventions)
Includes bibliographical references and index.
ISBN 978-1-138-82068-5 (hardback)
-- ISBN 978-1-138-82072-2 (pbk.)
-- ISBN 978-1-315-74372-1 (ebook) 1. International
relations--Social aspects. 2. Queer theory. I. Picq,
Manuela Lavinas. II. Thiel, Markus, 1973-
JZ1251.S48 2015
327.086'6--dc23
2014043131

ISBN: 978-1-138-82068-5 (hbk)
ISBN: 978-1-138-82072-2 (pbk)
ISBN: 978-1-315-74372-1 (ebk)

Typeset in Bembo
by Taylor & Francis Books

CONTENTS

LIST OF TABLES

LIST OF CONTRIBUTORS

Mehmet Sinan Birdal is currently Assistant Professor of International Relations at Işk University, Istanbul. He is the author of *The Holy Roman Empire and the Ottomans: From Global Imperial Power to Absolutist States*. His current research projects involve Turkish foreign policy, political economy of the BRICS countries, transitional justice, and comparative social movements. He is a frequent contributor to Turkish and international online and printed press on international security, Turkish politics, Middle East politics, and LGBT politics.

Michael J. Bosia's research on communities facing the pressures of globalization and marginalization has been published in *Globalizations, Perspectives on Politics, New Political Science, French Politics, Culture & Society*, and four edited collections. A founding member of the LGBTQA Caucus of the International Studies Association, he is Associate Professor of Political Science at Saint Michael's College in Vermont and was named a co-recipient of the Caucus Scholar Award in 2015. He has presented his research at conferences, colleges, and universities from Boston to Quito, Ecuador, to Madrid, UC Irvine to NYU Paris and Bija Vidyapeeth in Dehradun, India. Recent publications include two edited volumes: with Meredith Weiss, *Global Homophobia: States, Movements, and the Politics of Oppression* (University of Illinois Press, 2013); and *Globalization and Food Sovereignty: Global and Local Change in the New Politics of Food* with Peter Andree, Jeffrey Ayres, and Marie-Josée Massicotte (University of Toronto Press, 2014); his current project, from which this chapters draws, is based on field research on state homophobia and LGBT activism in France, Uganda, and Egypt.

Francine D'Amico is Associate Professor and Director of Undergraduate Studies in International Relations at the Maxwell School of Citizenship & Public Affairs in the College of Arts & Sciences of Syracuse University, where she teaches courses on international law, international organizations, global governance, and Latin America and serves on the University Senate LGBT Concerns Committee. Her recent research publications include: "Critical Feminism: Gender-at-Work," in *Making Sense of International Relations Theory* 2E, ed. Jennifer Sterling-Folker (2013). Dr. D'Amico received her PhD from Cornell University and joined the Syracuse faculty in fall 2000.

Sandra McEvoy is an Associate Professor of Political Science at Wheelock College. Before arriving at Wheelock, she served as Associate Director of the Consortium on Gender, Security, and Human Rights at the University of Massachusetts-Boston. Her research focuses on women's participation in political violence and gender-focused strategies that incorporate perpetrators of political violence into long-term conflict resolution strategies. Currently, she is preparing a book manuscript that documents Loyalist women's participation in paramilitary organizations in Northern Ireland during the 30-year conflict in that country. The manuscript draws on empirical data collected during field research in Northern Ireland over the last 14 years. She is active in several professional associations, including the International Studies Association, where she has served as Chair of the Women's Caucus and founding Chair of the Lesbian, Gay, Bisexual, Transgender, Queer, and Allies Caucus.

Anthony J. Langlois is an Associate Professor and Head of the Discipline of International Relations at Flinders University, Adelaide, Australia. He was educated at the University of Tasmania and the Australian National University. Langlois is the author of *The Politics of Justice and Human Rights: Southeast Asia and Universalist Theory* (Cambridge University Press, 2001) and co-editor of *Global Democracy and its Difficulties* (Routledge, 2009) and *Australian Foreign Policy: Controversies and Debates* (Oxford University Press, 2014). He has published many scholarly articles and book chapters and sits on the editorial advisory boards of *Ethics and International Affairs* and the *Journal of Human Rights*.

Manuela Lavinas Picq is Professor of International Relations at Universidad San Francisco de Quito, Ecuador. She has been a research fellow at the Woodrow Wilson Center, a Loewenstein Fellow at Amherst College, and a member at the Institute for Advanced Study. Her research at the intersection of Latin American politics and international relations emphasizes the significance of feminist and Indigenous perspectives for thinking the international differently. She has identified Indigenous women and Amazonia as sites to think an international realm beyond state sovereignty. Recent publications include "Decolonizing Methodologies in the Field of IR Theory" (*International Political Science Review*, 2013) and "Between the Dock and a Hard Place: Hazards and Opportunities of Legal Pluralism for Indigenous Women in Ecuador" (*Latin American Politics and Society*, 2012). She is a regular opinion contributor to Al Jazeera.

Momin Rahman is an Associate Professor of Sociology at Trent University and a Fellow of the Mark S. Bonham Centre for Sexual Diversity Studies at the University of Toronto, both in Canada. His current research is on the conflicts between LGBT citizenship and Muslim cultures. He has published over 20 chapters and articles, and books include *Homosexualities, Muslim Cultures and Modernity* (Palgrave Macmillan, 2014), *Gender and Sexuality* (with Stevi Jackson, Polity, 2010), and *Sexuality and Democracy* (Edinburgh University Press, 2000).

Laura Sjoberg is Associate Professor of Political Science with a courtesy affiliation in Women and Gender Studies at the University of Florida. She holds a PhD from the University of Southern California and a Juris Doctorate from Boston College Law School. Her research on gender and international security has been published in more than three dozen journals in political science, gender studies, and law. She is author or editor of nine books, including, most recently, *Gendering Global Conflict: Toward a Feminist Theory of War* (Columbia University Press, 2013) and a textbook called *Gender, War, and Conflict* (Polity, 2014).

Markus Thiel is Associate Professor in the Department of Politics and International Relations at Florida International University, Miami, and research associate at Miami-FIU's EU Center of Excellence. He graduated with a PhD from the University of Miami, and has published several EU-related articles and book chapters at the EU Center of Excellence as well as in *Journal of European Integration, International Studies Encyclopedia, Perspectives on European Politics & Society*, and others. In addition, his research on the political sociology of the EU produced a monograph, *The Limits of Transnationalism* (Palgrave, 2011), and three co-edited volumes on: *Diversity and the European Union* (Palgrave, 2009), *Identity Politics in the Age of Globalization* (Lynne Rienner/First Forum Press, 2010), and *European Identity and Culture: Narratives of Transnational Belonging* (Ashgate, 2012). Besides his focus on LGBT perspectives in IR, he is currently working on a book entitled *Civil Society and Human Rights Advocacy in the European Union* (forthcoming, University of Pennsylvania Press).

PREFACE

It all started with old friends looking at vacation photos. The pictures were from the first gay pride in the Amazon town of Benjamin Constant, Brazil. The two friends were once graduate students who were now professors of international relations in different parts of the world. It did not take long before the chat about Amazon sexualities evolved into a larger debate about the role of sexual politics in the study of international relations at large. The conversation around a glass of wine led to a panel, which then turned into a book.

This project concretely emerged at the International Studies Association 2013 in San Francisco (naturally!), when a number of contributors to this volume were wrapped up in discussion after our panel concluded. We noticed that despite our various geographical and sectoral foci, we all questioned traditional international relations concepts in similar ways. Moreover, we found it baffling that despite the increased salience of the topic in world politics, little theorization had been occurring thus far. The product of our ongoing online and in-person discussions is presented in this book, and it is our hope that this represents the opening, rather than the conclusion, of an ongoing intellectual project.

We hope this volume will influence academic debates. What is certain is that it has already fomented a community of scholars. The best part of making this book is that it was fun, with stimulating interactions every step of the way. It was a reiterated pleasure to engage with the contributors, from the first ISA panel when we had no idea a book would come out of it, passing through theoretical disagreements over the role of the state in the International Queering Paradigm Conference in Quito, to the last polishing stages before publication at an ISA-FLACSO panel in Buenos Aires after a night of tango out together. Friendships and ideas developed together, and their inextricability is perhaps this project's most valuable achievement.

There were many people involved without whom we would have not been able to publish our work: a special thanks goes to Cai Wilkinson and the current leadership of ISA's LGBTQ Caucus under Jack Amoreux, who initially put our panel on the conference program and subsequently supported this book project. Everyone interested in the topic should consider becoming part of the caucus!

Sonia Corrêa, Judith Stiehm, Laura Sjoberg, and Susanne Zwingel provided insightful comments at different stages of the project. A special thanks goes to them and to our contributors to this volume, a courageous and fun group of ground-breaking scholars. Jenny Edkins and Nick Vaughan-Williams, our Intervention series editors were supportive from the beginning, and the Routledge reviewers and editorial team (Nicola Parkin, Peter Harris) did their own part to bring this book to fruition. Last, but not least, Maristher Guevara, student of international relations and applied ecology at Universidad San Francisco de Quito, contributed reliable assistance in the formatting stages, and Eloisa Vladescu's constant support and careful review was invaluable.

Markus Thiel wants to thank his home department of Politics and International Relations and Rebecca Salokar for supporting his research. In addition, there are other individuals for whom he is grateful: Philip Ayoub and David Patternotte for driving area-specific LGBTQ research forward and the University of Miami and Florida International's Queer Studies Research Group for its stimulating colloquium. In addition, Lauren Wilcox, Paul Amar, Elizabeth Prügl, Amy Lind, Mike Williams, and most importantly, his collaborator and dear friend Manuela have all propelled this project forward one way or another. Lastly, he is grateful to his husband, Peter Garcia, who endured involuntary lectures in LGBTQ studies over the course of this project.

Manuela Picq is grateful for the support she received at the Institute for Advanced Study, where most of this book was completed. Joan Scott's intellectual encouragement and the careful feedback of colleagues in the Ethnography and Theory Seminar nurtured this project. She wishes to thank Universidad San Francisco de Quito and the individuals who made this research possible: Sarah Sarzynski took her to Amazonia (in every sense) and Ramiro Romaina made her return; Flavia Cunha invited her to the first Forum of LGBT Human Rights in Benjamin Constant; mentors and peers William C. Smith, Arlene Tickner, Momin Rahman, and Rahul Rao stimulated and polished different stages of her research. She is most grateful to the contributors, who provoked new debates with joy, irreverence, and care and showed not only that theory matters but that it can be fun. To Markus, who gracefully blends academia and friendship, *namaste*.

INTRODUCTION

Sexualities in world politics

Manuela Lavinas Picq and Markus Thiel

Russia's President Putin provoked worldwide upheaval when he tried to impose national law criminalizing homosexual behavior in the run-up to the 2014 Olympic Winter Games in Sochi. The "law against the propaganda of nontraditional sexual relations" came to the core of an international culture war over LGBTQ rights (Halper, 2013). On one hand, LGBTQ groups urged Western governments and the International Olympic Committee (IOC) to pressure Putin's government to withdraw the law. On the other, U.S.-based religious conservatives actively supported Russia's government on the issue. The Winter Games proceeded without policy change in support of gay rights in Russia. Yet sustained pressure from over 40 international NGOs led the IOC to include LGBT rights in its Charter's non-discrimination clause. Russia is one among various cases that illustrate the securitization of LGBTQ politics. Uganda's Anti-Homosexuality Act also triggered international outcry, whether in the form of conservative religious support or U.S. sanctions, reinforcing the idea that homosexuality calls for international intervention. This debate is further complicated by the fact that homophobe legislation in many postcolonial states was introduced by the British colonial administration (Gupta & Long, 2009).

Episodes such as these not only mark the formal politicization of sexuality but also highlight the international salience of sexual discrimination in domestic contexts. They show how rights for LGBTQ individuals have recently become embedded in the geopolitics of "the West," so much so that some theorists speak of the "Gay International" (Massad, 2007). They also signal that governments such as those in Russia, Uganda, or Egypt are "securitizing" sexual politics, i.e., framing populations that were invisible or vulnerable as societal threats or in contrast as threatened disempowered subjects to be saved by international intervention. Paul Amar (2013) noted that this angle of "securitized sexualities" continuously feeds the geopoliticization of sexualities. Moreover, these examples reveal the complexity of LGBTQ "intermestics," the pluralist interdependence of domestic and international as well as governmental and civil society actors in today's globalized advocacy. Yet these are not the only aspects showcasing the relevance of sexual politics for international relations: whether one thinks of the increasing devotion international organizations pay to the needs of LGBTQ individuals, or the international diffusion of marriage equality, the status of non-conforming sexualities has reached an unprecedented level of attention, both positive and negative.

As LGBTQ claims acquire global relevance, how do sexual politics[1] impact the study of international relations? This book argues that LGBTQ perspectives are not only an inherent part of world politics but can also influence IR theory-making. LGBTQ politics have simultaneously gained international prominence in the past decade, achieving significant policy change, and provoked cultural resistance and policy pushbacks. As of 2014, 78 countries had criminalized homosexuality and five of those even punished it with the death penalty (Itaborahy & Zhu, 2014), aside from the precarious situation of individuals subject to harassment and marginalization. Worldwide, LGBTQ populations seek protection and equal treatment, whether in the form of "negative" policies preventing hate crimes, repression, and persecution, or in the form of "positive" rights, such as legislation granting sexual and gender expression and fostering sexual equality.

Sexual rights language was introduced in intergovernmental norms by feminists during the 1994 United Nations (UN) Conference on Population and Development in Cairo, which then led to the Brazilian Resolution on human rights and sexual orientation presented to ECOSOC in 2003 (Girard, 2007). Sexual politics are far broader than LGBT rights, encompassing intense debates on sex work, abortion, and adolescent sexuality. In that sense, we must be cautious not to collapse LGBT rights and sexual rights, an association we later interrogate, even though they often intertwine in interstate negotiations. Sexual rights discourse became subsequently enshrined in transnational social movements as revealed by the dynamic presence of transnational human rights and LGBTQ activists, including but not limited to the International Lesbian and Gay Association (ILGA), the International Gay and Lesbian Human Rights Commission (IGLHRC), Human Rights Watch, the Sexual Rights Initiative, and relevant regional networks such as the Coalition of African Lesbians. In contrast, most international human rights declarations predate the emergence of LGBT claims, and thus exclude specific language on sexual rights. Yet LGBTQ rights are gradually mainstreamed into (inter)national policy, inscribed as rights to sexual equality in the South African constitution or same-sex partnership recognitions from Latin America to Europe (Tremblay et al., 2011). In an effort to frame LGBTQ rights as desirable human rights, research now quantifies the costs of homophobic legislation (World Bank, 2014). But the rise of LGBTQ politics also led governments across the globe to ignite conservative–homophobic resistance and culture wars against sexual claims, whether in complaints about intrusive homo-colonialization (Rahman, 2014) or by criminalizing homosexual behavior (Weiss & Bosia, 2013). The emergence of LGBTQ rights entails a complex history, and the backlashes of culture wars should not be simplified (Corrêa et al., 2008). For instance, the effects of President Bush's international policies removing language on "men who have sex with men" from UN texts linger today as poignant examples of deliberate state-led regressive sexual geopolitics (Girard, 2007).[2] LGBTQ rights became linked to developmental and other international negotiations that primarily are of a functional nature (Lind, 2010). In short, the diffusion of LGBTQ rights globally occurs unevenly and is beset with a number of ambiguous assumptions that, if theoretically unpacked, can provide more critical perspectives on the conduct of international relations.

This volume sheds light on the contribution of LGBTQ perspectives to IR theory and practice. Sexuality politics, more so than gender-based theories, arrived late on the theoretical scene in part because sexuality and gender studies initially highlighted poststructuralist thinking, which was hardly accepted in (North American) mainstream political science (Kollmann, 2009). Weber (2014) reinforced this argument by decrying the parochialism of standard international theory. That invisibility changed with emerging empirical work in LGBT studies, and the increasing relevance of trans/international discourses for LGBTQ individuals and groups. This book responds to Kollmann's call for more empirically motivated but also critical scholarship on this subject. It offers comparative case studies from regional, cultural, and theoretical peripheries to identify ways of rethinking IR. Further, it aims to add to critical theory, broadening the knowledge about previously unrecognized perspectives in an accessible manner. Being aware of Weber's preoccupation with the de-queering, disciplining nature of theory establishment in the social sciences, we critically reconsider IR concepts from a particular LGBTQ vantage point and infuse them with queer thinking. Considering the relative dearth of contemporary mainstream IR-theorizing, authors ask what contribution LGBTQ politics can provide for conceiving the political subject, as well as the international structure in which activism is embedded.

One could say that IR concepts and sexual politics have been historically divided. The advocacy that drives international politics of sexuality stem predominantly from the civil society sector, which lacks a customary home in the state-/system-centric grand theories of IR (particularly in realism, liberalism, and their neo-incarnations). LGBTQ politics start with the personal as analytical referent, in contrast to most mainstream IR scholars who eschew the "private" in favor of a focus on the assumed "public." They are also rooted in the contestations of dominant cultures, which include state institutions as core objects of study in IR. Few IR scholars traced the contentious evolution of sexual rights policies in the international arenas, highlighting their conflictive character but also the potential for transnational alliance building (García & Parker, 2006; Corrêa et al., 2008; Waites & Kollman, 2009). The indifference towards emerging sexuality issues is related to broader theoretical gaps that disconnect paradigmatic IR theories from the world it is supposed to understand. The lacking utility of traditional IR theorizing became further evident when the *European Journal of International Relations*, one of the field's most prominent outlets, dedicated a special issue to the 'End of IR Theory' in 2013. The editors asked contributors to comment on the crisis in current theorizing about world politics, and a number of prominent observers commented on the ever proliferating number of theories and remarked on the positivist–quantitative dominance. Their conclusion offered a view forward calling for an eclectic "integrative pluralism" (Dunne et al., 2013), and we aim to proceed in a similar fashion by highlighting the intersections of feminist, postcolonial, critical, and queer theory for the opening up of new vantage points on IR concepts and theories.

LGBTQ perspectives can invigorate IR theorizing through their particular perspective and the challenges they pose to generalizing accounts. They offer reflective views on international politics that are drawn from personal-yet-political experiences, are critical of assumed normalities, and add to existing theories in a pluralist manner. The changes initiated by LGBTQ claims concur with what many theorists (Waites, 2009; Sjoberg, 2012; Weber, 2014) see as the need to critically analyze the ossification of theories in IR. No matter if one talks about gender, sexuality, or identity, the discourse surrounding those categorizing concepts tends to reify fluid, developmental, and ambiguous states of being and expression. Just as "gender" or "LGBT" are increasingly contested positional–representative categories, IR concepts (e.g., war, international community, stateness) and paradigms (i.e., the grand theories and debates) are often taken for granted and reproduced so that they achieve almost hegemonic status without allowing for alternative viewpoints. For instance, critical feminist or queer theorists do not automatically characterize the current global trend of Western state and IGO support for LGBTQ populations as welcome, as it may foster the creation of binary sexual identities or lead to some form of homo–nationalism and neo–colonialisms (Puar, 2007; Corrêa et al., 2013). Critical and queer theorists argue against the reification of liberal Western ideas surrounding sexuality. If the purpose of social activists is to achieve change that is favorable for underrepresented groups and the objective of queer theorists is to highlight the negative implications of normativity, then research that probes us to reevaluate accepted norms is essential in order to keep the "discipline" of IR alive and relevant.

This book offers fresh LGBTQ perspectives on international politics to make two central contributions. First, chapters bring together case studies from different regional and policy avenues to expose the plurality of LGBTQ claims and approaches. From industrialized Europe to the Amazon region, sexual politics have been propelling rights claims grounded on local experiences and meanings while also translating international norms to respond to local claims. This double bind is crucial. Second, this volume uses case studies to argue that LGBTQ perspectives can impact theory-making in IR. Critical theories, from postmodern to feminist ones, crafted ontological perspectives that locate the subject in novel ways, developing epistemological insights that challenge core foundations of IR knowledge and critically reconceptualize concepts such as war and authority. This book explores the specific theoretical contributions of LGBTQ politics as a significant site from where to pursue critical IR. LGBTQ perspectives open avenues for a substantial reevaluation of IR practices and concepts. They also provide a terrain for attaining political objectives in a more narrow (group rights) or broader (social justice) view. By referencing established IR concepts when reconsidering these perspectives, we aim to build a dialog with mainstream views, something that is woefully neglected in today's theoretical silos.

In the following sections, we first clarify some terminological issues, then show to what extent LGBT perspectives extend feminist and queer theories, validate marginal perspectives for theory-building and, finally, highlight common elements particular to LGBT politics, such as positionality, normativity, and advocacy.

On terminology: explaining LGBTQ

A few words about terminology are in order to comprehend the complexities surrounding LGBTQ politics and perspectives. In the planning stages of this volume, a discussion occurred among contributors surrounding the "alphabet soup" issue identifying the subject of the book. Much international attention is drawn to G(ay) and L(esbian) advocacy politics, neglecting the B(isexual), T(ransgender), and "Queer" experiences in "LGBT." Some assemble a host of sympathetic allies under the extended "LGBTTIQQ2SA" umbrella (lesbian, gay, bisexual, transsexual, transgender, intersex, queer, questioning, 2-spirited, and allies – see the glossary at the end of this book). "Sexual orientation and gender identity" (SOGI) constitutes another term that avoids identity-based categorizations along LGBTQ lines, but at the same time has been criticized for being too essentialist (Waites, 2009) as it presupposes relatively stable sexual preferences and identities that are not present for many bisexual or transgender individuals. While we stand in solidarity with all non-conforming sexualities, we felt that most issues at stake in contemporary politics would best be captured by using the standard term LGBT, even with all its reductionist problems (from epistemological issues about the value of assigning fixed labels, such as gender or sexual orientation, to the fact that LGBT categories are neither universally recognized as many cultures do not subscribe to these Western identity-based concepts, nor or do they capture the full range of sexual diversity). Moreover, the alphabet soup forces people with different aims into one broad group – think of sexual rights claims of gays and lesbians (e.g., marriage equality) versus gender identity issues (healthcare, legal recognition) of transgender individuals. But it still is the most recognizable umbrella term; thus we opted for it in order to make our work more accessible.

We deliberately added queer to LGBT to highlight the inherent linkage between inclusionary and transgressive approaches towards sexual equality for all. The particular acronym "LGBTQ" may strike the informed reader as odd, given that there is some ideological distance between mainstream-oriented proponents of LGBT politics seeking equality and inclusion, and queer perspectives who contest the former approach as conforming to hetero- or homonormative objectives. Even scholarly works are discussing the division (as well as overlap) between gay and lesbian studies and queer theories (Lovaas, 2013). Yet in practice, some LGBT individuals adopt a queer identity, which speaks to the entanglement of both concepts. In contrast to activists and scholars emphasizing inclusionary LGBT politics, queer theorists eschew normative frameworks. But both highlight the ambiguous roles of positionality, normativity, and action, which we will review later. And while queer approaches are relevant in deconstructing essentialist understandings of gender and sexuality, it is recognized that in practice "law, policy and states appear to need identifiable categories to combat discrimination" (Waites & Kollmann, 2009: 13). Queers opt for alternative views and practices that are critical of mainstream society, including but not limited to many sociopolitical institutions such as mainstream democracy, neoliberal capitalism, etc. Queer movements are thus less apt in exploiting political opportunity structures and consequently, play a lesser role in (inter)national LGBT advocacy politics, although their views are intellectually enriching. This conceptual tension is also prevalent in this volume, as the contributors used slightly diverging terminologies that best suited their own characterization of the research subject(s).

This volume focuses on the impact of LGBTQ rights in international politics. That means that heterosexual, gender, or other sexual rights policies are largely left aside, although they serve as analytical counterpoints in this survey of the field. Our aim is to examine trends of non-mainstream sexual and gender expressions as they relate to the (re)construction of IR practice and theories. In doing so, we are concerned less with the various identity politics within this community and more with the degree to which their practice redefines the utility of conventional IR concepts. A debate about the use of "sexual orientation" and "gender identity" exists in the field, as some scholars question these notions emphasizing the rigid, binary reification of relatively fluid identity concepts (Waites, 2009), while others critique the implicit divergence between sexuality and gender: "LGBs have sex, while T&Is have gender" (Budhiraja et al., 2010: 138). One cannot neglect the group-external connotations relating to the choice of terminology, ranging from an internationally recognized engagement within the broader human rights discourse to the stigmatizing or stigma-managing embrace of categorical sexual identities (Wilkinson & Kirey, 2010). As Weeks (2000) so poignantly describes, "after Michel Foucault (1979) we have become accustomed to seeing 'sexuality' as an invented ensemble of related but disparate elements sometimes only contingently related to bodily needs or desires, and 'performed', as Judith Butler (1990, 1993) has suggested, in power-laden situations" (2). We thus recognize the contingent and fluid nature of sexuality which reflects ambiguously on the practice of LGBTQ politics and its repercussions on IR.

Through this volume, authors interchangeably use LGBT, LGBTQ, or LGBTIQ to refer to political movements, social theory, and the lived experiences of people who identify as LGBTIQ – or some combination of those identity markers. As editors, we left it to the authors to decide to use acronyms as they saw fit because no standardized "LGBT" exists. Some favor the LGBT acronym because it is the one used by activists in their case study or because the word queer can be a politically charged term associated with the Anglo-American experience. LGBT perspectives and queer theory, however, are used differently in this volume when it comes to theorizing world politics: some authors (e.g., McEvoy, Langlois, Bosia) directly frame their research argument within queer theory, while others present empirical work that pushes queer theory. This is a fundamental dimension of the relationship between theory and practice in this project. If this volume tackles LGBTQ claims at large, its goal is not only to advance queer theory but also to establish queer IR theory.

LGBTQ perspectives: beyond feminist and/or queer theories?

Feminist as well as queer theories have been fundamental for the development of LGBT perspectives on IR, just as they built solidarity alliances in the international struggle for sexual rights and gender equality. However, the feminist influence in LGBTQ politics does not impede significant tensions. While LGBTQ politics and perspectives have feminist roots, they may generate novel critiques. Falling under the labels of interpretivist or reflexivist IR theories, together with postmodern, critical, and postcolonial theories, LGBTQ perspectives share a number of meta-theoretical onto-logical (referencing the nature of being or reality) as well as epistemological (the experience and resulting knowledge of being) points. Depending on the stance of the observer, however, these viewpoints diverge on how or whether to codify sexuality. As such it is part of this project to examine how far LGBTQ perspectives add another enriching facet to the meta-theoretical points later.

Feminist gazes were fundamental to renovating IR themes and epistemologies. Feminist research was groundbreaking for introducing the idea of positionality to global politics. It expanded conventional understandings of what constitutes the international, for instance defining masculinity as a foreign policy issue (Enloe, 2005), contested core IR epistemologies such as security (Tickner, 1997) and introduced new research methodologies (Ackerly et al., 2006). Beyond showing how gender matters, feminist gazes shed light on other invisibilities, such as IR scholars' racist, colonial traits (Tickner, 2010). Together with postcolonial approaches, feminist insights permitted to establish the interaction of sexuality and race in the making of modern nation-states. The sexual dimension of colonialism, in particular, has been analyzed in depth by a fast expanding body of literature. Feminists tackled the question of the gatekeeper in depth. In fact, one of J. Ann Tickner's (2010) articles, "You may never understand," expresses the lingering difficulties encountered by feminist scholars trying to shift IR epistemologies. After breaking epistemological walls and expanding the legitimate content of world politics in theory and practice, many feminists have started to wonder whether their efforts can significantly renovate IR or if we will need "to kill the discipline," as Robbie Shilliam once claimed.

Feminist and LGBTQ approaches think IR from similar positions of sexual margin-ality and perceive of IR concepts and research as constitutive rather than causal (Tickner, 2005). Both perspectives share a commitment to redefining conceptual foundations of IR away from familiar gender-neutral, patriarchal narratives. Both denounce hierarchies based on sexual difference as well as the obscuring of such inequalities by patriarchal practices. They both seek to problematize theoretical assumptions founded on hegemonic masculinities. Each contests claims of universal knowledge based largely on the status of privileged men. Each seeks to bring sexual difference as fundamental to the understanding of global politics. But are they the same? Should we assume LGBTQ politics will make contributions similar to feminist inquiry, in which case they constitute a subcategory of analysis providing a different outlook on the same objects/subjects of analysis? Or can we conceive of LGBTQ to make larger contributions that challenge IR epistemologies beyond questions of (post)modernity, intersectionality, and hetero/homonormativity? Are LGBTQ perspectives merely a feminist extension? Recognizing the importance of feminist engagements, we suggest LGBTQ perspectives also constitute strategic sites for challenging disciplinary canons.

Sexuality-based perspectives differ not only from feminism but among themselves. There are significant differences between LGBT and queer stands that merit careful nuance. Queer theory was inspired by the HIV/AIDS activism that sprang up in the 1970s and early 1980s in San Francisco, New York, and other cities in the United States. The term itself was first coined by Teresa de Lauretis in the early 1990s at a conference at UC Santa Cruz. Theorists drew from literary criticism, as well as post-structuralist philosophy to emphasize deviance and unstable sexualities and question established norms, categories, and orders. They revolted against the minoritizing process of declaring non-conforming sexualities as being abject, citing Foucault's and Derrida's works on sexuality, knowledge, and power. Plummer (2003) posits that "Queer theory is really post-structuralism (and postmodernism) applied to sexuality and gender" (520). This initial direct connection to sexuality has been loosened as queer theory or more precisely, a diverse body of queer theories, has moved into a number of academic disciplines from literature to politics, and became an aggregate term for deconstructive, transgressive views on established positions, no matter where these may be located. Queer scholars contest simplistic normative and binary notions of, for instance, sexuality (hetero/homo), gender (male/female), class (rich/poor), race (white/non-white), and focus on the subjective bodily experience and in terms of sexuality, include desire as a preferred analytical lens. As a scholarly undertaking queer theory concerns "any form of research positioned within conceptual frameworks that highlight the instability of taken-for-granted meanings and resulting power relations" (Nash & Browne, 2012: 4). In providing a challenge for existing theories and approaches towards politics, queer theories have proliferated among elite intellectual, often academic, circles.

When thinking about parsing differences between queer theories and LGBT perspectives, it has become increasingly clear that queer theories highlighted and altered the discourse surrounding non-conformity, positionality, and (anti)normativity, although material inequalities of the unrepresented remain (ibid., 6). In particular bisexual and transgender populations experience bi/transphobia,-erasure and deriding assumptions and prejudices, as they are considered too gender and sexuality queer (even in lesbian and gay communities). And while transgender studies emerged as a hotly debated and contested subfield of queer studies and have made inroads into IR theorizing as well, a more defined and possibly "monolithic concept of trans would only enable its exoticization and fetishization, thus undermining the ability of trans to defy stabilization" (Elliott, 2012: 1). These tensions have impacts for how we conceptualize IR, and what issues we tend to highlight as opposed to the ones we neglect. What does it mean for awareness about sexuality issues globally, for example, if an online search on google.com for the word "gay" yields roughly 300 million results, while "lesbian" only 155 million results, "bisexual" 43 million, and "transgender" as well as "queer" a miniscule 12 million (The Advocate, 2014)?

Being a rather provocative way of conceptualizing social reality and stemming from industrialized countries, queer theory may be limited in the ways it can travel to different geographic, cultural, and social localities. Some scholars even identified the "normalization" of the queer, as well as exclusionary versions of queer theories based on identity differences (Sabsay, 2013: 86). Yet both LGBT studies and queer theory are concerned with issues of difference/exclusion, critiquing hierarchies (of order, status, etc.) and the pursuit of equality. Queer theory, as a progression of critical feminist theory, reinvigorated emancipatory ideas based on the human sexual experience. But it does not always align comfortably with the predominantly political strategies advanced in transnational feminist or LGBT rights policies, as the latter are viewed as conforming, normative, stereotyping, and even nationalistic. While queer tactics subvert heteronormative policies, LGBT advocacy is aimed at inclusion within existing forms of representation rather than the appreciation of difference, permitting state authority in the form of homocolonialism (Rahman, 2014). Ruffolo thus advocates the notion of 'post-queer' politics, signifying a de-essentializing of queer concepts themselves (e.g., the queer/heteronormative dualism) in the political agenda of such theories (2009).

The chapters in this volume highlight specific IR concepts and theories in an attempt to reconceptualize those, using LGBTQ experiences. These experiences result in different perspectives on IR from outside and below, and thus challenge traditional theories and concepts. We posit the LGBTQ perspective as useful for rethinking concepts of stateness and contest IR's theoretical core–periphery dichotomy.

Validating conceptual peripheries for theory

Much has happened since Stanley Hoffman (1977) defined IR as an American social science. Feminists accused the discipline of perpetuating masculine hegemonies, made feminist sense of war (Enloe, 2010), and proposed new methodologies to conduct feminist IR (Ackerly et al., 2006). Postcolonial scholars investigated IR's lasting imperialism and shed light onto silenced histories in an effort to break IR's euro-centrism (Hobson, 2012). Indigeneity challenged disciplinary markers (Beier, 2005; Shaw, 2008) while looking at race made visible how white supremacy is constitutive of the modern world system (Shilliam, 2010; Vitalis, 2010) and continues to inform most theoretical constructs (Henderson, 2007). Critical scholars expanded IR boundaries on methodological grounds (Jackson, 2011) or by engaging alternative forms of knowledge production like storytelling (Inayatullah, 2011). More recently, an emerging literature out of and about the non-core questioned the use of IR meta-theories outside the U.S. (Tickner, 2013), defending the validity of worlds "beyond the west" (Blaney & Tickner, 2013). These critics call for greater pluralism in terms of analysis, away from generalizable research towards a more context-bound and non-rational understanding of individuals' political experience. Even mainstream journals, despite their prevailing positivist and quantitative orientation, are publishing more non-paradigmatic work (Maliniak et al., 2011). This indicates dissatisfaction with the explanatory value of categorical and all encompassing foundational theories. Echoing these critics, this book engages LGBTQ perspectives to challenge central tenets of the discipline.

All contributions to this volume navigate the universal and the particular when relating LGBTQ experiences to the international system. The reader may wonder how Turkey's Gezi protests relate to reflexivity, what international organizations have to do with human rights theory, and end up de facto conceptually confused by the association of Muslim homosexuality with Amazon gay prides. A common thread that articulates chapters under the LGBTQ umbrella is an exploration of the tension between particularism and universalism. Birdal (Chapter 7) does it explicitly, indicating the universality of LGBTQ politics in Turkey, while Thiel (Chapter 4) underlines the particularism of various LGBTQ demands under the EU's supranational policies. Bosia (Chapter 2) confronts a globalization of homosexuality that flattens particularities against the diverse experience of local sexualities. LGBTQ claims are an emerging political language, whose various expressions appear as all being part of one global push towards bottom-up democratization, collectively disrupting narratives of contemporary governmental or neoliberal oppression. If LGBTQ claims are interreferencing, however, they also play different political roles in each and every context. This constant navigation suggests the need to particularize the universal and universalize the particular. With its tendency to universalize parochial insights, IR theory is ill equipped to grasp how sexual politics influence stateness in the non-core, as Bosia indicates. It even fails to offer an adequate account of how sexuality shapes mainstream institutions at the core, as D'Amico (Chapter 3) and Thiel (Chapter 4) suggest. This volume is more than a comparative project or a claim for the complementarity between local and global. It is recognition that the universal is parochial. All theory is parochial in the sense that it is inevitably enclosed in a local context (Roy & Bhan, 2013). Theories are parochial stories that travel cloaked as universal. The Comaroffs (2012) tackle this divide by thinking the north and the south as co-constitutive of the world order and relocating modernity southwards. This book too is an invitation to think the core as relational to the non-core. LGBTQ perspectives offer new methodologies that not only blur the borders between a theoretical core and periphery but, in doing so, provoke conventional understandings of the state.

One way to do so is to contest the lasting divide between theory and case study in the study of IR. Case studies are generally understood to be in the non-core, whereas the core produces political theory (Tickner, 2013). One of this book's objectives is to emphasize the importance of case studies from the political non-core, like LGBTQ claims, to generate theory together with the core. The contributors validate the role of various peripheries, political and sexual, as sites to frame theory. Scholars have tried to think IR from elsewhere, indicating that place matters for how we conceive the international and emphasized the difference in thinking from the non-core (Blaney & Tickner, 2013). Sexualities, in their various meanings and experiences, constitute such a location in the conceptual non-core that permits to unlearn established theoretical frames, using positionality and reflexivity to turn what is familiar into something strange. To think through an LGBTQ lens, however, is not simply to say that sexuality (like place) matters. To think from the non-core is an epistemological project. By the non-core we indicate more than those places in the global South defined as failed states that epitomize underdevelopment. The non-core is, as Roy and Bhan (2013) posit, what theoretical canons can only make sense of in dystopian ways. Our underlying idea is simple: new places foment new theories. Our aim is more than looking into practices that traditional IR does not consider relevant. We seek a reframing of relevant ontologies to overcome the traditional core as such. To take the non-core seriously is to use it in theory-making, whether we are talking about Amazonia or LGBTQ claims (or both). The chapters that follow reflect discontent with the limits of conventional IR theory to explain what world politics entails, challenge perceptions of the periphery as disconnected instead of fused with the core. One task they contribute to is simply to expand the repertoire of what constitutes the international with empirical case studies. Another task they tackle is the matter of what alternative sights of the international do to IR theory. These alternative understandings of the international challenge IR theory.

Another interrelated way in which LGBTQ perspectives question disciplinary foundations is by redefining the centrality of the state. What is the role of the state in the emancipation of LGBT individuals? Should LGBTQ advocates enter or exit the state? Why is the state a main symbol of modernity? Contributors suggest that emancipation can take unexpected forms and locations. Picq (Chapter 6) and Birdal (Chapter 7) show that expressions of LGBT emancipation emerge in unexpected places, such as Amazonia, and forms, such as park protests. Bosia (Chapter 2) and Rahman (Chapter 5) debunk myths of linear flows from the core to the non-core, explaining how the modern state does not always export sexual rights but also homonationalism, even describing the state as a psychopath that manipulates sexuality. D'Amico and Thiel (Chapters 3 and 4) show that the world's most influential international organizations in human rights, the UN and EU, are failing on LGBT mainstreaming because of their reliance on states. Sticking to theory, Langlois (Chapter 1) argues that disciplinary state centrism impedes queer theory. As it discusses sexuality, this volume challenges stateness as traditionally conceived, taking feminist and postcolonial theories to new realms. The analysis of LGBTQ dynamics in various geographical and conceptual peripheries offers more than insights to think international relations differently. It indicates the potential impact of a sexuality critique to foundational sites of IR theory. Such a non-conformist theoretical strand dares researchers to arrive at new ways of scholarly inquiry that go beyond deconstructing and relativizing.

Positionality, normativity, and action – critical elements of LGBTQ perspectives

> "Positionality, or the paradox that you can only get rid of oppressive dichotomies by affirming the subordinate form in order to challenge the hegemonic term is one that continues to haunt the radical agenda." (Weeks, 2000: 7)

Positionality expresses the assumption that the subjective outlook of an individual, as well as its ascribed role, influences how it experiences its surrounding reality. As such it is an indispensable concept originating in feminist theory, which argues that women's unique and often underprivileged positions in society enable them to evaluate their societal position in a gender-specific manner. It is also represented under the heading of "subjectivity" in queer theory/ies, implying an emancipatory stance to LGBT politics as well. While some feminist scholars examined the construction of the feminine as subaltern, the political implications of the gender binary remain a significant point of discussion. In contrast, LGBTQ individuals often find that their sexuality or sexual orientation is not necessarily an attribute that is obvious or easily attached to them. Thus positionality on an individual level depends on the degree to which a person identifies with their sexual and gender identity and is willing to deploy it in the public realm. Examples abound, as, for instance, the role of coming/being out, the ignorance surrounding bisexuality or the transitional passing of many transgender individuals evidence. Here, as well as in collective terms, the role of power relations is one that easily lends itself to analysis through a unique IR lens. This ambiguous ontological base also impacts broader IR epistemological claims of objectivity, rationality, agency, and distinct levels of analysis, which concentrate on what is visible and not hidden. And in terms of paradigmatic analyses, it questions generalizing assumptions of competition, collaboration, recognition, and exploitation found in major theoretical schools that perceive of the social environment as factual and stable.

Yet at the same time, a mainstream societal consensus is sought across countries in order to influence discourses and policies relating to LGBTQ groups in society. Queer contestations escape categorization. Depending on the degree of political inclusion, however, LGBT as a category may be stereotyped into a heteronormative copy of traditional societal structures, equipped with equal rights while recognized as being different, or defamed as an abject sexual "other" when speaking up. In reality, a spectrum of domestically differentiated roles are inhabited by and ascribed to LGBT individuals, who, in turn, need to reconcile the political need for an essentialized identity-based visibility with the wish to express themselves personally as neither hetero- nor homoconform individuals with a fluid and complex sexual identity. This balancing of LGBT mainstreaming is further complicated by the fact that societies across the globe vary in the ways in which non-conforming sexuality and gender expressions can be lived, from closeted bisexual behavior to the public acceptance of third genders. It is here that queer theory helps to raise awareness about the problematic identification with established sexual or gender role models. But, to cite Sabsay (2013), does such a Western mode of thinking allow for a meaningful application and contestation of current heteronormative thinking? Moreover, should the private experience be made part of the public–political in an attempt to attain rights even in those settings in which LGBTQ people are sometimes sheltered from discrimination precisely because sexuality is deemed private and thus, out of the reach of public control? The "private" is also where wrongs such as marital rape and sexual abuse occur (Brysk, 2013). Part of the rationale of this volume is to work out the value of such existing conceptualizations of position-ality for LGBT individuals' as well as queer political expression domestically and transnationally.

Normativity – ideology or ethical necessity?

"Sexual democratization implies that, in order to become democratic, governments as well as sexually progressive movements are obliged to adhere to these Western inter-nationalist models [...] the three hegemonic trends through which sexual rights have been articulated are: a) the politics of inclusion; b) the emergence of new homo-normativities that in some cases are complicit with new forms of nationalism; and c) the reduction of sexual rights to cultural rights." (Sabsay, 2013: 82)

At first sight, one would argue that the normative contents of LGBTQ political expressions criticize established, often heteronormative, norms and values. Whereas the realist and liberal schools of IR neglect normative considerations, the critical, con-structivist, and feminist theories firmly established this sort of critique. As for queer theory, it exhibits, as mentioned earlier, a strong anti-normative and maybe even anti-foundational ontological stance, in fact rejecting any sort of preconceived social realities. Such thinking is based on the oppressive nature of assumed "uni-versal heterosexuality" (Diamond, 2008), against which non-heteronormative individuals differentiate themselves personally and often, publicly. What can be done to recognize the existence of alternative sexual and gender expressions? How can the transcending of binary hetero- and homonormativities occur in (international) politics without a fixation on sexual norms? Normativity then is a crystallizing point around which differences between established modes of thinking (about society in general, or IR in particular) and the claims of LGBT politics become evident.

But it also makes the divergent perspectives on normativity in feminist theory, queer theory, and LGBT politics visible. Despite LGBT politics running counter to many mainstream societies, and often inciting a culture war over the morality of traditional heterosexual norms as opposed to alternative sexual expressions, LGBT advocates themselves profess a number of normative positions that relate to IR, such as the search for political power, autonomy, and protective order. These would certainly be criticized by queer theorists: the universalist–liberal stance by which LGBT inclusion is promoted by advocates, progressive states, and many international organizations, presupposes inherently normative conceptions of liberal governance. They claim that their ideals are better than alternative societal models (such as, for instance, egalitarian socialism or ethno-centric particularism), thereby actually essentializing and hegemonizing diverse sexual expressions as well. Normatively conducted advocacy politics then, in theory, can be just as totalitarian in outlook as the mainstream politics it tries to change. Normativity also comes into play when debating the value of marriage equality, particularly when challenged on grounds of suspected hetero- or increasingly, homonormativity. What, then, is the "logic of appropriateness" of LGBTQ politics in this complex subject area?

From discourse to action: agents and structure intertwined

"The truth is that the battle cannot be won primarily in the streets and conference halls in New York or Geneva but here in Lagos and Abuja. This is not to say that support from international NGOs, activists and diplomats is not important – far from that. The point being canvassed here is that local activists need to be empowered to drive the process." (Ugwu, 2013: 13)

In contrast to most grand IR theories, which either do not conceive of pluralistic political action at all or view it predominantly as state tools, LGBTQ claims necessitate public and political advocacy. For queer theorists who explore discourses as fundamental and determining factors and view politics as secondary, LGBT perspectives regularly point to the need to go beyond discursive positions. For LGBT activists, -friendly actors, and theorists alike, political advocacy has become not only an essential signifier of their own positionality, but also a critical part of their public raison d'être. In being a political actor, no matter if in domestic or international politics, they not only criticize but hope to transform the larger governance structure. In doing so, they reach for goals of equality and non-discrimination and embed their own struggle in the larger human rights movement. We agree with the view of Corrêa et al. (2008) that LGBT equality, because of its connection to socially constructed sexuality, and not only in order to build alliances, needs to be connected to a larger social justice cause. It is said that the gay rights movement is the civil rights issue of our time. But how should the diffusion of LGBT civic protest – a queer activity in itself – be compared to the largely Western-exported activities of international non-governmental organizations (INGOs) that possibly perpetuate homocolonialism? And how should the homophobic counter-mobilization be responded to?

Internationally, a similar volatility of strong notions of "gender" or "sexual orientation" in human rights discourse emerges. The Yogyakarta Principles sought to de-essentialize sexual discourse, favoring the understanding that everybody has a sexual orientation and a gender expression. Yet this is not necessarily how the language came to be used or interpreted afterwards. Waites (2009) emphasizes the centrality of those two notions in contemporary human rights discourses, but also highlights the problematic nature of these notions in reifying binary matrixes and thus, problematizing and securitizing relatively fluid identitive concepts (sexual "orientation," rather than an individual identity, or the use of "gender identity," presuming a clear identity), and excluding other important ones, such as bisexuality or transgender. In global forums such as the UN, a resulting split between the more tolerant countries and the more culturally conservative countries is visible on this issue (see D'Amico, Chapter 3), and becomes reinforced by the advocacy of liberal democracies, that then leads to a similar pushback by member states. Global queer politics by LGBT activists and human rights groups, then, should in this view move towards contesting the excluding and problematizing nature of such fixed, politically instrumentalized notions in the international community, including in the UN and the EU. While theoretically stimulating, it is questionable whether such flexibility is something that the majority of states globally would be open to.

To sum up, questions of positionality, normativity, and theory–practice linkage have much weight in the analysis of global sexual politics. The following chapters respond to one or more of these facets, interrogate established IR concepts, and add their own substantive regional or topical content to the larger debate about non-normative sexualities in IR. Thus, the emerging picture of the role of LGBTQ claims is intentionally assembled and hybrid to reflect better the incongruities and complexities of any social reality, and the international system in particular. No linear progress, certainty, or inherent logic exists in this area of human existence, but the following chapters challenge the reader to change perspectives on established IR concepts, perspectives, and theories. We seek not to advocate for a particular way of conducting LGBTQ advocacy politics, or to establish a single view of how sexuality impresses on IR. International action requires attention to local nuance, not interventionist Western action. For Blasius (2001), "LGBT movements (are successful when they) shape debate and advocacy about their same-sex loving and gender diversity across cultures through framing their specific cultural traditions within new ways of conceiving and enacting just governance" (220). How to find more nuanced and truly "glocal" solutions to the difficult global debate about sexual rights remains an open question. How exactly these novel rights approaches will look like is yet unclear and is unlikely to evolve as a standardized format, but it will certainly provide for more comparative theorization in the years to come.

Chapter preview

Each chapter analyzes a case study to reevaluate established IR concepts such as stateness, war and security, international organization, market, modernity, and relations between the core and the periphery. The volume contains a regionally and conceptually diverse set of cases ranging from the EU to the Middle East and from legal perspectives to cultural critiques. The authors show how LGBTQ approaches confront conventional paradigms to propose more critical and inclusive ways of practicing IR, something that has been seriously neglected in academic scholarship thus far.

The volume starts by discussing how LGBTQ claims matter to theory. Anthony Langlois takes a human rights approach to argue that international sexuality and gender politics are consequential for international theory. In "Human rights, LGBT rights, and international theory," he analyzes IR's recent interest for human rights and the significance of sexuality within it. Although sexuality and queer international theory is abundant, he points out, IR fails to sustain LGBTQ debates. Part of the problem is that human rights concepts and LGBTQ perspectives do not neatly map onto one another. Instead, his critical examination of the relationship between these two discourses highlights significant tensions. These include debates over the role of the state, the possibility of queer liberalism, and of performativity and positionality. Langlois shows that LGBTQ perspectives complicate human rights. He articulates where human rights theory may support LGBTQ political projects while also being cognizant of and critically responsive to those aspects of human rights discourses about which LGBTQ (particularly queer) theorists have consistently had reservations. The familiar is first made strange, then used to make strange ways of looking at international politics familiar once again. As the author advocates for an expansion of international human rights theory, he invites further LGBTQ insights to push critical IR to new levels.

Mike Bosia's theoretical critique probes the fundamental value of stateness. Without mincing his words, he posits the state as a psychopath; a self-interested entity suspended between domestic and global politics regulating sexuality and gender for statecraft. His chapter "To love or to loathe: modernity, homophobia, and LGBT rights" engages research in peripheries like Uganda to question whether the state as conventionally conceived in IR theories is a possible ally in winning human rights for sexual and gender minorities. He considers the regulation of sexuality as a lasting helpmate of the Western modernist project. Modernity, which decides the rule and the exception to the rule, is inextricably related to the Western state, its defining institution. Bosia conceptualizes state homophobia, historicizes sexual binaries, and explains how homonationalism might corrupt sexual liberation. He rethinks LGBTQ politics to move beyond processes of political and sexual modernization where the post-colonial state is the dominant figure in claims making and rights claiming, often above and before the need to recognize diverse identities and places for mobilization. This theoretically rich chapter resignifies the postcolonial state as exceptional, then, dismantles narratives of modernity – queer or otherwise – that fetishize the nation-state first and comprehend identities and rights only as products of it.

Two chapters then move from IR theory to the practice of world politics in international organizations. Francine D'Amico traces LGBT politics – or their neglect – at the UN. In her chapter "LGBT and (Dis)United Nations: sexual and gender minorities, international law, and UN politics," she analyzes the absence of "sexual minorities" from "universal" human rights law, stemming from the polarization of member-states votes. No legally binding global treaty explicitly protects the right of sexual groups to be free from discrimination, violence, and persecution and to be free to enjoy all the rights articulated in the Universal Declaration of Human Rights. In 2007, the Yogyakarta Principles provided a legal roadmap to address these exclusions, bypassing states blockage and keeping the topic alive in UN debates. But resistance remained. In 2008, the UN General Assembly considered a non-binding declaration on human rights, sexual orientation, and gender identity. Of 192 UN member states, only 66 endorsed the declaration, with support in Europe and Latin America and opposition across Asia, Africa, and the Middle East. The author also problematizes the lack of access of LGBTQI NGOs to the UN system. In her view, sexual diversity remains marginal in part because few NGOs representing sexual claims have accredited status with the UN's Economic and Social Council (ECOSOC). Liberal feminist perspectives on international relations offer little to bridge these divides, but critical and postcolonialist feminist IR theories may provide strategies for solidarity. D'Amico highlights the challenge contained in attaining sexual equality in the world's largest international organization.

Markus Thiel tackles politics of sexuality in the European Union (EU). He exposes the EU's political economy motives behind antidiscrimination policy to understand how LGBTQ experiences influence IR theory. In "Transversal and particularistic politics in the European Union's antidiscrimination policy: LGBT politics under neoliberalism," he shows how new research has contributed to uncovering the gendered and sexualized inequalities in EU politics, including within constituent member states, despite the normative–legal provisions set by the EU. The Union pursues a wide-ranging antidiscrimination policy inclusive of a variety of stances on LGBT (and other) rights, which, in certain instances, clashes with member states' conceptions and stimulates blowback from social conservative INGOs and other stakeholders. In its antidiscrimination regime, the EU pursues mainstreaming through a differentiated logic that produces a particularistic perspective as well as field of (policy) action in relation to the various marginalized populations. At the same time, the antidiscrimination directive applies only to employment-related discrimination, with activists aiming to broaden its application beyond this market-framed rationale. The questions that appear are whether and why gender and sexuality are treated differently in the development of antidiscrimination policies in a free market bloc. Inferences for novel IR theory-building are drawn from the experience of LGBT groups representing an amorphous, transversal movement inclusive of a wide array of identifications and expressions that ultimately contest the neoliberal supremacy of markets.

The volume then blurs the core–periphery borders with chapters that engage realities in so-called peripheral locations to challenge conventional theory at the core. Momin Rahman's theoretical exploration draws on his research on Muslim cultures. In "Sexual diffusions and conceptual confusions: Muslim homophobia and homosexualities in the context of modernity," Rahman argues that a modernization thesis underpins the current visibility and putative expansion of LGBTQ rights discourses. This thesis, he argues, contains conceptual confusions around sexual identities, non-Western identities, and the formation of modernity. His chapter assesses the credibility of the thesis that characterizes the contemporary diffusion of sexual diversity politics from Western countries to those outside the West as an inevitable and welcome consequence of modernization. Rahman argues that sexual diversity cannot develop in the same way in contemporary international contexts, largely because modernization processes in postcolonial contexts are historically and sociologically different from those in Western modernity. He cautions how sexuality is conceptualized in cross-national and historical context to avoid a politically essentialist assumption of sexual identity. He reconsiders core–periphery divides through postcolonial critiques that acknowledge the social construction of sexual identities. The rejection of Western frameworks of sexual politics ignores the contemporary connections in LGBTQ identities and strategies at the risk of reinstating euro-centric understandings of modern sexuality. As he challenges theoretical canons, he advocates work towards a more intersectional understanding of modernity when theorizing sexual diffusion in contemporary times.

Manuela Lavinas Picq takes an Amazonian viewpoint to evaluate the contributions of LGBTQ perspectives for critical IR. In "Amazon prides: LGBT perspectives on international relations," she explores gay prides in the Amazon to develop two arguments. She first sheds light on global dynamics of gender in peripheries where they tend to be overlooked. LGBT politics are all along the Amazon, revealing the extent to which the "local" and the "global" are permanently interacting with and redefining each other. Second, she looks at gender identities to shatter flattening generalizations about Amazonia. Gay pride activities depart from the imagination of an atemporal and homogenous Amazon to disclose instead a diverse, complex society, cosmopolitan rather than isolated from the global political core. Our research surprises are revealing of our assumptions. The surprise of "discovering" gay pride parades in Amazonia is embedded in the assumption that it is not supposed to be a place in which political modernity thrives. A queer gaze permits one to discover another Amazon that is more plural than often assumed. Similarly to feminist inquiries, Picq argues, an LGBTQ approach debunks conceptual assumptions of IR about the non-core. She proposes the Amazon as a case study in the South from where to propel dialogues between LGBTQ studies and postcolonial approaches, using that intersection to rethink the nation-state from distinctively alternative perspectives. Further, Picq questions whether sexuality is just another feminist gaze or whether it is a lightning rod of its own that may contribute to breaking free from IR's disciplinary straightjackets.

Mehmet Sinan Birdal brings evidence from LGBT politics in Turkey to engage theoretical debates between the universal and the particular. His chapter, "Between the universal and the particular: the politics of the recognition of LGBT rights in Turkey," traces the emergence of LGBT politics of recognition during the 2013 Gezi protests. His analysis shows how both opponents and proponents of LGBTQ rights resort simultaneously to universalizing and particularizing narratives to justify their arguments. Opponents base their arguments on a universalistic narrative emphasizing the rule of national sovereignty and non-interference. They underline the prevalence of homophobia in many societies as an indicator of its universal appeal, which would confirm the primacy of particularistic discourse and local culture in addressing the subject. Proponents, in turn, argue back that LGBT rights are human rights and that the global prevalence of homophobia is partly due to the colonial diffusion of sexual norms and international law. This chapter illustrates how this debate manifests itself in Turkey, where the political discourse of the incumbent Justice and Development Party (JDP) is also redefining Turkish identity by resorting to both a universalist–liberal discourse with an emphasis on democratic procedure and particularistic conservative premises that emphasize cultural traditions. This state ideology follows a pattern analyzed by Partha Chatterjee with regard to postcolonial nationalism broadly speaking. Birdal sees the growing role of the LGBT movement since the Gezi protests of 2013 as an interesting case for ongoing theoretical debates about the universality and particularity of LGBT rights in the context of postcolonial theories. He shows not only how LGBT-related human rights continue to be a divisive issue on the international agenda, but especially how a case study like Gezi bears important clues about how the LGBT movement can go beyond a politics of recognition and represent universality in its particularity.

Sandra McEvoy engages methodological peripheries to rethink IR canons. Her chapter, "Queering security studies in Northern Ireland: problem, practice, and practitioner," draws on interdisciplinary research methods to stimulate feminist conversations on the relationship between the identities of the researcher and the process of conducting research in post-conflict environments. Only recently has mainstream IR begun to consider the necessity of multi-methodological and interdisciplinary approaches in conflict resolution. Ackerly et al. (2006) highlighted what feminist researchers have been advocating for decades, namely, that effective research requires an ongoing commitment to self-reflection and engagement with Indigenous knowledges. Crucially, these authors also warned that the absence of reflexive praxis in inquiries that involve issues of global politics can be particularly grievous. It is this self-reflecting research aptitude that has improved the ethics of conducting research on delicate topics. Researchers should seriously consider the ethics of studying topics such as the use of sexual violence in armed conflict, female genital mutilation, but also, while still in its infancy, the experiences of LGBTQ men and women in conflict affected areas around the world. As scholarship continues to grow, researchers must consider the ways in which the sexuality (and other social identities) of the researcher shapes the research design process, influences data collection, and effects the process of meaning making. This is ever more true in states of insecurity and war.

In the conclusion, Laura Sjoberg reviews the contributions of the previous chapters, and relates these perspectives to feminist thought and queer theories more generally. By doing so, she aims at critically examining the potential novelty that LGBTQ perspectives may mean for the reconceptualization of established IR concepts and theories. Her view is that applying these new lenses to international relations adds an inclusive facet to what is already an increasingly pluralistic academic field. She questions the uniqueness of LGBTQ perspectives, given that they rather extend feminist and critical perspectives in their emphasis on positionality, normativity, and critical advocacy. Yet she welcomes the nuanced way in which the presented case studies further theoretical extensions of the lived experiences of LGBTQ individuals, and highlights the transformative potential of the chapter contributions in reconceptualizing subjects, processes and objects in IR. In sum, given the similar positions of a number of critical theoretical schools, she argues for an integrative approach combining the force of LGBTQ/queer/feminist/critical/postcolonial scholarship.

Notes

1 "Sexual politics" is used here in a narrow sense for the observation of LGBTQ politics' repercussions for IR (theory), not to provide a broad view of sex and politics. Much has been written on AIDS/HIV (Altman, 2001; Corrêa et al., 2008), on prostitution (Kempadoo & Doezema, 1998) and other issues of sexual politics issues already. Gay and lesbian studies relate well to the subject of this volume and are political in nature, but very seldom take into account the broader trans- or international repercussions of LGBTQ politics.

2 While banning gay marriage and promoting traditional marriage at home, the administration of President Bush joined Egypt, Iran, and Pakistan in resisting any text

mentioning stigmatized groups like men who have sex with men or sex workers from the Final Declaration of Commitments at the 2001 UN Special Session on HIV/AIDS.

Bibliography

Ackerly B, Stern M, and True J (2006) *Feminist Methodologies for International Relations.* Cambridge: Cambridge University Press.

Altman D (2001) *Global Sex.* Chicago: University of Chicago Press.

Amar P (2013) *The Security Archipelago: Human-Security States, Sexuality Politics, and the End of Neoliberalism.* Durham, NC: Duke University Press.

Beier M (2005) *International Relations in Uncommon Places: Indigeneity, Cosmology, and the Limits of International Theory.* Basingstoke: Palgrave Macmillan.

Blasius M (2001) *Sexual Identities, Queer Politics.* Princeton, NJ: Princeton University Press.

Browne K and Nash C (2010) *Queer Methods and Methodologies.* Farnham: Ashgate.

Brysk A (2013) Human rights movements. In: Snow D A et al. (eds.) *Wiley-Blackwell Encyclopedia of Social and Political Movements.* Malden, MA: Wiley.

Budhiraja S, Fried S, and Teixeira A (2010) Spelling it out. In: Lind A (ed.) *Development, Sexual Rights and Global Governance.* New York: Routledge.

Comaroff J and Comaroff L (2012) *Theory from the South: Or How Euro-America is Evolving Towards Africa.* Boulder, CO: Paradigm Publishers.

Corrêa S, Parker R, and Petchensky R (2008) *Sexuality, Health and Human Rights.* London: Routledge.

Corrêa S, Richard-Davis B, and Parker R (2013) Sexualities and globalities. In: Tolman D L & Diamond L M (eds.) *APA Handbook of Sexuality and Psychology, Vol. 2: Contextual Approaches.* APA Handbooks in Psychology. Washington, DC: American Psychological Association.

Diamond L (2008) *Sexual Fluidity: Understanding Women's Love and Desire.* Cambridge, MA: Harvard University Press.

Dunne T, Hansen L, and Wight C (2013) The end of IR theory. *European Journal of International Relations* 19(3): 405–25.

Elliott P (2012) *Debates in Transgender, Queer, and Feminist Theory: Contested Sites.* Farnham: Ashgate.

Enloe C (2005) *Masculinity as Foreign Policy Issue.* Washington DC: Foreign Policy in Focus.

——(2010) *Nimo's War, Emma's War Making Feminist Sense of the Iraq War.* Berkeley: University of California Press.

García J and Parker R (2006) From global discourse to local action: the makings of a sexual rights movement? *Horizontes Antropológicos* 26: 13–41.

Girard F (2004) Global Implications of US Domestic and International Policies on Sexuality. Sexuality Policy Watch Working Papers No. 1.

——(2007) Negotiating sexual rights and sexual orientation at the UN. In: Parker R, Petchesky R, & Sember R (eds.) *SexPolitics: Reports from the Frontlines.* Rio de Janeiro: Sexuality Policy Watch.

Gupta A and Long S (2009) This alien legacy: the origins of "sodomy" laws in British colonialism. Human Rights Watch. http://dspace.africaportal.org/jspui/bitstream/123456789/24321/1/Origins%20of%20sodomy%20laws%20in%20British%20Colonialism.pdf?1

Halper K (2013) Putin's war on gays: a timeline of homophobia. *Policy Mic.* http://mic.com/articles/58593/putin-s-war-on-gays-a-timeline-of-homophobia

Henderson E (2007) Navigating the muddy waters of the mainstream: tracing the mystification of racism in international relations. In: Rich W (ed.) *African American Perspectives on Political Science.* Philadelphia, PA: Temple University Press.

Hobson J (2012) *The Eurocentric Conception of World Politics: Western International Theory. 1760–2010.* Cambridge: Cambridge University Press.

Hoffmann S (1977) An American social science: international relations. *Daedalus* 106: 41–60.

Inayatullah N (2011) *Autobiographical International Relations: I, IR*. New York: Routledge.

Itaborahy L P and Zhu J (2014) *State-sponsored Homophobia: A World Survey of Laws: Criminalisation, Protection and Recognition of Same-sex Love*. Geneva: International Lesbian and Gay Association (ILGA).

Jackson P T (2011) *The Conduct of Inquiry in International Relations*. New York: Routledge.

Kempadoo K and Doezema J (1998) *Global Sex Workers: Rights, Resistance, and Redefinition*. New York: Routledge.

Knight K (2014) LGBTI rights – still not there yet. IRIN news. http://www.irinnews.org/report/100487/lgbti-rights-still-not-there-yet

Kollmann K (2009) *LGBT Rights: From Queers to Humans*. International Studies. A Compendium Project. Boston, MA: Wiley-Blackwell.

Lind A (2010) *Development, Sexual Rights and Global Governance*. New York: Routledge.

Lovaas K (2013) *LGBT Studies and Queer Theory: New Conflicts, Collaborations, and Contested Terrain*. New York: Routledge.

Maliniak D, Oakes A, Peterson S, and Tierney M (2011) International relations in the US Academy. *International Studies Quarterly* 55(2): 437–64.

Massad J (2007) *Desiring Arabs*. Chicago: University of Chicago Press.

Nyanzi S (2014) The paradoxical geopolitics of recriminalizing homosexuality in Uganda: one of three ugly sisters. *Sexuality Policy Watch Newsletter* 14.

Plummer K (2003) The flow of boundaries: gays, queers and intimate citizenship. In Downes D, Rock P, Chinkin C, & Gearty C (eds.) *Crime, Social Control and Human Rights: From Moral Panics to States of Denial, Essays in Honour of Stanley Cohen*. New York: Routledge.

Puar, J (2007) *Terrorist Assemblages: Homonationalism in Queer Times*. Durham, NC: Duke University Press.

Rahman M (2014) *Homosexualities, Muslim Cultures and Modernity*. Basingstoke: Palgrave Macmillan.

Roy A and Bhan G (2013) Lessons from somewhere. *Cityscapes* 4. http://www.cityscapesdigital.net/2013/11/18/lessons-somewhere/

Ruffolo D (2009) *Post-Queer Politics*. Farnham: Ashgate.

Sabsay L (2013) Queering the politics of global sexual rights? *Studies in Ethnicity and Nationalism* 13(1): 80–90.

Shaw K (2008) *Indigeneity & Political Theory*. New York: Routledge.

Shilliam R (2010) *International Relations and Non-Western Thought: Imperialism, Colonialism, and Investigations of Global Modernity*. New York: Routledge.

Sjoberg L (2012) Towards trans-gendering international relations? *International Political Sociology* 6(4): 337–54.

Tickner A B (2013) Core, periphery and (neo)imperialist international relations. *European Journal of International Relations* 19(3): 627–46.

Tickner A B and Blaney D (2013) *Claiming the International*. London: Routledge.

Tickner J A (1997) You just don't understand: troubled engagements between feminists and IR theorists. *International Studies Quarterly* 41(4): 611–32.

——(2005) Gendering a discipline: some feminist methodological contributions to international relations. *Signs: Journal of Women in Culture and Society* 30: 2173–88.

——(2010) You may never understand: prospects for feminist futures in international relations. *Australian Feminist Law Journal* 32: 9–20.

Tremblay M, Paternotte D, and Johnson C (2011) *The Lesbian and Gay Movement and the State: Comparative Insights into a Transformed Relationship*. Burlington, VT: Ashgate.

Ugwu D (2013) As the flames of homophobia burn around the world, understanding Nigeria's anti-gay bill. *African Perspectives*: 3–6.

Vitalis R (2010) The noble American science of imperial relations and its laws of race development. *Comparative Studies in Society and History* 52(4): 909–38.

Waites K and Kollmann M (2013) The global politics of lesbian, gay, bisexual and transgender human rights: an introduction. *Contemporary Politics* 15(1): 1–17.

Waites M (2009) Critique of "sexual orientation" and "gender identity" in man rights discourse: global queer politics beyond the Yogyakarta Principles. *Contemporary Politics* 15(1): 137–56.

Weber C (2014) Why is there no queer international theory? *European Journal of International Relations* (OnlineFirst): 1–25.

Weeks J (2000) *Making Sexual History*. Hoboken, NJ: Wiley.

Weiss M and Bosia M (2013) *Global Homophobia: States, Movements, and the Politics of Oppression*. Illinois: University of Illinois Press.

Wilkinson C and Kirey A (2010) What's in a name? The personal and political meanings of "LGBT" for non-heterosexual and transgender youth in Kyrgyzstan. *Central Asian Survey* 29(04): 485–99.

World Bank (2014) *The Economic Costs of Homophobia*. Report. http://www.worldbank.org/content/dam/Worldbank/document/SAR/economic-costs-homophobia-lgbt-exlusion-india.pdf

1

HUMAN RIGHTS, LGBT RIGHTS, AND INTERNATIONAL THEORY

Anthony J. Langlois

Introduction

It is only in recent decades that human rights have become an acceptable scholarly focus for theorists within the academic discipline of international relations – albeit an approval often dispensed as a reluctant concession. More recent (still halting and very hesitant) has been the acknowledgement of LGBT rights and sexuality and gender politics in general as legitimate interests for international theorists. A further claim, that these are consequential matters which might shape and guide our interpretations of international politics *itself*, is still a very *queer* claim. In this chapter, I propose to utilize this queerness and take advantage of the way in which this claim challenges, destabilizes and reorders analytical priorities for both human rights and international theory. The study of international sexuality and gender politics is shown to be consequential for international theory in general and human rights in particular.

International theory and LGBT politics

In an article from the late 1990s, Paul EeNam Park Hagland set out to bring together LGBT politics, human rights, and international relations theory (Hagland, 1997). His effort represents one of the earliest attempts to do this. Hagland's opening observations place his subsequent comments on the paucity of theoretical reflection on LGBT matters in context, by observing the slow pace at which human rights groups in general embraced LGBT issues. While notionally oriented towards the interests of the oppressed and marginalized, they paid scant attention to LGBT concerns. Little wonder, then, that states themselves did not respect the human rights of LGBT peoples: "there is not a single country which fully respects LGBT rights," Hagland observed in 1997 (Hagland, 1997: 357). The academy performed equally badly:

> Nor has international relations (IR) theory to date considered LGBT politics and human rights a topic worthy of interest or scrutiny: leading theorists have simply ignored LGBT rights as a concern, either normative or empirical. Hence the question of LGBT rights as human rights simply has not been engaged in any systematic fashion by mainstream IR theory. (Hagland, 1997: 357)

Hagland is intent on engaging with international relations and LGBT politics, but for his purposes, IR theory was to prove excruciatingly restrictive (not an uncommon view: Sylvester, 2007; see also Altman, 2001: 131). Hagland nonetheless uses IR theory to point to two factors: "the weakness of international institutions and international law" and "the state-centric bias of some traditional human rights approaches" (Hagland, 1997: 358). Hagland invokes realism and liberal institutionalism as the poles of the debate within IR theory, and rehearses this debate to complicate the optimism expressed by LGBT advocates regarding apparent advances. Hagland insists that, in the absence of enforcement mechanisms, declarations of rights while symbolically important lack efficacy. The internationalist fervor of human rights discourse notwithstanding, when it comes down to the matter of protecting vulnerable populations, the state is in the driving seat. Realism thus has its place: if a state does not have goodwill towards its LGBT populations, then there is very little that those populations can directly expect from the formal international institutions and legal structures of the human rights movement.

These lessons are well learnt; today, two decades after Hagland wrote, they are being taken up and articulated in different ways in the human rights literature (see, for example, Nash, 2011). What is interesting to observe about Hagland's piece, however, is the way IR theory fails him as a means for going any further than these elementary cautions. He is quite explicit about needing to turn elsewhere to pursue his questions about the constitution of sexuality politics and rights in international affairs: answers would have to be sought from social constructionism, feminism, and Foucauldian analyses (Hagland, 1997: 258). Two decades on, I suggest the project Hagland embarked on remains unfulfilled. In reaching "beyond IR theory," Hagland sought to develop a normative and strategic approach for thinking about LGBT rights as human rights. While it is the case that many of the theoretical resources to which Hagland turned have subsequently been incorporated into IR theory (cf. Reus-Smit & Snidal, 2010), the project itself has received little attention within formal IR (see also Foster et al., 2012; Smith & Lee, 2014).

To show this, I turn first to Cynthia Weber, who presses the matter further by asking why there is no *queer* international theory. While Weber does not discuss human rights directly, Ryan Richard Thoreson's account of the persecution and discrimination suffered by LGBT people, and the articulation of those experiences through the discourse of human rights, points us back to the questions Hagland raised about the construction of human rights and sexuality rights.

Queering IR?

While Hagland, writing in the mid-1990s, sought to emphasise the failure of "any … standard work in the literature" to seriously treat LGBT human rights issues (Hagland, 1997, note 2: 378), Cynthia Weber, writing after 25 years of queer theory, asks why the discipline of international relations has not "gone somewhat queer" (Weber, 2014: 1). This should be a pressing question for IR scholars: queer scholars themselves are well and truly at home on the familiar turf of the IR scholar. The war on terror, immigration, displaced people flows, transnationalism, global capital and labor, violence of various forms, surveillance – all of these and more are central subjects of study in IR; they are all *also* taken up and given masterful treatment by a wide range of queer scholars whom Weber lists. Global queer studies scholars contribute to the three core areas of traditional IR scholarship: "war and peace, state and nation formation, and international political economy." These contributions are not somehow marginal, but are top ranked in various disciplinary journals and books series – "But not in the field of IR" (Weber, 2014: 2).

Weber, playing on Martin Wight's famous question, "why is there no international theory?" (Wight, 1960), asks: why is there no *queer* international theory? In the end, Weber answers this question by stating that there *is* a lot of queer international theory. Some IR scholars do write on queer themes; there is an expanding body of work, which she cites, although most of this is not published in "IR outlets." This might give rise to the supposition that the work of these scholars is too interdisciplinary to qualify as "proper" IR work. But Weber argues that "the primary foci of most queer-themed work published by IR scholars are classic IR themes such as war, security, sovereignty, intervention, hegemony, nationalism, empire, colonialism, and the general practice of foreign policy" (Weber, 2014: 2). Weber continues:

> Of particular relevance to IR scholars are investigations that explore how failing hegemonic states perform queerness through their conduct of interventions and wars to solidify their hegemonic status, how states produce themselves and their citizens as pro-LGBT subjects in part to constitute other states, "civilizations" or peoples as national and global threats, how the articulation and circulation of global (economic) value through queer and racialized bodies supports the practices of empires, and more generally how "queer" is mobilized to designate some state practices as progressive and others as non-progressive as a mechanism to divide the world into orderly vs. disorderly (anarchic) spaces. (Weber, 2014: 2–3 citations omitted)

Queer international scholarship, then, is abundant; certainly, to refer back to Hagland's concerns, there is a lot of work being done about LGBT persons, their politics, and the rights discourses they invoke (Seckinelgin & Paternotte, forthcoming). Why is it, then, that this work fails to appear in the mainstream IR theoretic context? Or, as Weber puts it, "Why does there *appear* to be no Queer International Theory?" (Weber, 2014: 3). Weber's answer to this question helps us on two fronts. It directly helps us with the question regarding this case – the appearance that there is no queer IR theory. Weber's analysis also presents generalizable conclusions about the nature of IR as a discipline which can help us with a second consideration: why it is that IR does not consistently sustain the kinds of debate about human rights that could provide spaces for the discussion of LGBTQ concerns regarding human rights (although see here Symons & Altman, forthcoming). It is curious that human rights, which connects to all the main themes of "disciplinary IR," continues to occupy only a minor position, or is left for the international lawyers and philosophers.

The many scholars that Weber instances write about and engage in queer international politics. Weber's claim is that, for disciplinary IR, there is no route from queer international politics to queer international theory: attempts to join the dots here will be stymied by the core intellectual structures of the discipline. Such a claim is highly significant, given the purpose of a volume like this, which seeks to engage in theoretical reflection in IR from the positionality of various forms of sexuality and gender politics. For those not schooled in disciplinary IR, this desire for theoretical reflection may seem to be a natural, even overdue, development – making Weber's claim seem strange or perhaps implausible. However, it is an important argument that goes to the core of the identity of IR as an academic discipline. At the same time, it displays why Weber places the stress on the *appearance* that there is no queer international theory, rather there *actually* being none. In short: queer theories are seen to fail the discipline, and thus appear to be absent, having been replaced by theories that *do* get the disciplinary tick of approval (Weber, 2014: 18).

To show how this happens, Weber walks us through Martin Wight's famous homology: "Politics is to International Politics as Political Theory is to historical Interpretation." This homology first appeared in Wight's 1960 essay "Why is there no international theory?" (Wight, 1960). "Historical interpretation" appears in this equation where one might expect to find "international theory." This is necessitated by the failure of international theory to exist as a knowledge system parallel in content and function to political theory, which might tell the story of states and their relations, the state system and its survival, and the high politics of diplomacy.

Weber gives the famous essay this gloss:

> What Wight's essay offers IR is a cautionary tale about how *not* to produce failing international theory and a curative tale about how to successfully revive a discipline whose theoretical endeavors have led it astray. The power and influence of Wight's essay and the homology at its core are undeniable. Whether to embrace, debate, or refine it, Wight's argument is so rehearsed in IR through teaching and research … that his essay "has almost iconic status in IR so that in reading it one is reading the discipline itself." (Weber, 2014, citing Epp, 1996: 5)

This, in turn, naturalizes within the discipline certain assumptions about what theory is and how one should do it. The kinds of knowledge and theory that might emerge out of reflection on the international politics of sexuality and gender – the possibility of queer international theory – is commonly foreclosed by a disciplinary IR which defines theoretical failure in the terms applied by Wight to international theory. The methodological, epistemological, theoretical, ontological approaches such a theorist must use defy too many of Wight's "tidy boundaries" to *appear* as international theory (Weber, 2014: 8). To reach this point is merely to have reached the first staging post in Weber's detailed and complex argument, the end goal of which is to enable readers to see and recognise queer IR theory when they come across it, and to understand why it is that at first glance it might not *appear*, despite being very much present. My goal in moving on is to take advantage of this invitation to *see*, as we move our focus more narrowly to human rights.

Paradoxical rights

The question of theorizing rights for LGBT people is one that is hard to pick up in the IR theoretic context; Weber's discussion helps illuminate this. But theorizing human rights is crucial, given the idea's dominance and the role it increasingly plays in articulating the standing, legibility, and welfare of LGBT people in global affairs. Can human rights be theorized in a way which, while retaining a critical edge, articulates a *positive* role for them to play with respect to the international politics of sexuality and LGBT people? This is not as straightforward as some human rights enthusiasts might think. The extension of human rights to sexuality politics means the extension of conceptual, institutional, legal and political frameworks to matters of sexual orientation and gender identity. This process of extension creates normative standards that people are then expected to identify with, assimilate to, support, engage with (or in the "marginal cases," react against). And in so doing, this process further entrenches the existing institutions that govern our lives – institutions which, even when purporting to be emancipatory, often constrain freedoms, generate inequality and entrench injustice.

For Ryan Richard Thoreson, this plays out in three areas (Thoreson, 2011). First, when LGBT activists and professionals intervene in situations, and when their interventions are framed using the discourse of human rights, they bring with them ideas of humanity, citizenship and responsibility that reshape the pre-existing social fabric. There are many levels at which this will self-consciously be the case – indeed, it may be the whole point. But such a self-aware intervention will not qualify as a queer intervention if it is simply an attempt to replace one set of normativities with another.

Second: the critique of statism. Hagland's point was that the international recognition of LGBT protective norms required state support and sponsorship for activation. Thoreson emphasizes the statist *quid pro quo*, the cost of protection is recognition and assimilation by the state: "The violated subject may find voice for their suffering through the international arena and may productively bring pressure on the state apparatus to rectify its wrongs, but the process is ultimately focused on recognition and legitimation by a state apparatus that is often quite hostile to queerness" (Thoreson, 2011: 14). Benign ambivalence may not be such a good thing from the state either, allowing for "good queers" to be played off against others, in a broader conflictual politics of class, race, sex or gender, in which LGBT rights for some are used to butter the state's bread, playing up its power to control and manipulate LGBT subjectivities and politics.

This gives rise to another set of questions, and a third avenue of possible queer critique of the LGBT rights as a human rights venture: as human rights gains ground globally and becomes more efficacious as a driver of institutional and social change, it risks pushing aside other mechanism and modes of being – including forms of sexual orientation and gender identity and their expression. "With the strong prerogative to define and protect queer populations, the human rights project erases ambiguity by creating and imposing particular epistemologies regarding sex, sexuality, and sexual subjectivity" (Thoreson, 2011: 16) – L,G,B,T,I,Q (etc.) – as they have come to be identified. The theoretical paradox for a politics that seeks to queer human rights should be clear: human rights are about *establishing* particular normative boundaries; queer, if it is anything, is *anti-normative*. Establishing and policing boundaries is not supposed to be its brief.

The parallels with what happens in international relations theory are very clear. This is precisely Weber's point about the role of Wight's homology: it sets up a series of boundaries that then prevent the telling of queer international politics "as they really are" (Weber, 2014: 8). In the case of IR theory, the problem with queer international theory is that it has another story to tell in addition to the story that traditionally justifies or legitimates classification as IR – the story about the survival of the state and its system. Further, it tells this additional story in ways and with means other than those traditionally used by the discipline. This is the same problem that is faced by the story of "human rights as LGBT rights": the "human rights project" is not in any sense "neutral" or "objective" with respect to social reality and experience. Rather, it is both a way of articulating our moral and political relationships which trades on certain (often naturalized) traditions of understanding; and, it is a way of proposing to *do* politics – indeed, it is a politics in itself (Langlois, 2001). Using human rights – the concepts, the discourse, the institutions, the networks – is always to participate in that politics and necessarily (if critically and hesitatingly) to function within its framework.

It is very easy to become seduced by the rhetoric of human rights – its claims to universalism, its claim to being a global ethical movement – and to be blinded by the macro-level impact of the global human rights institutional architecture, centered on the UN. Thoreson points to the ways in which human rights at the local level are very different from what one might suppose them to be, if one were to take the rhetoric seriously and look only at the macro global institutions. (cf. Hopgood, 2013) This conclusion has long been supported by anthropologists. Mark Goodale, for example, speaks of human rights universalism as a kind of mirage: as we approach the sites of human rights practice, we find not "universal human rights" but practices of normativity that are hybridized, innovative, global and local (Goodale, 2013: 420) (cf. Merry, 2006; Goodale, 2014).

The ethnographic and anthropological work presented by Goodale and his colla-borators forces a critical deconstruction of human rights – and indeed, Goodale himself directly challenges the discourses of progress and the "project of humanity" that is central to much human rights rhetoric. However, this is not to put away the possibilities of emancipatory work being achieved through human rights. A line may be drawn between the critique and repurposing of human rights: parallel paths emerge in anthropology and queer theory. Goodale, reflecting on the progressive potential of human rights, argues for "the emergence of new forms of moral practice and at least the suggestion of collective transformation" (Goodale, 2013: 421). Thoreson is also hopeful, seeing the potential to "transform human rights into a vehicle for queer positivity" (Thoreson, 2011: 19). As Goodale indicates, certain ways of studying human rights lead to the destabilization of global or hegemonic norms about human rights. Queer pursues a similar end, even self-referentially: what is queer in the global north is not necessarily what is queer elsewhere; "queer solidarity" is a very slippery, perhaps contradictory, theoretical idea.

Both elements then, human rights and queer, have a destabilizing force. It is this potential to cut across established norms, expectations and identities that makes sense of a queer account of human rights: human rights "as the queer project of rendering the strange familiar and the familiar strange" (Thoreson, 2011: 20).

Theorizing queer human rights in critical IR

Now I want to take up the point that an engagement is going on within work on LGBT human rights that focuses on their specificity in time and place, and is critical of the universalism that is often seen as the core of the global human rights project. The kinds of question being raised by human rights scholars and practitioners, as they negotiate the global politics of sexuality rights, can do critical work on human rights – especially if that critique or queering is understood as destabilizing existing categories and forcing a focus on actual practices within the international (rather than only those practices our theories prefer us to observe, in only permitted observational spaces). Here, then, I survey four recent approaches to sexuality politics and rights that suggest a series of openings for further critical engagement.

Performativity

What do we *do* when we claim human rights? In particular, what happens in the many places and times we are told that we do *not* have rights? To insist that, yes, we do have rights, and to then engage in various forms of rights claiming activity is an increasingly observed outcome. These practices may involve ambit claims for rights, legal practices for redressing abuse, agitation for the creation of institutions that would ensure rights protection, and so on. In doing this, we engage in efforts to create a world that recognizes and responds to the rights claims we make (Langlois, 2014a, 2014b).

In Karen Zivi's *performative* analysis of rights, these practices of rights claiming that destabilize and reconstitute our world are of great interest: her examples come from the U.S. and South Africa and respectively concern same-sex marriage and AIDS policy concerning mother-to-child HIV transmission. She says, "I approach rights claiming as an activity or, rather, set of activities through which we shape – indeed, at times constitute – our world and our selves" (Zivi, 2011: 9). Zivi continues:

> A performative perspective on rights moves us from an almost exclusive focus on questions about what rights *are* to a more careful consideration of what it is rights *do*; from a tendency to treat rights as things or instruments we use to bring about a particular end to a recognition that rights claiming is a complex linguistic activity, the outcomes of which are quite often beyond our complete control. A performative perspective on rights, in other words, moves us beyond concerns about the formal definitions of rights and allows us to take seriously rights claiming as a social and political practice. (Zivi, 2011: 9)

In that social and political practice, rights claiming depends on established conventions and norms in order to be legible; but it need not be – indeed, perhaps, usually is not – identical with them. Breaking recognized rules "opens up the possibility of the new"; with the new come "forces and effects that exceed" established conventions and norms (Zivi, 2011: 19).

Zivi's performative approach may be attractive in the first instance because of the way in which it can shed light on the development and claiming of new rights – such as rights for LGBT people. It would be a mistake, however, to think that the purpose of this approach is simply to explain the way in which new, deserving constituencies manage to win and secure rights, bringing to an end debates sustained by opponents. Such "rights-as-trumps" approaches, which aim to produce clear and secure political winners, are antithetical to a performative approach. Rather – and this is where we see the very clear synergies with queer theorizing – messiness, contingency and indeterminacy need to be taken seriously. Rights claims play a key role; but we may be mistaken to think either that our political objectives will be established through successful rights claims, or that we can, in fact, control or define what a successful rights claim turns out to be. Rights claims, says Zivi, "are not trumps because they are not irresistible and irrefutable claims that promise particular results; they are, instead, claims of persuasion" (Zivi, 2011: 51).

Zivi's performative account of rights claiming enables a form of analysis generative of greater insights than those typically used in IR scholarship on human rights. In particular, it fosters what Thoreson argues are the virtues of queer critique as well: a critical approach to existing categories and a focus on the actual practice of human rights – on what it is that individual people, communities, and institutions do when they perform rights claims. Among other consequences, such an approach forces a thinking about the politics of rights and of those establishing rights systems. Rights are not just "there," not just natural rights – "spectral attributes" worn like amulets to ward off tyranny, in Dworkin's disparaging phrase (Dworkin, 1978: 176). They are, rather, political technologies that always engage and perform a broader political agenda. What that agenda is or can become is a moot point. For Zivi, the hope is that it is generative of a more radical democratic politics.

Positionality

Positionality, like performativity, can destabilize human rights and force an examination of their practice. In his recent book *Third World Protest*, Rahul Rao offers a deeply personal and analytically cogent discussion of the impact of Western discourses of LGBT rights on Third World societies. His "central preoccupation … is to find a language in which to criticize the hierarchies and supremacism that lurk within the cosmopolitan politics of LGBT solidarity without minimizing or ignoring the oppressiveness of communitarian homophobia" (Rao, 2010: 176) (see also Rao, 2014).

Rao's discussion first turns to the celebrated work of Joseph Massad (Massad, 2008), who is not fond of "Western LGBT solidarity politics." Massad criticizes its culturally imperialistic imposition of a Western sexual ontology on Arabs, in the process destroying Indigenous sexual subjectivities. He also argues that this Western solidarity has heightened the visibility of sexual minorities, inviting repressive government interventions. Rao is not so sure that this is an adequate response, given that many Arabs do appropriate Western style LGBT identities, and do rework them as they seek sexual self-determination. Surely, he argues, something is amiss when these people are dismissed as mere "native informants" to a Western LGBT movement: "In effect, in criticizing cosmopolitan rescue politics and its local interlocutors, Massad slips into a reinforcement of communitarian authenticity narratives that police how sexual preferences ought to be expressed" (Rao, 2010: 177). By contrast, Rao suggests we consider why there might be a genuine sense of grievance against "traditional" sexual ontologies, and then to ask whether there is any usefulness in the various politics of solidarity offered by the "Gay International."

"I suppose I am one of Massad's 'native informants,'" Rao comments, before spelling out some aspects of the grievance against a "traditional sexual ontology": "The physical, mental, and emotional costs that such an ontology exacts in the form of broken relationships, sham heterosexual marriages, suicides, lack of legal and social recognition of what are otherwise deeply fulfilling personal relationships, lack of access to health care, etc. are well documented in many countries, but remain unacknowledged in Massad's argument" (Rao, 2010: 178).

Rao's "antipathy'" to Massad's analysis stems from Massad's failure to account for these costs. Whether Western solidarity politics does any better is a moot point. Rao's survey of some high-profile cases in this field ends with the wry observation that "the Gay International is an extraordinarily fractious space. … It is united by a common Western sexual ontology, but its constituents disagree radically on whether, when and how to export this ontology to the rest of the world" (Rao, 2010: 189).

Disagreement about the politics of sexual self-determination is common among Massad's "native informants": activists, people of color, Third World queers resident in the West. These, says, Rao, are "sandwiched … between a coercive liberal solidarism supportive of Western hegemony, and a variety of authoritarian pluralisms" that contest such hegemony; "malevolent communitarian homophobia" on the one hand and "condescending cosmopolitan rescue" on the other (Rao, 2010: 192).

The broader theme of Rao's book is about protest sensibilities, and, in particular, he is concerned to address the question of protest sensibility in a context where there is "no singular locus of threat" – this is the experience of such people, and Rao's interview vignettes grant the reader some sense of the dilemmas faced. He says:

> Theirs is a protest sensibility underpinned by complex imaginaries of threat, in which the quest for self-determination has entailed a struggle against both homophobia within their communities as well as salvation by international or white LGBT allies. The latter struggle has been for power and resources but also, ironically, for recognition as equals. In part, what these activists have been trying to say to their purported rescuers is that they are not just gay, but other things as well – Palestinian, Arab, Muslim – and that gay liberation that does not respect those other identities is no liberation at all. (Rao, 2010: 192)

Rao writes about the positionality of the periphery, the Third World. But the same critical themes apply within the "core," where the practice of a "queer liberalism" has forgotten the radicalism of its gay liberationist past.

Queer liberalism

Writing about the contemporary state of gay politics in the U.S., David Eng has said "Our current moment is marked by a particular coming together of economic and political spheres that form the basis for liberal inclusion ... " (Eng, 2010: 26). Eng uses the phrase "queer liberalism" to articulate this coming together, particularly in the context of "citizen-subjects petitioning for rights and recognition before the law" (Eng, 2010: 3). (For an earlier gloss on "queer liberalism," see Phelan, 2000.) Eng notes that earlier radical critiques of the state, its oppression and its accounts of family, kinship and so on, have given way to the desire for *legitimization* by the state of same-sex attachments and associated relational structures. Eng's analysis centers around the 2003 US Supreme Court decision *Lawrence v. Texas*, which declared unconstitutional a Texas statute criminalizing sodomy.

Eng's distinctive reading of *Lawrence* is salutary here because it destabilizes the achievement that many see *Lawrence* to be, and raises critical questions about the rights politics invoked by the queer movement. In his usage, *queer liberalism* denotes the inclusion of queers into the liberal political project, but in doing so it shows the *costs* of this inclusion; by reviewing these costs, Eng enjoins us to adopt or return to a more radical politics. I read this account of queer liberalism as a *cautionary tale* for those using human rights as tools for their queer global politics.

The key cautions Eng identifies have to do with the disassociation of sexuality and race, and both of these from the impact of capitalist economics and neoliberal globalization. Queer liberalism, argues Eng, engages a "colorblind" moment in U.S. politics which sets queer freedom up as an achievement that comes *after* the "completion" of the "racial project." Queer freedom is set up as "the latest political incarnation of 'the rights of man'" (Eng, 2010: 4). By contrast, Eng argues that "the emergence of queer liberalism depends upon the active management, repression, and subsuming of race" (Eng, 2010: 17). The analysis of *Lawrence* is crucial in this respect. The case itself "begins as a story of racial trespass," with a caller to the police reporting (in racially offensive terms) a weapons disturbance on the part of a black man – one of the parties in the black–white "couple" of the case (itself actually a one-night stand). Eng asks, how is it that such a story "ends as a narrative of queer freedom?" (Eng, 2010: 17).

The right to privacy emerges as the key right in *Lawrence*; Eng's analysis places this right within its history as a racialized property right. Eng's reading is not confined to the histories of intimacy, privacy, and rights; neither is it confined to the ways "in which gays and lesbians are liberated precisely by proving that they can be proper US citizen-subjects of the capitalist nation state" (Eng, 2010: 30). Rather, "homonormativity collaborates with a neo-liberalism willfully blind to unequal structures of globalization and its increasingly international gendered division of labor" (Eng, 2010: 31).

> The turning away from a sustained examination of the vast political and economic inequalities in the state, civil society, and commercial life, marks the paradoxes of queer liberalism. A renewed queer studies must insist that problems of neoliberal political economy cannot be abstracted away from the racial, gendered, and sexual hierarchies of the nation-state, but must be understood as operating in and through them. (Eng, 2010: 34)

Eng's paradoxes of queer liberalism are writ large in the global human rights project. An emerging research agenda belatedly recognizes the critical intersection between neoliberal practice and human rights, and other critical takes on human rights are also proliferating (Golder, 2012; Holder & Reidy, 2013; Douzinas & Gearty, 2014; Lutz-Bachmann & Nascimento, 2014).

"Dating the state"

As Spivak has said, we cannot *not* want rights (Spivak, 2009). But rights do not come by themselves. As we were reminded by Hagland at the beginning of this discussion, the state is still the critical institution for the recognition and enforcement of rights claims. And, it turns out, it can be quite useful for the broader political purposes of states (especially on the international stage), to play on the fact that they *do* provide rights for sexual and gender minorities within their borders (Franke, 2012: 4–5).

Katherine Franke, citing Jasbir Puar, describes these as cases where "golden handcuffs" attach gay rights to the nationalist projects being engineered by state elites (Franke, 2012: 44; see also Peterson, 1999; Puar, 2007, 2012; Peterson, 2013). Franke looks at the way in which political elites in Israel, Romania, Poland, Iran, the U.S. and the EU system utilize the politics of gay rights for purposes that undermine the broader normative framework with which such rights would normally be identified. As she comments, it is worth paying close attention to the way in which "a state's posture with respect to the rights of 'its' homosexuals has become an effective foreign policy tool" (Franke, 2012: 3).

A key example here is the way in which human rights law becomes a key tool in the extension of other global political projects – such as the internationalization of neoliberal governance systems. The importance of human rights law in credentialing states as suitable members of economic and political communities (like the European Union) is fundamental here – and is also, as Franke bluntly puts it, "bankrupt." There are two senses in which this is the case. First, some human rights abuses rank higher than others: gay rights are the shibboleth; get that sorted and you are waved through, with other egregious abuses quietly ignored. Worse – especially when it comes to economic and social rights – such states end up hosting the human rights fallout of the West's neoliberal economic expansion (its "new markets" and their benefits to a select few).

Second, the articulation through this process of a "necessary relationship between identity formation, recognition, and rights ... makes an epistemic claim that risks a kind of violence in many contexts ..." (Franke, 2012: 31–32). Referencing the Yogyakarta Principles, Franke argues that while these are "seemingly progressive, inclusive, and dignity respecting," they nonetheless make claims about human sexuality and gender that do not leave room for alternative ways of being (cf. Thoreson, 2009; Waites, 2009).

Franke says she is concerned with "who and what is actualized when the LGBT subject is given a voice through the intervention of human rights." It is clear that when this intervention comes from states, "a 'gay right' is not a 'gay right' is not a 'gay right'" (Franke, 2012: 39). The gay whose politics and subject position, ethnicity and religion, suits the agenda of the state may find himself to be the "good citizen" who receives recognition, identity, and status. But at whose cost? Franke is unequivocal about this:

> Noting the duplicity of the state's homo-friendliness is not enough. Rather the "patriotized" rights-bearing LGBT subject and "its" movement have a duty to actively resist being mustered into nationalist projects undertaken in its name and purportedly on its behalf. (Franke, 2012: 40)

Gay rights instrumentalized as an oppressive tool of foreign policy seems a perverse legacy of gay liberation, and raises critical questions regarding how to theorize the politics of sexuality and gender rights in the international, as well as fundamental questions about the nature and performance of rights politics itself. If the usefulness of rights is in some sense linked to them being powers deployed by the state, how is it possible for us, as Franke puts it, to do a rights politics that resists occupation by the state? Queering our politics, then, demands "a refusal to take up the frames, and the identities those frames call up, which 'winning' our rights produces" (Franke, 2012: 46). More poignantly, it is to refuse the seduction and embrace of the state at that point when the state seems to come on side; it is to recognize the *queerness* of that point: a moment of deep danger as well as one of liberation; a moment destabilizing in its possibilities for both emancipation and requisition.

Conclusion

From this survey of international theory, global LGBT politics, and human rights, the salience of the queer claim that sexuality and gender politics might legitimately – even unavoidably – shape and guide our interpretations of international politics in general is evident. Both Hagland and Weber demonstrate ways in which, in this regard, conventional international theory is unable or has refused to critically engage with the complexities of its own subject matter. Many of these complexities can be apprehended when looking through the queer lens of international sexuality and gender politics. Doing so destabilizes conventional categories and approaches, illuminating a range of practices of the international that often go unremarked. Human rights examined through the complexity of global sexuality and gender politics make the familiar utility of a rights politics strange, by showing how its easy categories can fail its assumed emancipatory intent. It can also, however, make the strange familiar, as Thoreson reminds us: showing the ways in which the practices of global sexualities and gender identities, with their capacity to destabilize the standard categories we use to interpret international politics, nonetheless open spaces for different forms of critical emancipatory global politics.

In the second part of this chapter, I illustrated some of these "showings" by considering four different approaches to human rights. In each of these – performativity, positionality, queer liberalism, and state critique – the familiar is first made strange, and is then used to make strange ways of looking at international politics familiar once again – familiar, at least, to those engaged by critical, emancipatory desire. These nuanced and sophisticated accounts of practices within the global politics of sexuality and gender identity may seem queer and strange to conventional international and human rights theorists; in being so, however, they speak with enormous critical power to the most fundamental questions regarding the nature of the international today.

Acknowledgements

This chapter was completed while I was a visiting fellow at the Centre for Advanced International Theory at the University of Sussex, in 2014. I would like to thank the Director of the Centre, Beate Jahn, and its members for their generous hospitality, friendship, and intellectual camaraderie.

Suggested further reading

Altman D (2001) *Global Sex*. Chicago: University of Chicago Press.
Binnie J (2004) *The Globalization of Sexuality*. London: Sage.
Blasius M (2001) *Sexual Identities. Queer Politics*. Princeton, NJ: Princeton University Press.
Duggan L (2003) *The Twilight of Equality: Neoliberalism, Cultural Politics, and the Attack on Democracy*. Boston, MA: Beacon Press.
Wilkinson C and Langlois A J (eds.) (2014) Not such an international human rights norm? Local resistance to Lesbian, gay, bisexual, and transgender rights. *Journal of Human Rights* 13: 3.

Bibliography

Altman D (2001) *Global Sex*. Chicago: University of Chicago Press.
Douzinas C and Gearty C (eds.) (2014) *The Meanings of Rights: The Philosophy and Social Theory of Human Rights*. Cambridge: Cambridge University Press.
Dworkin R (1978) *Taking Rights Seriously*. Cambridge, MA: Harvard University Press.
Eng D L (2010) *The Feeling of Kinship: Queer Liberalism and the Racialization of Intimacy*. Durham, NC: Duke University Press.
Foster E, Kerr P, Hopkins A, Byrne C, and Ahall L (2012) The personal is not political: at least in the UK's top politics and IR departments. *British Journal of Politics & International Relations*. http://doi.wiley.com/10.1111/j.1467–1856X.2011.00500.x
Franke K (2012) Dating the state: the moral hazards of winning gay rights. *Columbia Human Rights Law Review* 44(1): 1–46.
Golder B (2012) *Re-reading Foucault: On Law, Power and Rights*. New York: Routledge.
Goodale M (2013) Human rights and moral agency. In: Holder C & Reidy D (eds.) *Human Rights: The Hard Questions*. Cambridge: Cambridge University Press.
——(2014) Human rights after the post-Cold War, reprint edn. In: Goodale M (ed.) *Human Rights at the Crossroads*. Oxford: Oxford University Press.
Hagland P E (1997) International theory and LGBT politics: testing the limits of a human rights-based strategy. *GLQ: A Journal of Lesbian and Gay Studies* 3(4): 357–84.
Holder C and Reidy D (2013) *Human Rights: The Hard Questions*. Cambridge: Cambridge University Press.
Hopgood S (2013) *The Endtimes of Human Rights*. Ithaca, NY: Cornell University Press.
Langlois A J (2001) *The Politics of Justice and Human Rights: Southeast Asia and Universalist Theory*. Cambridge: Cambridge University Press.
——(2014a) Human rights, "orientation", and ASEAN. *Journal of Human Rights* 13(3): 307–21.
——(2014b) Performing human rights: the meaning of rights in the ASEAN Intergovernmental Commission on Human Rights. In: Yeatman A (ed.) *The Aporia of Rights: Explorations in Citizenship in the Era of Human Rights*. London: Bloomsbury Academic.
Lutz-Bachmann M and Nascimento A (eds.) (2014) *Human Rights, Human Dignity, and Cosmopolitan Ideals: Essays on Critical Theory and Human Rights*. Burlington, VT: Ashgate.
Massad J A (2008) *Desiring Arabs*. Chicago: University of Chicago Press.
Merry S E (2006) Transnational human rights and local activism: mapping the middle. *American Anthropologist* 108(1): 38–51.
Nash K (2011) States of human rights. *Sociologica* 43(6): 1–20. http://www.sociologica.mulino.it/journal/article/index/Article/Journal:ARTICLE:455/Item/Journal:ARTICLE: 455
Peterson V S (1999) Political identities/nationalism as heterosexism. *International Feminist Journal of Politics* 1(1): 34–65.
——(2013) The intended and unintended queering of states/nations. *Studies in Ethnicity and Nationalism* 13(1): 57–68.
Phelan S (2000) Queer liberalism? *American Political Science Review* 94(2): 431–42.
Puar J K (2007) *Terrorist Assemblages: Homonationalism in Queer Times*. Durham, NC: Duke University Press.

——(2012) The golden handcuffs of gay rights: how pinkwashing distorts both LGBTIQ and anti-occupation activism. *The Feminist Wire*. http://thefeministwire.com/2012/01/the-golden-handcuffs-of-gay-rights-how-pinkwashing-distorts-both-lgbtiq-and-anti-occupation-activism/

Rao R(2010) *Third World Protest: Between Home and the World*. Oxford: Oxford University Press.

——(2014) Queer questions. *International Feminist Journal of Politics* 16(2): 1–19.

Reus-Smit C and Snidal D (2010) *The Oxford Handbook of International Relations*. Oxford: Oxford University Press.

Seckinelgin H and Paternotte D (forthcoming) "Lesbian and gay rights are human rights": Multiple globalizations and lesbian and gay activism. In: Paternotte D & Tremblay M (eds.) *The Ashgate Research Companion to Lesbian and Gay Activism*. Farnham: Ashgate.

Smith N J and Lee D (2014) What's queer about political science? *British Journal of Politics & International Relations:* 1–15. http://onlinelibrary.wiley.com/doi/10.1111/1467–1856X.12037/abstract

Spivak G C (2009) *Outside in the Teaching Machine*. New York: Routledge.

Sylvester C (2007) Whither the international at the end of IR1. *Millennium – Journal of International Studies* 35(3): 551–73.

Symons J and Altman D (forthcoming) International norm polarization: sexuality as a subject of human rights protection. *International Theory*.

Thoreson R R (2009) Queering human rights: the Yogyakarta Principles and the norm that dare not speak its name. *Journal of Human Rights* 8(4): 323–39.

——(2011) The queer paradox of LGBTI human rights. *Interalia: A Journal of Queer Studies* 6: 1–27.

Waites M (2009) Critique of "sexual orientation" and "gender identity" in human rights discourse: global queer politics beyond the Yogyakarta Principles. *Contemporary Politics* 15(1): 137–56.

Weber C (2014) Why is there no queer international theory? *European Journal of International Relations:* 1–25.

Wight M (1960) Why is there no international theory? *International Relations* 2(1): 35–48.

Zivi K (2011) *Making Rights Claims: A Practice of Democratic Citizenship*. Oxford: Oxford University Press.

2

TO LOVE OR TO LOATHE

Modernity, homophobia, and LGBT rights

Michael J. Bosia

Introduction

Hail ricocheted off the pavement outside the ill-fitting door. Beyoncé, founder of Transgender Equality Uganda, met us at her Kampala office in a state-owned compound once housing the Uganda AIDS Commission Secretariat. We found ourselves trapped by the sudden downpour, so we talked – her assistant working on the computer. I kept one eye on the water falling across the threshold and flowing slowly toward the bundle of electrical cables on the floor. Beyoncé was indifferent to the danger, instead consumed by her relationship with the compound's manager, which made her presence there precarious amidst an unfolding story about the complications of gender and sexuality in a context of extreme state homophobia.

The scene reveals the unevenness of modernity and the importance of relationships in the system of crony capitalism surrounding the dictatorship of longtime President Yoweri Museveni. It also illustrates that the Ugandan state is in the midst of a differently penetrating development project: the imposition of a modern conceptualization of homosexuality, and with it the consolidation of the gender and sexual binaries where Beyoncé now finds herself. Within two decades, the state has gone from purposeful near silence on the predominately pre-politicized same gender practices to a chorus of public and private voices singing the perils of Western LGBT rights in near perfect harmony, conjuring at the same time it condemns a weak but emergent LG rights movement Beyoncé feels distanced from because she identifies as a woman. President Museveni gives out SUVs to his favorite pastors and provides support to Christian churches preaching the dangers of the "gay agenda," international assistance for HIV/AIDS prevention for men who have sex with men is under attack, homosexuality remains criminalized, the tabloid press splays sexual accusations across newsstands and television, and same-gender marriage has been prohibited by constitutional amendment. The newest proposals provide life imprisonment in certain cases, bar advocacy for sexual rights, and require the public to inform on suspected sexual minorities (Bosia, 2013; Kaoma, 2013).

Uganda is not unique. State homophobia has been the helpmate of the Western modernist project since the British spread sodomy laws throughout their empire in the nineteenth century (Ramasubban, 2007; Human Rights Watch, 2008; Sanders, 2009), and the association of homosexuality with modernity continues well into the era of LGBT rights (Bosia & Weiss, 2013; Rahman, 2014). But it is not only in overt hostility that state homophobia exists. In France today, for example, we see a government embracing marriage equality to reconstitute lesbian and gay subjects within heteronormative family life while, at the very same time, denying these couples any right to procreation other than adoption.[1] To compound the irony, lesbian and gay couples must now officially recognize the primacy of childrearing in conjugal life in signing the marriage contract at city hall.

In this chapter, I consider the regulation of homosexuality writ large as a process of state as part of the literature on the deployments of modernity as racial trope in the West and as a kind of self-righteousness among activists anticipating inevitable progress toward universal rights – theirs being a "sexual modernization theory" (Bosia & Weiss, 2013). While present in the challenge of LGBT activists (and a few states) in the West to those developing countries where remarkably similar homophobic rhetoric and laws are part of a toolkit drawn from to solidify rule, it is also within the West, where homophobia is considered an aspect of "tradition" inevitably to be overcome. Both affirm a nativist discourse about national superiority and modernity in the present. Here, I look to the state as the animator of progress, entering the debate over modernity as a unique set of social conditions emanating from the West that mark the modern from the premodern or "backward." Taking sexuality and gender as both productive and controlling because these systems are produced *as the modern*, I examine them as they serve the state through either repression or rights. In essence, the state's motivation is not homophobia per se, but an array of processes of "homosexualization" (Roscoe, 1997) as statecraft within the state's sovereign interest in rule as a process of war. In this way, the state is revealed as the universal stamp of modernity and a psychopath indifferent to questions of sexuality outside their effect on state building.

Homosexualization can range in degree from vociferous condemnations to seductive embraces with partial (or strategic) recognition. Excepting a few consensus-oriented small democracies, changes in legal status have produced much less change in rhetoric, often instead provoking more vociferous debate and a spike in private violence. In Paris, for example, access to marriage occurred in the context of intra-partisan contestation on the right, which exacerbated rising nationalist and xenophobic discontent, followed swiftly by an outburst of anti-gay and lesbian violence unseen in years. As well, "homonormative" discourses about marriage equality (Duggan, 2002) incapacitate other sexual minorities through the authorization of same-gender unions, denying civil status to not-going-to-marry lesbians and gay men as well as bisexual and transgender individuals, culminating in the emergence of a racialized homonationalism coincident with the War on Terror (Puar, 2007). More pronounced as antipathy, a heteronormative imperative or hegemony (Berlant & Warner, 1998) privileges a gender binary, but even as it denies significant recognition to homosexuality as a parallel sexual orientation, I note it also allows recognition of certain individual civic or market rights, such as employment or housing, in ways obscuring the social relationships of lesbians and gay men. Heterosexism or compulsory heterosexuality (Rich, 1994; Boellstorff, 2004) authorizes only explicit heterosexual family and social relationships while enforcing legal or social prohibition against lesbians, gay men, bisexual or transgender individuals, and other sexual minorities. These categories can exist simultaneously, often differentially empowered across time and between or within elite circles as in France, or heterosexism can exist as the primary ideology of state and social actors, as is emerging in Uganda.

Still, legal and social repression – carried on waves of neoliberalism, evangelism, and conflict (Bosia, 2013) – is shaping a Western gay menace as a preferred trope in statecraft as far afield as Russia and Uganda. Especially with HIV prevalent and prevention support necessary, homosexuality becomes overtly political, a process magnified in states in which the alternatives for legitimizing rule, like targeting ethnic groups or chastising foreign economic interests, would do more to undermine from below or destabilize from above. In these climates, police enforcement is heightened against activists and organizations who seek simple modifications of state practice, like the provision of HIV prevention materials. Arrest is followed by media exposé – one Ugandan transgender woman was forced to strip inside a police station and again outside in front of a crowd; the scene was broadcast on television that evening.[2] In the wake of revelation, those identified lose housing and employment, and face vigilantes, as another activist eventually finding refuge in Paris told me.[3] After his name was published, his life spiraled out of control: his family abandoned him, his business closed, and he was evicted by his landlord. He moved into a room in a slum on the outskirts of Kampala, far from social support, and lived on aid from friends. He was soon joined by others in similar circumstances, and, with growing harassment from neighbors, he was eventually able to claim exile in Europe with the support of AIDS activists. When the arrest is not made public, police extract a payoff in exchange for freedom, as part of a cycle of enforcement augmenting inadequate salaries, so the sanctioning of blackmail against sexual minorities amounts to state organized redistribution of resources.[4]

This evidence grounds my conceptualization of "state homophobia" as such rhetorical, legal, and physical attacks, largely structured as Western deviance, in places as disparate as Paris, Cairo, Moscow, and Kampala. Although "homophobia" is a troublingly raced and gendered Western word (Manalansan, 2009) that insinuates a particular sexual and gender order widely unfamiliar globally until recently, the term (as modified with "state") captures a particular set of policies, practices, and rhetoric deployed by state actors, allies, contenders, or proxies, who around the world speak of "gays," "lesbians," "men marrying men," "homosexuality," and even a U.S. or European "gay agenda." It seems appropriate if the form of oppression draws so explicitly from the West, then the term we use to analyze it should provoke those

Western origins. At the same time, I am not concerned with sexual oppression in terms of private beliefs, religion, or tradition as constraining, because I see the power of the state in its ability to manipulate and transform beliefs, religion, and tradition. Similarly, to speak of LG/LGBT rights or activists recognizes a particular set of more-or-less institutional settings where political identities, claims, and rights are framed and propagated even if practitioners themselves might personally (or domestically) prefer a localized terminology such as "kuchu" while they use LGBT internationally.

Homosexualizing modernity

While others interrogate LGBT rights as a marker of *Western* modernity universalized (Massad, 2007; Puar, 2007; Rahman, this volume), I instead examine the saturation of modernity with state homophobia that gives life to the very notion of homosexuality it seeks to abort. The values privileged within and through the categories of homophobia more often presage or at least trace the rise of LGBT rights (Bosia & Weiss, 2013); indeed, modernity first produces homosexualization – the idea of the homosexual as deviant – and then the reaction to this process from sexual minorities. Today, sexuality is wholly and variously linked with the neoliberal and imperial needs of the post-millennial state (Bosia, 2013), where the globalizing and neoliberal impulse fostering both homonormativity and homophobia arises in and is pushed by an Anglo-American West that sees itself as singular and uncontested modernity, against a variety of "easts" in Europe and across a world it constitutes in anticipation of liberation.

Similarly, where some imply nation as predominant in modernity's racializations and homosexualizations (Puar, 2007), I consider the sovereign state as it concretized and is concretizing all modernities – the ubiquitous political form enacting the universal and the exceptions it characterizes as backward arising in Anglo-American "sexual modernization." It is the Western state preceding and carrying the nation; the state promising progress in bureaucracy, capitalism, and neoliberalism; the state enabling and profiting from empire; the state preceding and carrying what many mistakenly consider the source of its own demise – globalization; and, it is the state structuring sexuality through both its regulatory and cultural power: as normative, exceptional, differentiated, national, and foreign. If we look at how Western modernity has shaped the world, we can find no force as powerful or universally embraced as the state; it is an obvious fact that the state, despite differences in governance, capacity, and territoriality, claims sovereignty nearly everywhere.

Perhaps its very ubiquity and banality renders the state often invisible in analyses of modernity when devoid of its hyphenated modifier (nation-), preoccupied as such analysis might be with cultural dimensions or economic masters of the state instead of sovereign rule as the source of empire or resistance. In contrast, I draw from Peterson in describing the state as a "bearer" of things (1992) – nation, gender, sexuality, etc. – and modernity as the beneficiary of early state consolidation. While Peterson considers the "mutually interactive projects characteristic of modernity" to include the state (14), I see the sovereign state as uniquely marking modernity, because it creates proprietary and discrete interests and practices informing the norms and expectations of empowered actors and so gives force to modernizing impulses. The state, constitutive of internal actors, allies, proxies and contenders for state power who animate it, is both a historical creation, deriving its interests and practices over the *longue durée*, and a group of *bricoleurs* who apply the modes of analysis and action inherited from the past and innovated in the present.[5] As global and local, they are situated between domestic and international actors[6] who cooperate or are in conflict. And while sexuality and gender are deep and durable facets of governing regimes, like racial formations they are subject to revision and resistance (Winant, 2000), which enables today's *bricoleurs* to deploy a state homophobia more impromptu, cascading, strategic, and purposeful than it is hegemonic, disembodied, or unreflexive.

With the state's bellicose origins and training distinctly Western – even if in other parts derived from beyond the West – and over time adopted or imposed and indigenized outside the West, the state is the ultimate "globalized localism" (Santos, 2006): rooted firmly in Europe, paradigmatic everywhere. Likely a result of this ubiquitous indigeneity crafted by state actors themselves, scholars and activists critical of the state more often than not overlook its Janus-like impulses – to love or to loathe with equal indifference – which indicate its psychopathological nature. Arendt, for example, called our attention to the deprivation of rights suffered by those rendered outside the state (1979) – seeming to call for a politics of state intervention – and the most ardent contemporary critics of the state, like Scott, see in the human experience some way to master the psychopath (Scott, 1998). My perspective suggests the state yields to no master and is faithful ally to none, so claims to the state for rights are precarious scaffolding balancing on the interests of actors who animate an institution formed for other preoccupations.

If the scene with Beyoncé hints at state homophobia, there are a variety of existential reasons for state actors, allies, contenders, and proxies to make this move: from strategic utility in the course of challenges from above or below (Bosia, 2013) to the management of development or security (Johnson, 2004; Canaday, 2009; Lee, 2011), to inscribing or resisting global or domestic dominance (Puar, 2007; Rahman, 2014). Sometimes, policy change and debate might seem haphazard and impromptu, with the rhetoric of homophobia underdeveloped and recombinant. Often, however, the precise content of rhetoric cascades across borders as it is embraced with or without regard to local understandings and traditions (Weiss & Bosia, 2013). Sexual minorities are then reconstituted ("homosexualized") as homosexual or LGBT subjects and targets of state action, even as these new subjects might cast about on the internet or learn from tourists about gay worlds beyond. It seems to me obvious that it would be difficult to seek out LGBT identities in such climates if the homosexualizing force of state homophobia did not give life to them in the first place.

The relative but seemingly uniform dispersal of heterosexism from state to state across the West since the nineteenth century, with its medicalization and criminalization of homosexuality, blurred its multiple points of origins in ways naturalizing and *de*-historicizing the emerging sexual binary. It also made the subsequent spread of LGBT activism across Europe and out from the U.S. appear to scholars not as a response to state homophobia but as *deus ex machina* in need of structural explanations such as economic transformation (Adam, 1985) or the forces of cultural globalization (Binnie, 2004; Murray, 2007). With much focus in the social sciences on either the local origins of LGBT activism or the transnational linkages between activists, the concerted and purposeful embrace of homophobia by state actors, allies, contenders, and proxies was largely ignored (Bosia & Weiss, 2013). And as the emergence of multiple LGBT or homosexual communities coincided with wider opportunities for travel and communication, it appeared as if singular geographic points in the U.S. marked the origins of a wave of change (Puar, 2007; Bosia, 2009). This same emphasis on movement (and now broadly Western origins) continued when the study of LGBT rights and identities expanded beyond the West, as if LGBT identities came out of European and North American struggles on a wave of tourism, scholarly research, and global human rights activism (Massad, 2007).

Such approaches undervalue the inextricable link between Beyoncé's life and the statecraft of President Yoweri Museveni seen in his growing invocation of homosexuality as a foreign menace in order to craft or solidify constituencies supporting the state's modernizing project. Even after early HIV/AIDS activists, policy advocates, and providers had put sexual rights and recognition on the prevention agenda globally (Altman, 1999; Weiss, 2006; Peacock et al., 2009), in Uganda, the effect on sexuality was minimal, and same gender sexual expression among men remained unspoken throughout the 1990s and even within the primary AIDS organization, TASO.[7] This did not stop Museveni from launching his campaign against homosexuality in 1998, which began with his denying there was any homosexuality in Uganda and continued as Museveni was embraced by the Bush administration and U.S. evangelicals as a second front in the War on Terror. For Beyoncé, the emerging climate meant few opportunities and, turning to sex work, frequent harassment from police. Today, she speaks about her experiences as a transgender woman as very different from those of gay and transgender men. She has been able to maneuver around the vociferous homophobia by calling attention to her gender identity, explaining to me that she eventually bonded with the government's manager at the office compound because she insisted she is a woman and not homosexual.

The state and Western modernity

Transformational capacity is the fundamental aspect of Western modernity, as modernity is shaped by rearrangements of time and space through which the local is no longer imagined as constricting and history is crafted as linear and progressive (Anderson, 1983; Giddens, 1990). This rearrangement makes possible the "disembedding" of social systems in order to universalize them, and scientific knowledge classifies social relationships so they might be reordered and improved as an ongoing process (Giddens, 1990: 17). Modernity sees itself as progressive and imperial, surpassing its own premodern superstitions to improve the human condition, and so uniquely qualified to instruct others while building the future – instruction in the superior nature of rational enlightenment in conflict with the traditions of an imagined Orient the West itself defined in the colonial era and continues to refine and define (Said, 1979).

The disruptive practices of transformation must be cast in terms of the exclusive character of modernity, deciding the rule and the exception to the rule. Modern institutions and modern reason give no ground to alternatives unless such alternatives are derived and authorized within the modernist paradigm. For Santos, modernity – in its monocultural formulations of scientific classification, universality, historical time, and capitalist efficiency – effaces all other varieties of knowing not authorized (2006). This knowledge empowered sets out to apprehend the particular within the global, then universalizes human experience in ways producing either the absence or insignificance of those modes of life incompatible with modern universality. The peculiar eccentricity of the modern is in describing, transforming, and discarding in one motion, creating what it means to be modern at the same time it creates a desire for the modern (Appadurai, 1996).

Yet, a variety of social practices, knowledges, and actors from locations around the world *inform* modernity: either alongside or preexisting modernity in the West, "borrowed," or as contrasting and reinforcing Western superiority along a linear notion of progress and development. So, modernity is decidedly local, arising in a particular European ferment around the Enlightenment and addressing the specific challenges of situated historical moments (Giddens, 1990). Its aspirations are always global outside the West and local within, rendering social practice legible within the West at the same time it subjects the non-West to the same transformations and erasures (Scott, 1998), animating modernity from its metropoles across a variety of peripheries (see Lebovics, 2004, on Paris, its provinces, and empire). In the nineteenth century, economic and political development as well as conquest, scientific expedition, and empire affirmed modernity as a European project with North American implications. After the First World War, Europeans in exhaustion and disillusionment ceded centrality to the U.S. (Hobsbawm, 1994).

The Western state made the Enlightenment possible, and the state is the animating and defining empowered institution (even if some say alongside capitalism) of modernity (Giddens, 1985, 1990). The process of statecraft as Europeans consolidated territory under sovereign rule formed new imperatives for the state and new demands on society requiring new ways of thinking and understanding. The sovereign state first questioned the spiritual by rendering the church subservient to the sovereign, and the sovereign state needed to order trade and accumulate capital, regulate provinces and colonies, produce armaments and wage war, settle peace, and legitimate rule. Later, as the colonial subject sought to oust the master, liberation turned to the state to do so (in the case of French West Africa, after demanding the Rights of Man instead).

European statecraft was embedded in contestation between rulers, and between the rulers and the ruled, as Europe fought its way out of the decentralizing and overlapping authorities of feudalism. Even prior to the Enlightenment, sovereign authority sought to eliminate internal competition at the same time it sought to consolidate and expand territory, two characteristics supported through a sovereign protection racket as a system of organized extraction (Tilly, 1985). The state defined the enemy, and then promised security against the enemy for the subject, even if security was against the predations of the state itself. As the technologies and extent of warmaking and security increased, production and wealth did as well, fueling more centralizing, warmaking, and extraction. Only when the state apparatus was seen as excessive did subjects negotiate limits on the state's authority.

As they consolidated, European states were never satiated. So the Enlightenment emphasis on knowledge and classification was uniquely suited to the state, enabling authorities to see society, population, and geography through means matching their expansive need for revenues, soldiers, and internal security (Scott, 1998). As Scott explains, states developed systems of classification and measurement enabling the radical transformations making diverse phenomena more precise, ordered, and clear. Everything from land tenure to family names, language to urban planning, weights and measures – the realms of physical and social governance enabled by modernity – were transformed from localized, differentiated and incomprehensible from the out-side, to standardized, uncomplicated, and universally accessible (ibid.). Similarly, the capabilities of modernity were put to good use as states implemented, refined, and globalized the mechanisms of capitalist market economies and later sought to protect themselves from the transformations they had unleashed (Polanyi, 1957).

These modernist assumptions enabled and compelled the transformation of sexual identities in order to cultivate reproductive social relations that the state can apprehend and regulate (Canaday, 2009; Lee, 2011). I see this both as directly in service of state power and as a means for consolidating governing coalitions. Indeed, the regulation of homosexuality emphasizes the modernist vision and the pragmatic amalgamation of knowledge and authority. Although sodomy was pro-hibited across Europe long before modernity, and decriminalized in France during the Revolution, it is well known that homosexuality as a status of being is a product of scientific knowledge and its exploitation over the course of the nineteenth and twentieth centuries (Greenberg, 1988). Through state administrative and policing powers as well as new modes of psychiatric treatment, same-gender sexual practices were redefined as homosexuality, an illness, and the homosexual who resulted was subject to the collaborative enforcement power of the state and medical establish-ment. As pragmatic bricolage, sexuality as a system of social regulation went hand in hand with state building through the creation of a sexed population (Rubin, 1993; Najmabadi, 2005; Peterson, 2013). In fact, homosexuality was never cured. Like the statecraft empowering particular ruling coalitions at the center of the state through racial regulation (Marx, 1998), homosexuality became a very public object of state building, framed through political contestation over state authority in national terms, sometimes to emphasize foreign or domestic dangers (Fejes, 2000) and at others to craft seditious conspiracies only a strong security apparatus could unveil (Johnson, 2004).

With this powerful creative capacity in mind, we must realize the state is not morally neutral; it is above and before morality: first, as it is the precursor to law and to the authority to institute and localize law; and second, as it exercises its power to shape the polity and the space where the polity is constituted through exception (Agamben, 1998). Not only does the sovereign state have the capacity to decide who is within the law and the others who can be extinguished through but outside the law, it also describes both the crisis and the state of exception feeding on times of crisis so that it is possible for the sovereign to regularize, as law, the extralegal and irregular (Agamben, 2005). In my mind, this is where the state is best revealed: a fundamental nature not imposing order, but masking order to craft disorder and consolidate power against it. The state, then, enacts a series of motivations to inspire a constitutive bargain, building acquiescence to and participation in rule as sovereign against lives (and people) whose existence as exceptional renders the bargain uncontested. The excepted, outside the state and so outside the modern, are rendered stateless and modern-less in order to seal the contrast with an advanced society well governed by a modern state. This process is devoid of morality, because the moral perspective of sovereignty can only be obtained within the ordering of sovereign communities against the exception defining such exclusions as morally grounded (ibid.).

To consider the state as psychopath draws from clinical manifestation in a standard set of symptoms: like the psychopath, the state has no other interests than its own, devoid of empathy or truthfulness, but at the same time attractive and even charming (Cleckley, 1988). The psychopath's suicidal tendencies are mirrored in the state's claims of existential threat always imminent; lacking irony, the state inspires a faith in its immortality at the same time it cultivates a sense of its precarity. Hence, it is the state's character – as the product of the Western – without which modernity could not have made universal that which is uniquely particular, in the exercise of its power to transform natural and social life so as to improve the productive capacity of the earth and society for its own sovereign ends, and its ability to transform the "other" into the excepted. The result has been, at times, what Scott (1998) calls the "high modernist" projects so ambitious that they bring misery in their failure. If the twentieth century is the "age of massacres" (Hobsbawm, 1994), and the first light of the twenty-first century demonstrates a "state of exception" (Agamben, 2005), it is because the Western state, as Freud wrote in the first months of war 100 years ago, "has forbidden to the individual the practice of wrongdoing, not because it desired to abolish it, but because it desires to monopolize it" (Freud, 1915).

The state and homonationalism

With the state's capacity to generate sexualities through authorization and prohibition, the development of an LGBT identity occurs definitively in reaction to the consolidation of sexual deviance, with rights claims responding to the prohibitions established by state action: antidiscrimination, for example, because employment is blocked. As Duggan and Hunter (1996) demonstrate, initial claims to privacy in the U.S. come as state and media collaboration renders the homosexual publically legible, just as similar collaboration is doing today in Uganda. Later, as the state bars the "promotion of homosexuality," LGBT activism shifts to the right to speak. A set of Western LGBT rights, then, is produced in response to repression as part of the state's agenda, and the globalization of this model occurs most effectively where state homophobia imposes the model as a gay bogeyman, in advance of LGBT rights organizing on the ground – or at most while such work is embryonic (Bosia & Weiss, 2013). Repression and liberation are effectively twin aspects of modernization.

In Puar's work (2007), "homonationalism" links LGBT rights in the West and the War on Terror's imperial, missionary impulses inside and outside the West, revealing the consequences of a state-centered claim to rights. LGBT organizations normalize homosexuality through the endorsement of marriage and access to the military, the latter in particular magnified in the racialized and gendered reaction to September 11 as gay rights goes global. While attentive to the genealogy of homosexuality, Puar focuses primarily on the cost of these moves in terms of their reinscription of both U.S. and global narratives of white and heterosexual privilege, in part through a neoliberal privatization of sexuality and its concomitant deradicalization. Like Massad (2007), Puar seeks to challenge the specificity of LGBT rights as known in the U.S. – as historical progress and an attribute of modernity used to create racial hierarchies excluding other states from the benefits of modern state sovereignty.

Where Massad (2007) creates an empowered international actor out of a yet to be globalized LGBT movement in reality hobbled by AIDS, conservative ascendancy, and the revival of religious politics, Puar is more sensitive to the complications of U.S. conservatism and the LGBT reaction, including the twin pillars of the Bush administration after 2001: vigorous defense of heterosexual marriage and the War on Terror. Nevertheless, like Massad, she selectively reads LGBT politics. In contrast, paying closer attention to LGBT rights claims responding to racial and sexual rubrics of state homophobia in the context of neoliberal globalization in particular, provides a more complete understanding of how homonationalism might corrupt sexual liberation, as does a broader examination of LGBT rights globally. In France, for example, many LGBT leaders were initially indifferent to the elite drive for marriage access on the left in 2012 – wary of a moderate left embracing aspects of neoliberal reform. Indifference yielded to outrage, however, as the conservative party ended a flirtation with LGBT moderates and endorsed a growing movement among religious and nationalist organizations opposed to the law. Similarly, proposals for a civil union law in the 1990s were met with demands for access to marriage in order to outflank a government activists had been fighting over the expulsion of immigrants for most of its tenure. These same activists organized against the war in Afghanistan in 2001, marching under banners that indicated more people died every day from AIDS than had died on September 11 in New York. In Uganda, the first engagements with the government addressed the need for access to HIV-related services that the government refused to extend to a population rendered invisibly foreign by the president. Only later after a process of homosexualization under evangelical auspices did activists begin to define themselves in terms of LGBT identities deserving of specific protections.

Finally, when Puar and others (see Rao, 2010) suggest homonationalism's essentializing "rescue" discourse serves to bolster the modernizing mission under-girding the War on Terror, their argument points to "colonialism, nation formation, and empire" (Puar, 2007: 49) exclusive of the universal state with its Janus-like multiplicities. This neglects a full understanding of the populations to be rescued and the forces they need to be rescued from. LGBT Ugandans, for example, are objects of rescue because of both localized state homophobia that renders homo-sexuality decidedly Western and the legacies of the Bush administration's injection of evangelical politics from the West (Kaoma, 2013). On one level, in the West we do see slippage over time from normalization to the embrace of empire; never-theless, Uganda remains at the forefront of both empire's War on Terror and in a battle between U.S. evangelicals and LGBT advocates.

Seeing the state: loving or loathing

It is ironic to use a diagnostic term from a field with such complicated relationships to modernity and homosexuality, and purposefully so. My argument is that this psychopath – LGBT loving or loathing – is a self-interested entity suspended between domestic and global politics, so enticing as the universal love object in political struggle, even if unintendedly. This argument drives my understanding of the state as uniquely positioned and empowered to animate modernity and the pro-cesses, procedures, and knowledges unleashed as the modern, for its own sustenance and development. *Seeing the state* focuses our attention on empowered actors, allies, proxies, and contenders for state power to illuminate the manipulations of and contestations over the national imaginary through the construction of belonging from the top down and empire from the metropole out (Anderson, 1983). This is how, in fact, the state, dressed up in national drag, becomes a siren whose call is as tempting to the excluded as it is to the included, so those marginalized by race (or for us gender or sexuality) are constituted through the terms of citizenship they also struggle against (Marx, 1998).

It also means all states by nature are unreliable, and the nexus of homo-sexualization and the psychopathology of the state requires our suspicion of even apparently pro-LGBT policies. We can draw conclusions about homophilia by applying Marx's comparative study of race politics (1998) serving to craft and consolidate constituencies. In the same way, we see the Obama administration's sudden embrace of global LGBT rights after 2011 as both constituency affirmation at home – in the context of leftwing and youth disillusionment – and susceptible to the geopolitical security interests of the world's primary superpower abroad. Similarly, this is a much better explanation for the shift of the administration from anti- to pro-LG marriage than assuming one was the President's honest belief and the other a political charade.

The LGBT rights agenda, then, is now tethered to the global interests of the U.S. On Russia, for example, the President chastised Vladimir Putin for his country's anti-LGBT legislation at the same time he condemned the grant of asylum to

National Security Agency whistleblower Edward Snowden, and the next day announced he was cancelling a meeting with Putin over the latter dispute but not the former. The most significant effort against Russia has been the composition of the U.S. Olympic Team sent to Sochi, and all efforts on LGBT rights were trumped by Russia's role in both controlling Syrian chemical weapons and the crisis in Ukraine. Elsewhere, U.S. condemnations of Uganda over a similar law have been complicated by a deep relationship on national security and development. With some military support delayed or cancelled, the administration did issue the first direct actions targeting any government over LGBT issues in U.S. history. However, unlike the moves taken against Russia during the annexation of Crimea, the efforts against Uganda were not described in their entirety as "sanctions," and in fact the announcement only used the word sanction in terms of actions targeting specific individuals, and not the government. Neither did they name the individuals targeted, as they did for those in Russia.[8] And the list published by Ugandan media[9] includes no top allies of Museveni, but instead only a few religious leaders notorious for inciting Western-style homophobia and a short list of parliamentarians and government officials of such low stature or who have been a problem for President Museveni even before some of them conspired to bring the anti-homosexuality bill to a vote without his knowledge. As "pinkwashing," the official announcement of the actions against Ugandans was posted on the White House website the same day the President said he was sending up to 300 military advisors back into Iraq. But it is also important to note that the administration's first action was against a close ally with strong ties to the U.S. evangelical community cultivated during the Bush administration, and not Egypt, another ally and the largest Arab country, where similar oppression has been growing.

Conclusion

Since the state is actualized within and through Western colonization and resistance to the west, as Rahman's analysis (2014) would suggest, examining how the state uses sexuality to contest binaries of power/disempower and modern/traditional helps elucidate the complications of Western modernity as state project, the racialized negation of some peoples as pre-modern, the nearly universality of homosexualization, and so the necessity as well as the problematics of intervention on behalf of sexual minorities under threat. Although homoprotectionist policies consolidate technics of and constituencies for rule, they have promoted identity-based solutions mapping state interests through LGBT status imposed on diverse and disparate experiences of sexuality. Even the two collaborative statements of principles developed by activists – in Montreal and Yogyakarta – are problematic in their identification of LGBT rights (the former) or the seeming neutrality of terms such as sexual orientation and gender (Kollman & Waites, 2009), which still enumerate rights predicated on the modernist assumption that all people have a gender and a sexual orientation integral to their personality (Waites, 2009). So the Obama administration's embrace of global LGBT rights homosexualizes same gender sexuality through the same modernist imperatives as the state-deployed homophobia in Iran. In the U.S., this process, as Rahman demonstrates, affirms domestic LGBT identities as secure against the oppression sexual minorities suffer elsewhere. Globally, it buttresses the modernizing justifications of U.S. empire the Obama administration has never disavowed but the U.S. public increasingly does. But it is not a call to do nothing.

Moreover, LGBT rights as global follows globalization's initial complication of diaspora, where once nationally oriented state ethnicities "are no longer tightly territorialized, spatially bounded, historically unselfconscious, or culturally homogenous" (Appadurai, 1996). After 2001, however, the possibility of a post-*national* order of disembedding and globally circulating meanings gave way to the state's occlusion of possibilities beyond itself within both the War on Terror and its neoliberal cousin. Wide-ranging and disparate exertions of war and restructuring met to mobilize a vast machinery out of proportion to military threat actually to assert state power across deterritorialized sovereignty and secure loyalty against the deterritorialization of community. At this moment, states sought to consolidate sexual and national difference, with universals pushing against more diverse conditions of sexual being once unpenetrated by Western understanding (see, for example, Broqua, 2013). The state – impossible without a reproductive function – now almost everywhere overwhelms sexual diversity and naturalizes a binary rendering reproduction legible through heteropatriarchal marriage (Peterson, 2014). Sexuality transforms along modernist imperatives (as the modern is imposed alongside a desire for it – Apparadurai, 1996) and is innovated along dimensions of heterosexism, heternormativity, and homonormativity in crafting ruling coalitions.

Rahman's homo*colonial* closures draw our attention to Western and Muslim sexual discourses by granting agency to the homophobia of Muslim state actors and to the imperial pretensions of Western actors (2014). I add that homophobia and Islamophobia suggest a state-provoked erasure in their entirety of the experience of *alternative* sexualities. So, to say state practices inside or outside the West are homophobic is to recognize nearly all states imposing a modern Western sexual binary; but to model these accusations, as LGBT rights activists often do, through notions combining essentialized and historicized understandings of sexuality, is to say that the modern homosexual always already exists in the premodern bodies of sexual minorities everywhere. Working arm-in-arm with the psychopathic state, then, is a modernizing project of local and global rescue, so that nothing is left ungoverned by the state's cognition of (homo)sexuality except what has yet to be "outed" as within it.

Notes

1 French law precludes medically assisted procreation outside heterosexual marriage and prohibits surrogacy in all cases.
2 I heard this story from multiple sources.
3 Author's interview, February 2013.
4 Sources in Cairo and Kampala spoke of these threats.
5 Following Peterson's reading of Migdal et al. (Peterson, 1992: 4).
6 See Gourevitch 1978.
7 Author's interviews: Paris, France, 2008, 2013; Kampala, Uganda, 2013.

8 http://m.whitehouse.gov/blog/2014/06/19/further-us-efforts-protect-human-rights-uganda accessed 7/6/2014
9 http://evibe.ug/shocking-list-of-ugandans-banned-from-entering-usa/

Suggested further reading

Lind A (ed.) (2010) *Development, Sexual Rights, and Global Governance*. New York: Routledge.
Najmabadi A (2005) *Women with Mustaches and Men without Beards: Gender and Sexual Anxieties of Iranian Modernity*. Berkeley: University of California Press.
Peterson V S (2003) *A Critical Rewriting of Global Political Economy: Integrating Reproductive, Productive, and Virtual Economies*. London: Routledge.
Rao R (2010) *Third World Protest: Between Home and the World*. Oxford: Oxford University Press.
Weiss M and Bosia M (eds.) (2013) *Global Homophobia: States, Movements, and the Politics of Oppression*. Champaign, IL: University of Illinois Press.

Bibliography

Adam B (1985) Structural foundations of the gay world. *Comparative Studies in Society and History* 27(4): 658–71.
Agamben G (1998) *Homo Sacer: Sovereign Power and Bare Life*. Stanford, CA: Stanford University Press.
——(2005) *State of Exception*, trans. K Attell. Chicago, IL: University of Chicago Press.
Altman D (1999) Globalization, political economy, and HIV/AIDS. *Theory and Society* 28(4): 559–84
Anderson B (1983) *Imagined Communities*. New York: Verso.
Appadurai A (1996) *Modernity at Large*. Minneapolis: University of Minnesota Press.
Arendt H (1979) *The Origins of Totalitarianism*. San Diego, CA: Harcourt, Brace, Jovanovich.
Berlant L and Warner M (1998) Sex in public. *Critical Inquiry* 24(2): 547–66.
Binnie J (2004) *The Globalization of Sexuality*. Thousand Oaks, CA: Sage.
Boellstorff T (2004) The emergence of political homophobia in Indonesia: masculinity and national belonging. *Ethnos* 69(4): 465–86.
Bosia M J (2009) AIDS and postcolonial politics: acting up on science and immigration in France. *French Politics, Culture & Society* 27(1): 69–90.
——(2013) Why states act: homophobia and crisis. In: Weiss M L & Bosia M J (eds.) *Global Homophobia: States, Movements, and the Politics of Oppression*. Champaign, IL: University of Illinois Press.
Bosia M J and Weiss M L (2013) Political homophobia in comparative perspective. In: Weiss M L & Bosia M J (eds.) *Global Homophobia: States, Movements, and the Politics of Oppression*. Champaign, IL: University of Illinois Press.
Broqua C (2013) Male homosexuality in Bamako: a cross-cultural and cross-historical comparative perspective. In: Epprecht M & Nyeck S (eds.) *Sexual Diversity in Africa: Politics, Theory, Citizenship*. Montreal: McGill-Queen's University Press.
Canaday M (2009) *The Straight State: Sexuality and Citizenship in the Twentieth-Century America*. Princeton, MA: Princeton University Press.
Cleckley H (1988) *The Mask of Sanity: An Attempt to Clarify Some Issues about the So-called Psychopathic Personality*. Augusta, GA: Emily S. Cleckley.
Duggan L (2002) The new homonormativity: the sexual politics of neoliberalism. In: Castronovo R & Nelson D (eds.) *Materializing Democracy: Toward a Revitalized Cultural Politics*. Durham, NC: Duke University Press.
Duggan L and Hunter N (1996) *Sex Wars*. New York: Routledge.
Fejes F (2000) Murder, perversion, and moral panic: the 1954 media campaign against Miami's homosexuals and the discourse of civic betterment. *Journal of the History of Sexuality* 9(3): 305–47.

Freud S (1915) *Thoughts for the Times on War and Death.* http://www.panarchy.org/freud/war.1915.html

Giddens A (1985) *Contemporary Critique of Historical Materialism, Vol. 2: The Nation, State and Violence.* Cambridge: Polity Press.

——(1990) *The Consequences of Modernity.* Stanford, CA: Stanford University Press.

Gourevitch P (1978) The second image reversed: the international origins of domestic politics. *International Organization* 17(4).

Greenberg D F (1988) *The Construction of Homosexuality.* Chicago, IL: University of Chicago Press.

Hobsbawm E (1994) *The Age of Extremes.* New York: Pantheon Books.

Human Rights Watch (2008) *This Alien Legacy: The Origins of "Sodomy" Laws in British Colonialism.* http://www.hrw.org/en/reports/2008/12/17/alien-legacy-0

Johnson D K (2004) *The Lavender Scare: The Cold War Persecution of Gays and Lesbians in the Federal Government.* Chicago, IL: University of Chicago Press.

——(2014) America's Cold War empire: exporting the lavender scare. In: Weiss M & Bosia M (eds.) *Global Homophobia: States, Movements, and the Politics of Oppression.* Illinois: University of Illinois Press.

Kaoma K (2013) The marriage of convenience: the U.S. Christian right, African Christianity, and postcolonial politics of sexual identity. In: Weiss M & Bosia M (eds.) *Global Homophobia: States, Movements, and the Politics of Oppression.* Illinois: University of Illinois Press.

Kollman K and Waites M (2009) The global politics of lesbian, gay, bisexual and transgender human rights: an introduction. *Contemporary Politics* 15(1): 1–17.

Lebovics H (2004) *Bringing the Empire Back Home: France in the Global Age.* Durham, NC: Duke University Press.

Lee J C H (2011) *Policing Sexuality: Sex, Society, and the State.* New York: Zed Books.

Manalansan M F IV (2009) Homophobia at New York's gay central. In: Murray D A B (ed.) *Homophobias: Lust and Loathing Across Time and Space.* Durham, NC: Duke University Press.

Marx A (1998) *Making Race and Nation: A Comparison of South Africa, the United States, and Brazil, World Politics.* New York: Cambridge University Press.

Massad J (2007) *Desiring Arabs.* Chicago, IL: University of Chicago Press.

Murray D A B (2007) The civilized homosexual: travel talk and the project of gay identity. *Sexualities* 10(49): 49–60.

——(ed.) (2009) *Homophobias: Lust and Loathing Across Time and Space.* Durham, NC: Duke University Press,

Najmabadi, A (2005) Mapping transformations of sex, gender, and sexuality in modern Iran. *Social Analysis* 49(2): 54–77.

Peacock D, Stemple L, Sawires S, and Coates T J (2009) Men, HIV/AIDS, and human rights. *Journal of Acquired Immune Deficiency Syndromes* 51(Supp. 3): 119–S125.

Peterson V S (1992) Introduction. In: Peterson V S (ed.) *Gendered States: Feminist (Re) Visions of International Relations Theory.* Boulder, CO: Lynne Rienner.

——(2013) The intended and uintended queering of states/nations. *Studies in Ethnicities and Nationalism* 13(1): 57–68.

——(2014) Sex matters. *International Feminist Journal of Politics.* http://www.tandfonline.com/doi/abs/10.1080/14616742.2014.913384#.U_DmbsVdX-Y

Polanyi K (1957) *The Great Transformation: The Political Origins of Our Time.* Boston, MA: Beacon Press.

Puar J (2007) *Terrorist Assemblages: Homonationalism in Queer Times.* Durham, NC: Duke University Press.

Rahman M (2014) *Homosexualities, Muslim Cultures and Modernity.* New York: Palgrave Macmillan.

Ramasubban R (2007) India – culture, politics, and discourses on sexuality: a history of resistance to the anti-sodomy law in India. In Parker E, Petchetky R, & Sember R (eds.)

Sex Politics: Report from the Front Lines. Sexuality Policy Watch. http://www.sxpolitics. org/frontlines/book/pdf/sexpolitics.pdf

Rich A (1994) Compulsory heterosexuality and Lesbian existence. In: *Blood, Bread, and Poetry.* New York: Norton Paperback.

Roscoe W (1997) Precursors of Islamic male homosexualities. In: Murray S O & Roscoe W (eds.) *Islamic Homosexualities: Culture, History, Literature.* New York: New York University Press.

Rubin G (1993) Thinking sex: notes for a radical reading of the politics of sexuality. In: Abelove H & Barale M (eds.) *The Lesbian and Gay Studies Reader.* New York: Routledge.

Said E (1979) *Orientalism.* New York: Vintage Books.

Sanders D (2009) 377 and the unnatural afterlife of British colonialism in Asia. *Asian Journal of Comparative Law* 4(1). http://www.bepress. com/asjcl/vol4/iss1/art7

Santos B S (2006) *The Rise of the Global Left: The World Social Forum and Beyond.* London/ New York: Zed Books.

Scott J (1998) *Seeing Like a State: How Certain Schemes to Improve the Human Condition Have Failed.* New Haven, CT: Yale University Press.

Tilly C (1985) War making and state making as organised crime. In: Evans P, Rueschemeyer D, & Skocpol T (eds.) *Bringing the State Back.* New York: Cambridge University Press.

Waites, M (2009) Critique of "sexual orientation" and "gender identity" in human rights discourse: global queer politics beyond the Yogyakarta Principles. *Contemporary Politics* 15(1): 137–56.

Weiss M (2006) Rejection as freedom? HIV/AIDS organizations and identity. *Perspectives on Politics* 4(4): 671–78.

Winant, H (2000) Race and racial theory. *Annual Review of Sociology* 26: 169–85.

3

LGBT AND (DIS)UNITED NATIONS

Sexual and gender minorities, international law, and UN politics

Francine D'Amico

Introduction

Until recently, sexual and gender minorities[1] have been absent from discussions about "universal" human rights, and the United Nations has neglected their concerns. While many issues important to sexual and gender minorities are now on the UN agenda, LGBTIQ-identified people and their particular concerns remain largely marginalized for several reasons. First, no legally binding global treaty explicitly recognizes the right of sexual and gender minorities to be free from discrimination, violence, and persecution and to enjoy all the rights articulated in the Universal Declaration of Human Rights. This includes subsequent human rights treaties, including the rights to marry, to free choice of employment, and to freedom of thought, conscience, religion, opinion, and expression. Second, differences between Western views of international law, which focus on the rights of the individual, and alternative views of international law, which focus on the rights of the community, hold sexual and gender minorities hostage in the debate over whose version of rights should be made "universal." On these issues, the nations remain (dis)united. Finally, few nongovernmental organizations (NGOs) representing sexual and gender minorities have received consultative status to enable them to advocate for change inside the UN system, and to obtain formal access to UN venues. These NGOs have had to moderate their message and to police their members. This effectively constrains their voices, limiting the potential for change in law, policy, and practice.

In 2006, the Yogyakarta Principles provided a roadmap to address these legal omissions and exclusions and to raise LGBTIQ concerns in the framework of the international human rights regime, but UN politics have blocked this road. The United Nations General Assembly considered a non-binding declaration on human rights, sexual orientation, and gender identity (SOGI) in 2008. However, only 66 of the then 192 UN member states – mainly in Europe and Latin America – initially endorsed the declaration. The United States later added a 67th endorsement. Many developing countries in Asia and Africa endorsed instead a counter-statement condemning same-sex relationships and transgender individuals. Subsequent efforts to raise these concerns have met with increased division at the global level and backlash at the domestic level. This pattern of increasing polarization makes a legislative strategy unlikely to bring change, suggesting that mainstream perspectives on international relations offer little hope to bridge this divide. However, a critical analysis drawing from feminist and queer theories provides strategies for solidarity to promote positive change. This chapter reviews the status of sexual and gender minorities in current international human rights law, analyzes the polarization of UN member states on issues of concern to sexual and gender minorities, and examines the access of LGBTIQ-focused NGOs to the UN system. The chapter concludes with a series of recommendations for LGBTIQ advocacy groups and public officials.[2]

Do current human rights instruments offer adequate legal protection to sexual and gender minorities?

To date, no global human rights instrument has explicitly guaranteed human rights protections to individuals or groups based on sexual orientation or gender identity. The Universal Declaration of Human Rights or UDHR articulated a set of norms with regard to how states ought to treat their citizens: "Everyone is entitled to all the rights and freedoms set forth in this Declaration, without distinction of any kind, such as race, colour, sex, language, religion, political or other opinion, national or social origin, property, birth or other status" (1948: Article 2). Subsequent codification in the International Covenant on Civil and Political Rights (1966) and International Covenant on Economic, Social, and Cultural Rights (1966) makes respect for these rights legally binding. Other treaties ban genocide (1948), apartheid (1973), torture (1984), apartheid in sports (1985), discrimination based on race (1966) or gender (1979), and enforced disappearance (2006). Several recent treaties extend human rights protections to people based on their identity group or personal situation or status, including minors (1989), migrant workers (1990), and persons with disabilities (2006). Yet none of these documents specifically identifies sexual and gender minorities as entitled to these protections, and several contain language that may be used to justify discrimination and violence against sexual and gender minorities. For example, UDHR Article 29.2 states: "In the exercise of his rights and freedoms, everyone shall be subject only to such limitations as are determined by law solely for the purpose of securing due recognition and respect for the rights and freedoms of others and of meeting the just requirements of *morality, public order and the general welfare* in a democratic society" (1948, emphasis added). This "morality and public order" discourse is frequently used in legislation criminalizing same-sex and transgender relations, behaviors, and identities.

In *Ask No Questions*, Mooney Cotter (2010) argues that these international human rights instruments might provide an adequate legal foundation for sexual and gender minorities to claim standing to challenge discrimination based on sexual orientation and gender identity. She contends that sexual and gender minorities may employ the ambiguous "other" status in these documents as legal grounds for antidiscrimination challenges in national, regional, and international courts (Mooney Cotter, 2010). However, even if the "other" status in these treaties were interpreted to extend protections to sexual and gender minorities, states objecting to such an interpretation could simply claim an exception. Under international law, states may express *reservations* to treaties, claiming exemption from particular rules deemed incompatible with their own legal system or cultural beliefs. In addition, states may issue *declarations* regarding how treaty provisions will be applied. For example, many states refuse review of their compliance with treaty obligations by the International Court of Justice or by treaty bodies established for this purpose, asserting their sovereign right to decide for themselves if they have kept their treaty promises. These practices ensure that states objecting to human rights protections for sexual and gender minorities may lawfully continue to commit or to permit discrimination and violence against LGBTIQ-identified people within their territory's jurisdiction.

There is some evidence to support Mooney Cotter's argument (2010) in the European and American contexts, but only when legislative change accompanied litigation.[3] While national and regional laws have been invoked at the domestic or regional level to challenge discrimination, "universal" international human rights law has not. Moreover, there is currently no "global court" venue where such "universal" claims can be pressed. The International Criminal Court has no jurisdiction beyond genocide, war crimes, crimes against humanity, and aggression as defined in the Rome Statute, and the International Court of Justice can at best offer an advisory opinion to other UN organs, such as the General Assembly or Security Council, regarding the interpretation and application of international human rights law. While no extant human rights treaty explicitly prohibits discrimination or violence targeting people because of perceived sexual orientation or gender identity, the identity- or status-based treaties may provide models for a future treaty protecting sexual and gender minority rights.

I argue that a litigation strategy based on current law alone will not succeed at the global level because the "universal" human rights instruments create necessary but not sufficient conditions for success in challenging *de jure* systemic bias. This bias was first analyzed by LaViolette and Whitworth in their 1994 article, "No safe haven: sexuality as a universal human right," which documented the extent to which human rights mechanisms failed to offer adequate protections or legal redress to sexual and gender minorities. The absences and silences in international human rights law have led other identity groups claiming special status – that is, seeking additional rights protection in the face of persistent discrimination on the basis of age, dis/ability, or other vulnerable status – to pursue explicit codification of their "other" status as protected, with varying results. Sexual and gender minorities and their allies must therefore embrace a dual strategy of both legislative change and litigation challenge. Legal challenges brought at the national and regional levels may eventually advance claims for nondiscrimination at the global level as the political opportunity structure shifts. In the interim, national and regional protections in some contexts and more welcoming asylum policies may at least provide "safe havens" for sexual and gender minorities from the most overt and lethal *de jure* forms of heterosexism and homophobia in their home countries.

How did LGBTIQ issues emerge in the UN agenda?

Social movement theory observes that political opportunity structure, framing, and mobilization resources and structures affect the potential for success for groups organizing for social change (McAdam et al., 1996). First, the appearance of LGBTIQ issues on the global agenda from the mid-2000s on resulted from positive and negative changes in the political opportunity structure. This was propelled in part by the success of domestic organizing from the 1960s on. These local initiatives promoted legislative change and pursued litigation at the national and regional levels in many countries. Strategies and organizational structures that succeeded at the local level were then used, replicated, or combined to advance the movement transnationally. Additionally, in this age of economic globalization, many multinational corporations began offering partner benefits to same-sex couples. These companies have become unexpected allies in creating openings in both domestic and international political opportunity structures, reaching beyond what state representatives in intergovernmental organizations have been able to accomplish through tangible material support to sexual and gender minorities. The ability to speak out without losing one's job or to support a movement financially provides additional resources for mobilization. At the same time, increasing violence and complete closure of some domestic political arenas led to a crisis requiring collective response, pushing transnational community mobilization when domestic doors were slammed shut. For example, in Uganda, media "outings" inciting vigilante hate crimes and "gay dragnets" resulted in an international outcry to protect gay rights activists and punish violations; in the United States, a rash of teen suicides in which bullies taunted victims because of perceived sexual orientation and gender identity differences prompted greater attention to LGBTIQ issues.

Second, transnational advocacy groups have long grappled with the question of how to frame the rights claims they are making: are individuals in this situation seeking rights like any other person or is there some need to protect this group collectively from rights violations for which they are uniquely targeted? As critical feminist and queer theorists point out, a key problem with a "same rights" principle applied in practice would mean, for example, that hate crime laws could not impose additional penalties for assaults in which victims were targeted precisely because of their perceived sexual orientation or gender identity (Leckey & Brooks, 2010). Cultural and religious objections to same-sex relations present additional challenges for selecting a successful frame for rights claims by sexual and gender minorities. From a critical legal perspective, another key problem is that international human rights law treats sexual and gender minorities as atomized individuals rather than as members of a social group with a "visible" collective identity, like race or ethnicity, that makes them subject to targeted violence and eligible for special protective status (MacKinnon, 2007). Domestic and transnational organizing focus around three goals: decriminalization, nondiscrimination, and liberalization or inclusion. None of these goals challenges the basic conceptualization of individual rights on which the international human rights regime is founded (Leckey & Brooks, 2010).

Third, mobilization resources and structures are also in flux. Faster communication through computer and internet facilitates transnational connections across state borders – at least for advocacy groups and activists with access. The advent of advocacy groups focused on transnational organizing around LGBTIQ concerns as well as growing solidarity work and support for sexual and gender minorities from mainstream human rights groups have expanded LGBTIQ movement resources. Two challenges for mobilizing LGBTIQ individuals collectively to advocate for change are self-imposed invisibility and societally imposed criminalization. Closeting is a strategy of self-protection from discrimination and violence, but the invisibility of closeted sexual and gender minorities inhibits efforts to organize collectively for change, and criminalization of same-sex relations makes public acknowledgement of an LGBTIQ-identity personally and professionally risky or even dangerous (Dufour, 1998; Von Wahl, 2012). As legislative changes and litigation victories have enabled more sexual and gender minorities to identify openly, mobilization resources have expanded. To summarize, changes and challenges in domestic and international political opportunity structures, issue framing, and mobilization resources and structures have brought LGBTIQ issues to the global agenda.

Sexual and gender minorities began mobilizing to advocate for change at different times in different countries and contexts. For example, in the United States, police harassment of patrons at a gay night club in New York City, the Stonewall Inn, in June 1969 sparked street demonstrations, mobilized rights activists, and generated media and public attention (Carter, 2004; Kuhn, 2011). By the early 1970s, LGBTIQ activists began to organize transnationally to advocate national decriminalization of sexual minority status. In 1978, the International Lesbian and Gay Association (ILGA) was established. This NGO federation, now called the International Lesbian, Gay, Bi, Trans, and Intersex Association, connects hundreds of civil society groups in over 100 countries (ILGA, 2014). Through the 1980s, LGBTIQ advocacy groups mobilized both locally and transnationally to demand national and global attention to the HIV/AIDS epidemic.

The decade of the 1990s brought the end of the Cold War and reduced focus on security issues, opening political space for increased East-West LGBTIQ transnational organizing. In 1991, LGBTIQ activists in San Francisco incorporated the International Gay and Lesbian Human Rights Commission (IGLHRC) as a U.S. non-profit and began transnational activism initially *vis-à-vis* Russia, Canada, and Argentina. In that same year, the World Health Organization deleted homosexuality from the *International Codex of Diseases*. Amnesty International recognized LGBTQ-identified people as "prisoners of conscience" in its report, *Breaking the Silence* (1997). Perhaps the world's best known human rights organization, Amnesty International, finally acknowledged that the criminalization of sexual and gender identity violated basic human rights. Both ILGA and IGLHRC attended the UN World Conference on Human Rights at Vienna, Austria, in 2003, where a draft resolution on "Human Rights & Sexual Orientation," also known as the Brazilian resolution, was presented. Joining Brazil as co-sponsors were Canada and 18 countries in Europe. The draft resolution was sent to the Commission on Human Rights 59th session (2004), where it was tabled by opponents, effectively blocking further action in that venue of the UN system.[4]

At the national level, several noteworthy changes occurred during the 1990s. Denial of asylum to sexual and gender minorities was a widely used exclusionary practice exacerbated by the global AIDS pandemic (Goldberg, 1993). The Clinton administration quietly shifted US asylum policy to allow refugee status for sexual and gender minorities. US Attorney General Janet Reno began interpreting the requirement for a "well-founded fear of persecution" to apply to sexual and gender minorities fleeing physical violence and legal prosecution in countries where penalties for LGBTIQ status included imprisonment or execution (AP, 1996). This policy shift shows that LGBTIQ rights claims may be incorporated into the international human rights regime via "soft law" policy processes, but this kind of policy change may easily be undone by the next executive officer. South Africa became the first country in the world to include explicit protection for sexual and gender minorities in its constitution during the transition to majority rule. This elicited a backlash on the continent, led by Robert Mugabe, president of Zimbabwe, who condemned homosexuality as "unAfrican" and "a perversion imported from the West" (Reid, 2013). This critique of sexual and gender minority rights as a form of cultural imperialism is particularly problematic because laws criminalizing homosexuality were imposed under European colonial rule, as Michael Bosia notes in Chapter 2 and Momin Rahman explores in Chapter 5 of this volume. The perception that antidiscrimination rules for sexual and gender minorities are being imposed from the outside rallies nationalist sentiment in defense of "tradition" and "community values," while local activists continue to challenge this perception (Reid, 2013).

The new millennium brought additional progress toward the LGBTIQ movement's main goals of curbing violence and promoting decriminalization to address *de jure* discrimination. For example, the International Commission of Jurists, an "expert" NGO comprised of legal scholars and practitioners established in 1952 to promote the rule of law, "began documenting UN references to violations experienced by LGBT individuals in 2003 and issued its first UN compilation in 2005" (2014). The International Commission of Jurists or ICJ – not to be confused with the UN's International Court of Justice or "World Court" of the same acronym – now maintains a searchable UN SOGI database, including UN documents, official statements, and meetings relevant to LGBTIQ concerns (ICJ, 2014).

At the International Conference on LGBT Human Rights held in Montreal, Quebec, Canada, in July 2006, participants drafted and endorsed the Declaration of Montreal, which calls for active protection of sexual and gender minorities from both state and private violence, full freedom of expression, assembly, and association for sexual minorities, and decriminalization of private consensual adult same-sex activity. According to the conference conveners, over 1,500 citizens from 100 countries attended this conference, which was held in conjunction with the 1st World Outgames. The Declaration, published July 29, 2006, was "unanimously adopted by the International Scientific Committee, consisting of 37 LGBT activists and experts from all over the world" intended as an advocacy tool "to summarize the main demands of the international LGBT movement in the broadest possible terms" and to promote political dialogue on the issues and concerns of sexual and gender minorities (International Conference LGBT, 2006). Subsequently, in November 2006, international human rights scholars, jurists, and practitioners met in Yogyakarta, Indonesia, to draft a set of principles to guide the development of national and international legal standards regarding the protection of human rights for sexual and gender minorities. The Yogyakarta Principles include, *inter alia*, rights to equality and nondiscrimination, recognition before the law and effective remedies and redress (Yogyakarta Principles, 2006; O'Flaherty & Fisher, 2008).

The Declaration of Montreal and the Yogyakarta Principles provide a normative framework and explicit discourse for the future codification of LGBTIQ human rights

This discourse was further articulated in the proposed Declaration on Human Rights, Sexual Orientation, and Gender Identity (hereafter SOGI Declaration) presented to the UN General Assembly on December 18, 2008. The measure, sponsored by France and the Netherlands and presented by Argentina, was also supported by the European Union and other states in the UN-designated Western Europe and Other Group (WEOG), such as Australia, Canada, and New Zealand. However, the United States, then under the Bush administration, did not support the SOGI Declaration in December 2008. This position was reversed by the Obama administration, which took office in January 2009, indicating a desire to signal "our collective support of the statement's main objective – the condemnation of human rights violations based on sexual orientation and gender identity, just as we condemn any other failure to protect human rights and fundamental freedoms" (Pollack, 2009). Queer theorists note that this "same rights" discourse constrains LGBTIQ advocacy to seek "tolerance" rather than "justice" (Puar, 2007).

The 2008 SOGI Declaration was vocally opposed by Russia, China, and the Holy See (Vatican), as well as members of the Arab League and the Organization of the Islamic Conference. In response to Argentina's presentation of the Declaration, 57 UN member states supported a counter-statement, sponsored by Syria, asserting domestic jurisdiction over matters relating to sexual orientation and claiming that the proposed declaration undermined the framework of international human rights and risked legitimizing "deplorable acts" such as pedophilia. Interestingly, self-identified human rights advocate South Africa remained silent on the issue, although Archbishop Desmond Tutu expressed support for human rights protections for sexual and gender minorities (IGLHRC, 2014). Ultimately, one-third of UN member states (67 of 192) supported the SOGI Declaration; another one-third (57 of 192) opposed the declaration and joined the counter-statement, and the final third (67 of 192) were silent on the question. Such extreme polarization is rare for an informal General Assembly declaration, which has even less normative force than a nonbinding Assembly resolution.

Which countries supported, which opposed, and which neither supported nor opposed the 2008 UNGA SOGI Declaration?

The main support for the SOGI Declaration came from the Western Europe and Other Group (WEOG) and Eastern Europe (EEUR) Group, followed by about one-third of the countries of the Americas Group (Grupo Latino e Caribeño – GRULAC). Of 33 states in the Americas, 12 supported, one (St. Lucia) opposed, and 20 – many Anglo-Caribbean states – made no statement. Of 23 countries in the Eastern Europe (EEUR) Group, 18 supported, none opposed, and five made no statement, including the former Soviet Republics of Azerbaijan, Belarus, Moldova, and Ukraine, along with the Russian Federation. Of 29 countries in the Western Europe and Other Group (WEOG), 27 supported, and just two – Monaco and Turkey – made no statement. The main opposition came from countries in the Africa and Asia-Pacific Groups. Of 54 countries in Africa, only six supported the declaration, while 31 endorsed Syria's counter-statement, and 17 made no statement. Of 53 countries in Asia, four supported the declaration, 25 opposed, and 24 made no statement (see Table 3.1).

Thus, of the 67 countries supporting the SOGI Declaration, 45, or two-thirds were in EEUR/WEOG, and most of the final one-third mainly in the Americas.

Critical legal theory reads the contentious debate over this declaration as one of the latest battlegrounds in the fundamental tension of the international legal system between the rights of states and the rights of people. The Universal Declaration of Human Rights or UDHR (December 10, 1948) represented the first normative challenge to the Westphalian system's central principles of state sovereignty and nonintervention. The UDHR thus began a process of decentering the logic of Westphalia underlying the international legal system, much like Copernicus' heliocentric model challenged the long-accepted Ptolemaic logic of a geocentric universe. This potentially seismic shift in the international legal system's logic is far from complete, but the fact that LGBTIQ concerns are now being debated suggests that further progress is possible, and that people-centered transnational human rights organizations should continue to push both state governments and intergovernmental institutions like the United Nations to engage with the issues.

Another round of the state-centric vs. people-centric international legal debate transpired in December 2010 as the UN General Assembly considered a resolution condemning extra-judicial and summary executions. The Human Rights Committee, which oversees implementation of the International Covenant on Civil and Political Rights (1966), deleted language that referred explicitly to sexual orientation and gender identity before submitting the draft resolution to the full General

TABLE 3.1 UNGA SOGI Declaration, 2008

	UN MEMBERS by REGION		
	FOR	AGAINST	NEUTRAL
AFRICA = 54 STATES	Cape Verde, Central African Republic, Gabon, Guinea-Bissau, Mauritius, Sao Tomé and Principe (6)	Algeria, Benin, Cameroon, Chad, Comoros, Côte d'Ivoire, Djibouti, Egypt, Eritrea, Ethiopia, Gambia, Guinea, Kenya, Libya, Malawi, Mali, Mauritania, Morocco, Niger, Nigeria, Rwanda, Senegal, Sierra Leone, Somalia, Sudan, Swaziland, Togo, Tunisia, Uganda, UR Tanzania, Zimbabwe (31)	Angola, Botswana, Burkina Faso, Burundi, Congo, DR Congo, Eq. Guinea, Ghana, Lesotho, Liberia, Madagascar, Mozambique, Namibia, Seychelles, South Africa, South Sudan,* Zambia (17)
ASIA = 53 STATES	Cyprus, Japan, Nepal, Timor-Leste (4)	Afghanistan, Bahrain, Bangladesh, Brunei Darussalam, DPR Korea (North), Fiji, Indonesia, Iran, Iraq, Jordan, Kazakhstan, Kuwait, Kyrgyzstan**, Lebanon, Malaysia, Maldives, Oman, Pakistan, Qatar, Saudi Arabia, Solomon Islands, Syria, Tajikistan, Turkmenistan, UAE, Uzbekistan**, Yemen (27 - 2 = 25)	Bhutan, Cambodia, China, India, Laos, Marshall Islands, Micronesia, Mongolia, Myanmar, Nauru, Palau, Papua New Guinea, Philippines, Republic of Korea (South), Samoa, Singapore, Sri Lanka, Thailand, Tonga, Tuvalu, Vanuatu, Vietnam (22 + 2 = 24)
EEUR = 23 STATES	Albania, Armenia, Bosnia and Herzegovina, Bulgaria, Croatia, Czech Republic, Estonia, Georgia, Hungary, Latvia, Lithuania, Montenegro, Poland, Romania, Serbia, Slovakia, Slovenia, FYR Macedonia (18)		Azerbaijan, Belarus, Moldova, Russian Federation, Ukraine (5)

TABLE 3.1 (CONTINUED)

	UN MEMBERS by REGION		
	FOR	AGAINST	NEUTRAL
GRULAC (AMERICAS) = 33	Argentina, Bolivia, Brazil, Chile, Colombia, Cuba, Ecuador, Mexico, Nicaragua, Paraguay, Uruguay, Venezuela (12)	St. Lucia	Antigua and Barbuda, Bahamas, Barbados, Belize, Costa Rica, Dominica, Dominican Republic, El Salvador, Grenada, Guatemala, Guyana, Haiti, Honduras, Jamaica, Panama, Peru, St. Kitts and Nevis, St. Vincent and Grenadines, Suriname, Trinidad and Tobago (20)
WEOG = 29 STATES****	Andorra, Australia, Austria, Belgium, Canada, Denmark, Finland, France, Germany, Greece, Iceland, Ireland, Israel, Italy, Liechtenstein, Luxembourg, Malta, Netherlands, New Zealand, Norway, Portugal, San Marino, Spain, Sweden, Switzerland, United Kingdom, United States of America (27)		Monaco, Turkey***

*South Sudan was not a UN member state in 2008

**Krygyzstan and Uzbekistan were initially listed as signatories of the Syrian counter-statement but declared they did not sign

***Turkey consults in the Asia Group but is enmuerated in WEOG for representation and voting in the UN system

****The United States consults in WEOG but does not vote; it is included in WEOG count

Assembly for consideration. The U.S. Permanent Representative to the United Nations, Ambassador Susan Rice, introduced an amendment to restore the deleted language. The amendment passed 93-55-27, and the amended resolution was adopted with 122 in favor, one against, and 62 abstentions (ISHR, 2010; Snow, 2010). The polarization evident in the debate over the 2008 UNGA SOGI Declaration persisted here, with most African and Asian member states either abstaining or absenting themselves from the vote.

In 2010, South Africa introduced a draft resolution on sexual orientation and gender identity for consideration by the UN Human Rights Council (HRC). The vote was taken June 17, 2011, after South Africa's term expired. With 47 countries on the HRC, the resolution passed with 23 in favor, 19 against, and three abstentions, with two states' representatives not present for voting. Significantly, the only African state to support the resolution was Mauritius. Burkina Faso and Zambia abstained, and nine African states voted against the resolution. Both Angola and Ghana, which had neither supported nor opposed the 2008 UNGA SOGI Declaration, and Gabon, which had supported the declaration, voted against Resolution 17/19 in the Human Rights Council. Libya's representative cast no vote. The non-profit Center for Human Rights and Humanitarian Law notes that 36 African states not only opposed this resolution but also enacted homophobic domestic legislation, including Mauritania, Sudan, and parts of Nigeria and Somalia, where same sex relations are "crimes punishable by death" (Salisbury, 2011).

Intriguingly, several states shifted from neutral on the 2008 UNGA SOGI Declaration to support HRC 17/19 in 2011, including the Republic of Korea and Thailand from the Asia-Pacific Group, Ukraine from the EEUR Group, and Guatemala from GRULAC. All eight GRULAC states and all seven WEOG states on the Council supported the measure, while EEUR split, with four – Hungary, Poland, Slovakia, and Ukraine – in favor and two – Moldova and Russia – against. Three Asian states – Japan, Republic of Korea, and Thailand – were in favor and eight opposed, including Bahrain, Bangladesh, Jordan, Malaysia, Maldives, Pakistan, Qatar, and Saudi Arabia. China abstained, and the representative from Kyrgyzstan did not vote. The moves from neutral positions in 2008 to either for or against a SOGI-related measure in 2011 suggest a slightly increased polarization of views during this period. This increased polarization is likely to prevent explicit legal codification of sexual and gender minority rights in an international treaty for some time to come. To paraphrase MacKinnon (2007), if we ask, "Are gays, lesbians, and other sexual and gender minorities human?" that is, "Are they entitled to international human rights protections?", then UN members remain starkly (dis)united on their answers.

Despite this contentious disunity, the UN system, prompted by LGBTIQ transnational advocacy groups, continues to put the rights question on the agenda in various venues. The 2011 report of the Office of the High Commissioner for Human Rights, Discriminatory Laws and Practices and Acts of Violence against Individuals Based on their Sexual Orientation and Gender Identity, documents systemic and systematic *de jure* and de facto discrimination against sexual and

TABLE 3.2 LGBTIQ-focused NGOs with UN ECOSOC consultative status

NGO	Headquarters	Applied	Granted	Status	Website
International Wages Due Lesbians	San Francisco, CA, USA	1998	1998	Roster	
Coalition of Activist Lesbians – Australia (COAL)	Lennox Head, New South Wales, Australia	1999	1999	Special	http://www.coal.org.au
European Region of the International Lesbian & Gay Federation (ILGA-Europe)	Brussels, Belgium	2006	2006	Special	http://www.ilga-europe.org/
Lesbian & Gay Federation in Germany (LSVD)	Cologne, Germany	2006	2006	Special	http://www.lsvd.de
LGBT Denmark – National Organization for Gay Men, Lesbians, Bisexuals, & Transgendered People (formerly Danish Association for Gays & Lesbians)	Copenhagen, Denmark	2006	2006	Special	http://www.lbl.dk
Swedish Federation of Lesbian, Gay, Bisexual, & Transgender Rights (RFSL)	Stockholm, Sweden	2̂007	2007	Special	http://www.rfsl.se
Federación Estatal de Lesbianas, Gays, Transexuales, y Bisexuales (FELGTB) – Spanish Federation of Lesbians, Gays, Transexuals, & Bisexuals	Madrid, Spain	2008	2008	Special	http://www.felgtb.org
Associação Brasileira de Gays, Lésbicas, Bissexuais, Travestis, e Transexuais (ABGLT) – Brazilian Association of Gays, Lesbians, Bisexuals, Transvestites, & Transexuals	Curitiba, Paraná, Brazil	2007	2009	Special	http://www.abglt.org.br
International Gay & Lesbian Human Rights Commission (IGLHRC)	New York, USA	2008	2010	Special	http://www.iglhrc.org
International Lesbian, Gay, Bisexual, Trans, and Intersex Association (formerly International Lesbian & Gay Association) (ILGA)	Brussels, Belgium	2006	2011	Special	http://ilga.org
Homosexuelle Initiative Wien (HOSI-WIEN) – Homosexual Initiative of Vienna	Vienna, Austria	2011	2013	Special	http://www.hosiwien.au
Australian Lesbian Medical Association (ALMA)	Fitzroy North, Victoria, Australia	2010	2013	Special	http://www.almas.org.au/

gender minorities, including: rape and sexual assault, torture, and killings, both state sanctioned and extra judicial; denial of employment, education, and healthcare; violations of the rights to free expression, association, and assembly; and denial of asylum, the right to form a family, and the right to participate in their community. To discuss this report, the Human Rights Council convened an expert panel on "Ending Violence and Discrimination against Individuals based on their Sexual Orientation and Gender Identity" in 2012. In a video message to the panelists, UN Secretary-General Ban-Ki Moon condemned "violence and discrimination against individuals based on their sexual orientation and gender identity as a monumental tragedy for those affected and a stain on the collective conscience" and urged the panel to make specific recommendations to address the situation (UNHRC, 2012). Significantly, several government delegations "signaled their opposition to any discussion of sexual orientation and gender identity by leaving the Council chamber at the start of the meeting," and a number of those who remained "voiced their opposition on cultural or religious grounds or argued that sexual orientation and gender identity were new concepts that lay outside the framework of international human rights law" (UNHCR, 2012). This prompted the panel moderator, Ambassador Abdul Minty of South Africa, to urge a less confrontational, more conciliatory approach on LGBTIQ issues. The panel report concluded: "No new rights or special rights were needed for LGBT people; rather, existing human rights standards needed to be applied so that LGBT people could enjoy the same rights as everyone else" (UNHRC, 2012: 4). This suggests sexual and gender minorities ought not claim "special rights" or protections, despite the very particular group identity targeting and violations they experience, such as "corrective rape" and enforced medical treatment to "cure homosexuality," which the report documents. LGBTIQ concerns remain constrained by UN politics.

In the face of rigidifying polarization, UN human rights agencies continue to articulate norms and to recommend policies and practices to address violence and discrimination against sexual and gender minorities. In September 2012 the UN Office of the High Commissioner for Human Rights published *Born Free and Equal: Sexual Orientation and Gender Identity in International Human Rights Law*, which identifies five core legal obligations of states with regard to LGBTIQ individuals. These are, in brief, obligations to: protect sexual and gender minorities from homophobic and transphobic violence; prevent and punish torture, cruel, inhuman, and degrading treatment in detention; repeal laws criminalizing "private sexual conduct between consenting adults"; prohibit and punish discrimination; and safeguard freedom of expression, association, and peaceful assembly for sexual and gender minorities (UNHCHR, 2012). At the same time, the United Nations High Commissioner for Refugees published "Guidelines on International Protection No. 9: Claims to Refugee Status based on Sexual Orientation and/or Gender Identity" (HCR/GIP/12/09), expanding on its previous "Guidance Note on Refugee Claims relating to Sexual Orientation and Gender Identity" (November 2008).

To engage civil society in the discussion, UN-sponsored regional seminars in Kathmandu, Paris, and Brasilia, and consultations with both open and clandestine advocacy groups in African countries were held in 2012 and early 2013 to discuss rights violations against sexual and gender minorities and to consider how to redress these violations. Reports from these seminars were presented at an International Conference on Human Rights, Sexual Orientation, and Gender Identity, held April 15–16, 2013, in Oslo, Norway. The conference was co-chaired by representatives from Norway and South Africa and attended by some 200 official government representatives and rights activists from 84 countries. The conference outcome document recommends "the establishment of a relevant mechanism ... to study and document in a comprehensive and recurrent manner trends, developments, challenges and opportunities in relation to human rights, sexual orientation and gender identity" (ICHRSOGI, 2013). The recommendations also include: "encouraging good practices, enhancing understanding of the application of international human rights law in this area, and promoting constructive and informed dialogue"; working collaboratively with other UN agencies to mainstream these issues throughout the UN system; presenting reports to the Human Rights Council; and offering "technical assistance to States to assist them in strengthening human rights protection on these grounds" (ICHRSOGI, 2013). Implementation of these proposals would institutionalize UN system attention to rights violations against sexual and gender minorities.

Who speaks for sexual and gender minorities in the UN system?

The United Nations Economic and Social Council (ECOSOC) oversees and coordinates all UN initiatives on human rights and determines which nongovernmental organizations (NGOs) receive "consultative status" to participate in meetings of UN agencies. NGOs with consultative status may submit reports, speak on the record, or organize events on UN grounds or in UN facilities. Applications for consultative status are made to the ECOSOC Committee on Nongovernmental Organizations (hereafter NGO Committee). The NGO Committee, comprised of 19 members chosen on the basis of the principle of geographic representation, approves about one-third of hundreds of applications reviewed each year (UN ECOSOC, 2013). ECOSOC is the UN system's "civil society" gatekeeper. Since 1946, when ECOSOC first granted consultative status to a civil society organization, thousands of NGOs have sought and obtained UN accreditation through ECOSOC. Few of these accredited NGOs have been explicitly committed to advocacy for the rights of sexual and gender minorities, and some LGBTIQ NGOs have been repeatedly deferred or outright denied accreditation, deliberately excluding them from venues where human rights issues are discussed, treaties drafted, and points of law decided.

According to the ECOSOC website, some 4,165 NGOs had consultative status as of July 30, 2014. A 2013 report indicated that 147 organizations had general consultative status, 2,774 had special consultative status, and 979 others were accredited for particular purposes, such as attendance at the UN Conference on Sustainable Development (RIO + 20) held in 2012 (UN ECOSOC, 2013). Of 42

LGBTIQ-focused NGOs registered in ECOSOC's Integrated Civil Society Organizations System (iCSO) database, only 12 have received consultative status; seven of these are based in Western Europe, two in the United States, two in Australia, and one in Brazil.[5] In other words, 11 of the 12 NGOs with ECOSOC consultative status are from countries in the UN-designated Western Europe and Other Group (WEOG). According to the iCSO database, one LGBT NGO was placed on the ECOSOC Roster in 1998, one was granted ECOSOC Special Consultative Status in 1999, three received consultative status in 2006, one per year from 2007 to 2011, none in 2012, and two in 2013. Of these, the International Lesbian and Gay Association (ILGA) waited the longest: ILGA applied to the NGO Committee for ECOSOC consultative status in 2006 and was repeatedly deferred; ILGA finally received consultative status in 2011 (see Table 3.2).

Not yet listed in the database is Canada-based ARC International, which was established in 2003 and received UN ECOSOC consultative status on July 15, 2014. ARC International maintains an office in Geneva, Switzerland, seat of several UN human rights agencies, to facilitate strategic planning around LGBT issues internationally and to advance LGBT issues within the UN human rights system. ARC International claims credit for successfully "engaging the support of the UN High Commissioner for Human Rights, ensuring that the records of all UN States on LGBT issues are subjected to international scrutiny, and bringing international support to the work of NGOs in countries around the world" (2014).

Gendering and queering human rights law

Mainstream theories of international relations, such as realism, liberalism, and constructivism, offer few insights into this polarized disunity and few paths forward. Realist theorists consider human rights issues relevant only in the ability of powerful states to coerce less powerful states to behave in particular ways and in terms of the exercise of sovereignty within a state's territory. Liberalist theorists advocating the rights of the individual and constructivists tracing norm contests in the development of current human rights instruments and practices focus our attention on improving the existing system, as Anthony Langlois observes in Chapter 3. Postcolonialist, feminist, and queer theoretical perspectives offer more critical and potentially transformative interpretations. From these critical perspectives, state advocacy for sexual and gender minority rights can be read as a "marker of modernity" in a globalizing world in which Western cultural values are presented and imposed as universal norms and the state is increasingly empowered to define and to regulate the lives of citizens, as was also seen in the move to secularism, the rejection of the veil, and the critique of female circumcision (Puar, 2007). Critical perspectives read this move to "homonationalism" as grounded in mainstream theories that defend the status quo power hierarchies of class/caste, race/ethnicity, gender, and sexual identity. These homonationalist state policies have three problematic consequences. First, they allow state leaders to hijack the political agenda from domestic and transnational groups who have long advocated LGBTIQ rights.

Second, they fuel more vociferous and violent backlash, polarizing and mobilizing opposition in global South countries such as Uganda, actually increasing targeting and risk to sexual and gender minorities. Third, this expropriation of the LGBTIQ agenda by some governments muzzles the domestic movement in countries in which calls for justice are silenced by comparison with the more dire situations of sexual and gender minorities at risk of loss of life and liberty elsewhere.

Feminist perspectives on international law turn our attention to the gendered power structures behind state decisions and ask how social constructions of gender shape the principles and practices of international law (Charlesworth, 1999; Charlesworth & Chinkin, 2000; MacKinnon, 2007). Critical feminist perspectives reveal the masculinist bias of international law and international legal institutions and reveal the absences and silences resulting from the androcentric standards and patriarchal practices of the legal system. Every point of feminist critique of the international legal system can be applied to LGBTIQ rights and representation, although few feminist scholars attempt to do so. If we ask the key critical feminist question, "Whose law is it?" we find a subtle, insidious, and invisible heterocentric bias. To paraphrase a description of feminist approaches in international law from Charlesworth et al.: "Our [LGBTIQ] approach requires looking behind abstract entities of states to the actual impact of rules on [sexual and gender minorities] within states ... both the structures of international lawmaking and the content of the rules of internal law privilege [heterosexuals]; if [sexual and gender minorities'] interests are acknowledged at all, they are marginalized. International law is a thoroughly [heterocentric and homophobic] system" (1991: 614–15). Yet few feminist scholars attend to questions concerning sexual and gender minorities in their analyses, themselves demonstrating a heteronormative bias. For example, only three of the 10 chapters in the recently published anthology *Gender in Transitional Justice* (Buckley-Zistel & Stanley, 2012) address or even mention LGBTIQ issues or lived experiences; one of these chapters focuses on gay men in the Nazi Holocaust (Von Wahl, 2012), and the other two chapters contain brief passages concerning "corrective rape" of lesbian and transgender individuals (Sigsworth & Valji, 2012; Studzinsky, 2012). Following standard publishing conventions, these passages are indexed under the term 'homosexual', a term which many LGBTIQ-identified people find pejorative. So even in feminist analysis focused on gender, sexual and gender minorities remain marginalized, silent, and invisible.

The distinction between the LGBTIQ agenda and the feminist agenda becomes apparent when advocates for "women's rights" wrongfully assume that all women are similarly situated or recognize but willingly compromise or sacrifice the needs of sexual and gender minorities to gain access to education, employment, and non-gender traditional professions qua "women," constructed as straight, normal, safe – that is, non-threatening to the current patriarchal order – *viz.*, "You may enter with permission, but only if you agree to abide by the institutional rules and regulations pre-determined by those with the power to construct the edifice." Like the subaltern in an Orientalist system, the "woman" who accepts this institutional bargain in a patriarchal system is constructed as "Other" and exists in the institution only by the grace of and in opposition to the "Self" with the power to admit or deny her. This gatekeeping power to admit or to exclude ensures that only the "woman" who understands and accepts her place in socially constructed gender roles and heterosexist hierarchy – and helps to police that institution against unauthorized intruders – will be allowed to stay. So, too, for LGBTIQ-focused NGOs seeking UN ECOSOC consultative status: they must be "tame" (rather than "flame") enough to pass muster, first, with the state representatives in the NGO Committee to be recommended for consultative status, and, second, with the 54 state representatives in ECOSOC itself.

That this "taming" results in silencing and marginalization was evident in the case of the International Lesbian, Gay, Bisexual, Trans, and Intersex Association's gain, loss, and regaining of UN ECOSOC consultative status. ILGA, as a transnational nongovernmental organization, brings together multiple LGBTIQ-focused NGOs to advocate for change at the global level. ILGA was first granted UN ECOSOC consultative status in 1993 but was suspended in 1994 in response to allegations that ILGA supported pedophilia because some of its constituent members advocated consensual sexual relations regardless of the age of the parties. In response to this UN suspension, ILGA members at the next annual conference voted to expel several constituent members, including NAMBLA (the North American Man/Boy Love Association). ILGA sought reinstatement of its consultative status in 2000, but the NGO Committee declined, expressing concern that ILGA's constituent member list was no longer being made public, so they could not prove that groups advocating pedophilia had been purged. ILGA contended that this policy of confidentiality was to protect its members from persecution and prosecution in countries where same-sex relations or status were still criminalized. ILGA's application for consultative status was rejected again in 2003 and 2006. ILGA reapplied in 2009 but was deferred until July 25, 2011, finally passing in ECOSOC with a vote of 30 in favor, 13 against, and five abstentions (ILGA, 2011). The vote reflected the pattern of polarization already noted earlier.

Conclusion: a way forward

Advocates for increased rights protections for sexual and gender minorities must continue to support litigation to redress grievances and to push for broader interpretation of extant human rights law. To clarify that rights protections extend to all, activists should demand that national, regional, and international human rights laws explicitly include sexual orientation and gender identity as grounds for such protection, rather than relying on the ambiguous "other status" currently found in treaties. Further, LGBTIQ groups should continue to advocate for additional punishment under hate crime statutes in domestic and international law for violence targeting sexual and gender minorities as well as inclusion of sexual orientation and gender identity as grounds for seeking asylum and refugee status in law and in practice. Other legislative change proposals would be to remove heteronormative language and values from international human rights treaties. For example, language echoing the "morality, public order, and general welfare" exception in the Universal Declaration of Human Rights (1948: 29.2) has been used time and again by governments to violate the rights of sexual and gender minorities. The Nazis committed acts of genocide and crimes against humanity against Jewish people because of their group identity; the Nazis also targeted sexual and gender minorities for imprisonment and extermination, and this, too, must be legally recognized as genocide against a group of people because of their identity – in this case, who they are is whom they love. Acts of genocide and crimes against humanity targeting LGBTIQ-identified people are committed daily by governments and individuals around the world. The Rome Statute of the International Criminal Court must be amended to reflect this reality and to enable prosecution of these heinous violations.

LGBTIQ-focused NGOs should continue to apply (and reapply) for ECOSOC consultative status to ensure a diversity of views and a more inclusive dialogue. Advocacy groups and their allies in UN member state delegations might press for a change in the process for obtaining consultative status, such that any organization that meets the objective criteria for said status will automatically go to a vote of the full ECOSOC rather than be blocked in the NGO Committee. The UN High Commissioner for Human Rights and the UN High Commissioner for Refugees must work in tandem to assist sexual and gender minorities with asylum claims to find safe havens. UN member states and UN agencies must train all personnel, in particular security and law enforcement officers, educators, and counselors, to respect the rights of sexual and gender minorities and to report violations. So-called "gay-bashing" – both verbal and physical – should be grounds for professional sanctions, including immediate dismissal from public service. Anti-bullying campaigns must explicitly condemn harassment based on perceived sexual orientation and gender identity. Finally, activists must advocate for an International Convention on the Rights of Sexual and Gender Minorities to address the most heinous rights violations particular to this identity group, such as imprisoning HIV+ people who have committed no crime, banning pride marches, and executing people for engaging in consensual same-sex relations. These incursions on the system's terms will continue to decenter but sexual and gender minorities must also mobilize to confront the hierarchy, else we enable a "global gay apartheid" (Puar, 2007) because "the master's tools will never dismantle the master's house" (Fanon, 1961). However, these tools can be used to expose the homophobic and heteronormative biases in contemporary human rights legal principles and practices and to open space for more dialogue and understanding.

But these acts within and through the current system are not enough. The end goal is neither tolerance nor acceptance: it is, quite simply, freedom. LGBTIQ-identified people need more than a "right to privacy" or a "right to marry." These heterocentric standards grant limited permission for sexual and gender minorities to be more like the dominant group and to conform to their norms of behavior, not to be who they are and to live that identity openly, freely, and joyfully. Ultimately, LGBTIQ-identified people must demand a "right to be queer." What would that look like? A world in which people act, talk, dress, and love as they please. A world in which all may display affection openly in public – not just during pride marches but in their everyday lives – without fear of being beaten, arrested, sexually assaulted, or executed or of losing their jobs or their homes. A world in which police, lawyers, judges, teachers, politicians, neighbors – everyone – stand up to defend the right of sexual and gender minorities to be who they are and to censure or punish those who deny that right. It would, in short, be a very different world than the one we live in today.

Notes

1 I use the term "sexual and gender minorities" to refer collectively to people who identify as gay, lesbian, bisexual, transsexual, transgender, intersexual, queer (LGBTIQ), or other varieties of sexuality or gender identity not conforming to the hegemonic identities of heterosexual masculinity or femininity dominant in a given society. The term reflects the political position of subordination of LGBTIQ-identified people *vis-à-vis* the dominant sex–gender paradigm and the power relations between and among these groups.

2 Many thanks to Syracuse University undergraduate student research assistants Grace Choi, Jaime Peca, Grace Davis, and Tikkara Cooper for their help on this project.

3 Mooney Cotter's analysis (2010) reviews legislation and litigation from English-language resources available on: Australia and New Zealand, South Africa and the African Union; Canada, Mexico, and the United States; the North American Free Trade Agreement; the United Kingdom, the Republic of Ireland, and the European Union. Significantly, all litigation claims she reviewed were based on national law or regional agreements, not the "universal" human rights in the UN-catalogued treaties listed here.

4 The co-sponsors for draft resolution E/CN.4/2003/L.92 were Austria, Belgium, Brazil, Canada, Czech Republic, Denmark, Finland, France, Germany, Greece, Ireland, Italy, Lichtenstein, Luxembourg, Netherlands, Norway, Portugal, Spain, Sweden, and the United Kingdom.

5 Methodology note: I reviewed the iCSO database using the title search function and found 29 NGOs with the term "gay" in their official title, seven additional "Lesbian"-only NGOs, two "queer," two "transgender," one "homosexual," and one "sexual minorities." The terms "gender minorities," "transsexual," "intersexual," and "hermaphrodite" returned no additional organization names. Colloquial terms used as epithets in some cultural contexts, such as "queen," "fag," and "dyke," also returned no LGBTIQ-focused NGO names in the iCSO database search function. The term "sexuality" returned a list of four organizations, but each of these was concerned broadly with sexual and reproductive issues or focused more on women's rights than the rights of sexual and gender minorities per se.

Suggested further reading

Leckey R and Brooks K (eds.) (2010) *Queer Theory: Law, Culture, Empire*. New York: Routledge.

MacKinnon C (2007) *Are Women Human? And Other International Dialogues*. Cambridge/London: Harvard University Press/Belknap Press.

Mooney Cotter A (2010) *Ask No Questions: An International Legal Analysis on Sexual Orientation Discrimination*. Burlington, VT: Ashgate Publishing.

Reid G (2013) *How to Be a Real Gay: Gay Identities in Small-Town South Africa*. South Africa: University of KwaZulu-Natal Press.

Sheill, K (2009) Losing out in the intersections: Lesbians, human rights, law and activism. In Kollman K & Waites M (eds.) The global politics of LGBT human rights. *Contemporary Politics* 15(1): 55–71.

Bibliography

Amnesty International (1997) *Breaking the Silence: Human Rights Violations Based on Sexual Orientation.* London: Amnesty International UK Print.

Associated Press (1996) U.S. grants political asylum to gays. December 7, reprinted in *The Finger Lakes Times* (Geneva, NY), December 8.

Buckley-Zistel S and Stanley R (eds.) (2012) *Gender in Transitional Justice.* New York: Palgrave Macmillan.

Carter D (2004) *Stonewall: The Riots that Sparked the Gay Revolution.* New York: St. Martin's Press.

Charlesworth H (1999) Feminist methods in international law. *American Journal of International Law* 93(2): 379–94.

Charlesworth H and Chinkin C (2000) *The Boundaries of International Law: A Feminist Analysis.* Manchester: Manchester University Press.

Charlesworth H, Chinkin C, and Wright R (1991) Feminist approaches to international law. *American Journal of International Law* 85(4): 613–45.

Dufour C (1998) Mobilizing gay activists. In: Costain A & McFarland A (eds.) *Social Movements and American Political Institutions.* Lanham, MD: Rowman & Littlefield.

Fanon, F (1961) *The Wretched of the Earth [Les damnés de la terre].* New York: Grove Press.

Goldberg S (1993) 'Give me liberty …': political asylum and the global persecution of Lesbians and gay men. *Cornell International Law Review* 26(3): 605–23.

Human Rights Watch (2008) UN: General Assembly statement affirms rights for all. December 18. http://www.hrw.org/en/news/2008/12/18/un-general-assembly-statement-affirms-rights-all

International Commission of Jurists (2014) Sexual Orientation and Gender Identity. http://www.icj.org/sogi-un-database/

International Conference on Human Rights, Sexual Orientation, and Gender Identity (2013) Oslo, Norway: April 15–16. http://www.hrsogi.org/

International Conference on Lesbian, Gay, Bisexual, and Transgender Human Rights (2006) Declaration of Montreal. Montreal, Quebec, Canada. http://www.declarationofmontreal.org

International Lesbian, Gay, Bisexual, Trans, and Intersex Association (2011) *LGBT Voices at the United Nations: ECOSOC Council Vote Grants Consultative Status to ILGA.* Geneva, Switzerland: July 25. http://ilga.org/ilga/en/article/n5GebHB1PY

——(2014) http://ilga.org/.

International Service for Human Rights (2010) UN Secretary-General and US Government Pledge to Champion LGBT Rights at the UN. December 16. http://www.ishr.ch/general-asssembly/978-un-secretary-general

Kuhn B (2011) *Gay Power! The Stonewall Riots and the Gay Rights Movement 1969.* New York: 21st Century.

LaViolette N and Whitworth S (1994) No safe haven: sexuality as a universal human right and gay and Lesbian activism in international politics. *Millennium: Journal of International Studies* 23(3): 563–88.

Leckey R and Brooks K (eds.) (2010) *Queer Theory: Law, Culture, Empire.* New York: Routledge.

McAdam D, McCarthy J, and Zald M (eds.) (1996) *Comparative Perspectives on Social Movements, Political Opportunity Structures, Mobilizing Structures, and Cultural Framings.* Cambridge: Cambridge University Press.

MacFarquhar N (2008) In a first, gay rights are pressed at the UN. *New York Times,* December 19. http://www.nytimes.com/2008/12/19/world/19nations.html

MacKinnon C (2007) *Are Women Human? And Other International Dialogues.* Cambridge/London: Harvard University Press/Belknap Press.

Mooney Cotter A (2010) *Ask No Questions: An International Legal Analysis on Sexual Orientation Discrimination.* Burlington, VT: Ashgate Publishing.

O'Flaherty M and Fisher J (2008) Sexual orientation, gender identity, and international human rights law: contextualizing the Yogyakarta Principles. *Human Rights Law Review* 8(2): 207–48.

Pillay N (2010) How we can fight back against homophobia. *Washington Post,* October 23: A15. http://www.washingtonpost.com/wp-dyn/content/article/2010/10/22/AR201 0102205450.html

Pollack M (2009) *Acting Deputy Assistant Secretary of State for the Bureau of Population, Refugees, and Migration*. USUN Press Release #2064, March 31.

Puar J K (2007) *Terrorist Assemblages: Homonationalism in Queer Times*. Durham, NC: Duke University Press.

Reid G (2013) *How to Be a Real Gay: Gay Identities in Small-Town South Africa*. South Africa: University of KwaZulu-Natal Press.

Rothschild C, Long S, and Fried S (eds.) (2005) *Written Out: How Sexuality Is Used to Attack Women's Organising*. International Gay and Lesbian Human Rights Commission and Center for Women's Global Leadership. https://iglhrc.org/content/international-written-out-how-sexuality-used-attack-womens-organizing-updated.

Salisbury S (2011) African Opposition to the UN Resolution on Sexual Orientation and Gender Identity. *Human Rights Brief*, Center for Human Rights and Humanitarian Law, November 10. http://hrbrief.org/2011/11/african-opposition-to-the-un-resolution-on-sexual-orientation-gender-identity/

Sigsworth R and Valji N (2012) Continuities of violence against women and the limitations of transitional justice: the case of South Africa. In: Buckley-Zistel S & Stanley R (eds.) *Gender in Transitional Justice*. New York: Palgrave Macmillan.

Snow A (2010) Gay rights row breaks out over amended UN resolution. *The Guardian (Manchester)*, December 21. http://www.guardian.co.uk/world/2010/dec/21/gay-rights-row-un-resolution

Studzinsky S (2012) Neglected crimes: the challenge of raising sexual and gender-based crimes before the extraordinary chambers in the courts of Cambodia. In: Buckley-Zistel S & Stanley R (eds.) *Gender in Transitional Justice*. New York: Palgrave Macmillan.

Trevelyan L (2008) UN split over homosexuality laws. *BBC News*, December 19. http://news.bbc.co/uk/go/pr/fr/-/2/hi/europe/7791063.stm

United Nations Economic and Social Council (2013) List of non-governmental organizations in consultative status with the Economic and Social Council as of 1 September 2013. E/2013/INF/6. http://esango.un.org/civilsociety/documents/E_2013_INF_6.pdf

United Nations General Assembly (2008) Joint Statement on Human Rights, Sexual Orientation, and Gender Identity. December 18. http://www.hrw.org

United Nations High Commissioner for Refugees (2012) Guidelines on International Protection No. 9: Claims to Refugee Status Based on Sexual Orientation and/or Gender Identity. HCR/GIP/12/09. http://www.unhcr.org/509136ca9.pdf

United Nations Human Rights Council (2011) Human Rights, Sexual Orientation, and Gender Identity. HRC/RES/17/19: June.

——(2012) Human Rights Council Panel on Ending Violence and Discrimination against Individuals based on their Sexual Orientation and Gender Identity. Geneva, Switzerland: UNHRC, March 7.

United Nations Office of the High Commissioner for Human Rights (2011) Discriminatory Laws and Practices and Acts of Violence against Individuals Based on their Sexual Orientation and Gender Identity: Report of the High Commissioner for Human Rights to the United Nations General Assembly. A/HRC/19/41: November 17.

——(2012) Born Free and Equal: Sexual Orientation and Gender Identity in International Human Rights Law. New York/Geneva: United Nations. http://www.ohchr.org/Documents/Publications/BornFreeAndEqualLowRes.pdf

United Nations Treaty Collection (2014) Status of Treaties: Multilateral Treaties Deposited with the Secretary-General. Chapter IV: Human Rights. https://treaties.un.org/

Von Wahl A (2012) How sexuality changes agency: gay men, Jews, and transitional justice. In: Buckley-Zistel S & Stanley R (eds.) *Gender in Transitional Justice*. New York: Palgrave Macmillan.

Yogyakarta Principles (2006) The Application of International Human Rights Laws in Relations to Sexual Orientation and Gender Identity. http://www.yogyakartaprinciples.org/

4

TRANSVERSAL AND PARTICULARISTIC POLITICS IN THE EUROPEAN UNION'S ANTIDISCRIMINATION POLICY

LGBT politics under neoliberalism

Markus Thiel

Introduction

In the 28-member bloc of the European Union (EU), gender and sexuality rights are highly regarded as part of the catalog of fundamental rights available to EU citizens, and the EU is viewed as a vanguard in promoting LGBTQ rights internationally. In effect, the EU as a regulatory institution superordinate to the state in economic and related matters "queers" traditional domestic politics in significant ways. Yet, recent research is split on the effects of the EU rights regime on sexual rights. While some view the region developing in a generally progressive direction (Paternotte & Ayoub, 2012), others have commented on the expectations–capabilities gap resulting from normative-legal provisions and "soft" law, i.e., the intergovernmental, voluntary agreement to best practices in the absence of comprehensively mandated gender equality (Kantola, 2010; Mazur & McBride, 2012). In her provocatively titled book *Why Europe is Lesbian and Gay Friendly (and the US Never Will Be)*, Wilson similarly weighs the EU impact, stating that "the construction of the EU did present windows of opportunity in which inclusive policies could be framed as economically beneficial" (2009: 3). Another socioeconomic analyst, Scharpf, was more critical when he wrote about the EU's "fundamental asymmetry between policies promoting market efficiencies and those promoting social protection and equality" (2002: 17).

This chapter, however, highlights another ambiguous aspect deduced from the EU's economic origin: the predication of sexual rights on neoliberal market policy creation. LGBTQ[1] politics are a comparatively young field of policy action and analysis, and the bloc's general antidiscrimination agenda covering gender and sexual orientation specifically in employment results from the fact that all EU law has to be justified in relation to the liberalization of the single market. The EU passed an employment-based antidiscrimination legal directive on various (gender, religious, sexual orientation, disability, age) grounds in 2000. In 2008 it proposed a more comprehensive 'horizontal' antidiscrimination directive going beyond employment. But member state governments in the EU Council continue to block ratification. Poland or Lithuania cite cultural incompatibilities, while Germany feels that the implementation would be too costly for businesses. Not only are LGBTQ individuals disadvantaged compared with heterosexual majority populations, but a particular group-/identity-based differentiation through the EU's approach towards inclusion may reinforce the potential discriminatory impact of state governance in these fields. And it lays bare the volatile limits of sexual rights affirmation under the pretext of neoliberal market integration.

In this chapter, I take a closer look at the "politics of sexuality." I explore how the construction of sexual differences conditions the work of LGBT advocates in regional markets in the context of the EU's rights policy discourse, which has at least normatively been broadened to include all major ethnic and social minorities. In time, it became a discursively mainstreamed approach towards policy-creation and-revision. Theoretically, transversal politics, i.e., a negotiation among stakeholders in which notions of difference are mediated and encompassed in broad equality provisions (Yuval-Davis, 1999), is preferable over any particularistic approach. A group rights approach may stigmatize specific populations, create competitive binaries or conflict with the equality-for-all agenda of political liberalism in Western democracies. With respect to the EU's potentially beneficial impact on sexual rights, the regional integration process "offers marginalized groups the opportunity to destabilize predominant (*domestic, added*) discourses and to project alternative narratives and interpretations" (Kamenou, 2011: 33). Yet the EU struggles with the tension between providing supranational equality to all member state citizens based on its market-oriented legal prerogatives, the particularism of specific gender or LGBT group demands, as well as of member states' policies and their political cultures. A look at the underlying societal mechanisms aids in explaining the ambiguous positioning of the EU when advocating limited equality provisions. Why do the EU and its member states treat gender and sexuality differently in the development of common supranational antidiscrimination policies? What public LGBTQ identity markers may be responsible for such differences that create such a binary? How does a neoliberal EU policy orientation impact the attainment of LGBT human rights? Lastly, given this contentious policy field, what inferences for critical IR theory building can be drawn from the experience of LGBT groups representing marginalized minorities on the one hand, and from queer theory, on the other?

The emergence of gender and LGBT equality policies in the EU

Social movement literature and queer social theory supply the theoretical backgrounds on which these multilevel interactions play out. Scholarly works in mainstream as well as critical international political economy (IPE) are largely silent on the question of the compatibility of neoliberal policies, i.e., policies emphasizing liberalization, privatization and competitiveness, and the rights claims of LGBTQ populations.

Such a gap has become more problematic since the Eurocrisis revealed that marginalized populations are more severely affected by crisis-induced repercussions than the general population (Thiel, 2013). Social movement literature emphasizes the opening of opportunity structures for claim making and agenda setting by movements and the framing of issues in a way that makes claims more receptive to other stakeholders. Scholars detailed the organizational-framing aspects of gender and LGBT civil society groups (Tremblay & Paternotte, 2011; Ayoub & Paternotte, 2014), whereas queer theory added a critical perspective to the binary conceptions of gender, hetero–homo relations, and the "queering" of the national through the EU's supranational involvement in policy processes (Kamenou, 2011). Queer theory is a diverse body of literature, but in the narrow focus applied here, it relates to activism that grapples with tensions on the transversal–particularistic spectrum of "single-issue activism" (by lesbians, gays, transgender, HIV/Aids groups) as opposed to a unifying umbrella conception that lays bare the dichotomy between a queering universality of rights and a homonormative minoritization (Yekani et al., 2013). It also exposes the alleged attempts at "normalization," on which much of the equality movement discourse in Europe and elsewhere is based and which queer movements generally resent in their desire to remain alternative or different in society. Queer theory adds a critique of neoliberal consumption and normalization that is sorely lacking in mainstream IPE (Duggan, 2004; Binnie, 2014). Thus, I combine one applied body of movement literature with more theoretical queer theory to open new venues for analysis regarding the interactions of these groups and probe those in regards to neoliberal assumptions about rights attainments. Feminist literature is tangentially important insofar as it serves as comparator to the LGBT advocacy analyses and queer theory.

I focus primarily on external representations of those groups (differences) and the resulting repercussions, rather than on their intrinsic characteristics. This avoids identitarian reifications of gender and sexuality roles and stereotypes. Instead, by capturing the dynamics between claim making, representation and political outcomes, I hope to uncover if transnational LGBT advocacy is different from gender-related politics (even though both are to a certain extent socially constructed), and how certain characteristics determine policy outcomes at the EU level based on neoliberal, rather than normative rights-based considerations. Both are heavily intertwined, however: it is fairly uncontested, for example, that "women's rights and lesbian rights are inextricably linked in substantive way, not least because the defense of lesbian rights is integral to the defense of all women's rights to determine their own sexuality" (Elman, 2007: 118). But gender and sexuality rights groups continue to experience different standings within the EU rights regime, with ensuing consequences for policies and rights attainment. A look at the construction of such advocacy politics in a neoliberal regional market system such as the EU yields insights into a critical reformulation of some IPE tenets as well.

As for gender politics in the EU, Woodward (2012), in a summary article, highlights four areas that are relevant for research and policy on this topic: representation of women in decision-making; EU gender equality policies; the European welfare state; and the international gender experience. Whereas the first two aspects are fairly straightforward success stories given the pan-European increase in female politicians and the mainstreaming of EU-mandated gender equality directives (although the latter has been viewed as soft law and thus, too easy to avoid by national governments given that pay differentials continue to exist), the last two are more problematic, as welfare state reforms were particularly detrimental for women. As for the final international criterion, although the EU seeks to export gender justice through development aid, the transformative momentum diminishes when no concrete membership incentives exist. Applied to LGBT advocacy in the EU, there are theoretical differences between political representation as an advanced status and antidiscrimination as a more basic one. Few guiding principles transferable to policy practice exist, whether with regards to LGBT representation in the EU – except for the European parliament's LGBT intergroup made up of legislators from various countries and parties, no other institutional representation exist; or with LGBT policy effects on welfare states and even less so with the EU's international advocacy of LGBT rights in third countries (sometimes termed "homocolonialism" for its liberal-interventionist impact on postcolonial societies). With regards to the latter, the Union has certain leverage over aspiring member countries that want to join the bloc and thus are required to integrate existing antidiscrimination clauses. Once states have acceded, however, they sometimes retreat on rights provisions: six months after accession in 2013, Croatia imposed a same-sex marriage ban by popular referendum (although a year later, parliament countered with the passing of a civil union law). Moreover, the explicit LGBT-friendly rhetoric of the EU in more distant regions elicits increasing pushback by, for instance, African or Asian states that decry such homocolonialist discourse. By these four policy benchmarks, then, the success of the women's movement has relatively few incentives for emulation by the LGBT movement.

The EU's history of antidiscrimination policies emerged based on the single market legislation, and as such automatically narrows legal rights against discrimination to employment- or market-related issue areas. Swiebel's (2009) comprehensive account of LGBT rights in the EU highlights that proposals to combat discrimination against homosexuals in employment were drafted as early as 1984. Brussels appropriated neoliberal policies early on. It is the area where the EU is strongest in terms of policy initiation, through the European Commission, and supervision through the Court of Justice. Of the four existing antidiscrimination directives (the Racial Equality, Employment Equality Framework, Sex Amendment and the Goods and Services ones) – the EU's most stringent legal instruments – the last two specifically aim at the equal positioning of men and women in the workplace and private law. The 2000 Employment Equality Framework directive is most significant because it encompasses a variety of intersectional grounds such as disability, age, religion, and sexual orientation, albeit only in the narrow employment area. In the case of the comprehensive horizontal antidiscrimination directive covering all EU policy areas, the European parliament is overwhelmingly in favor of this legislation but needs to rely on the state-led EU Council that prevents it from passing. In contrast, legal cases that have in the past few years appeared in front of the European Court of Justice, led to a subsequent gradual expansion of LGBT rights through the provision of civil union rights on equal status with marriage rights, asylum claims based on sexual discrimination, and in other non-employment-based areas.[2] On a broader societal level, hundreds of LGBT associations and INGOs can be found across EU member states that aim in a two-track way to influence national and EU-level public attitudes and legislation. These national and regional organizations are linked up with umbrella organizations in Brussels (such as the in LGBT affairs dominant International Lesbian and Gay Association, ILGA-Europe) to lobby major EU institutions, especially the Commission as the EU's executive. Their work, while difficult to measure in terms of legal or political output, advances through auxiliary input measures on both the state and EU level the acceptance of said minorities. While the EU can generally be classified as progressive in LGBT affairs, the legal limitations of the single market, and the pushback by member states, remain obstacles to the achievement of substantive antidiscrimination and equality.

Research on the progression of LGBT movements and policies tends to focus primarily on the fairly strong impact that movements have on political decision-makers – few of which are openly LGBT, either on the national or European level – and resemble more closely the women's movement of the 1970s. Back then, the LGBTQ movement was just emerging, whereas the feminist movement had already experienced various "waves" of political activism. What emerged in San Francisco and New York resembled for the most part earlier feminist attempts of societal emancipation: mainly driven by white, heteronormative men, it largely aimed more at inclusion and representation than the appreciation of difference. This changed only with the AIDS crisis, when the "gay disease" declared non-heteronormative sexualities as abject by the majority population and in turn, queer activists vocalized their differences with an exclusionary mainstream society. It seems ironic that today's largest LGBT activist groups seem, as Stein (2012) perceives it, to advocate "normalization as the price and ticket to success" (189), i.e., the inclusion of marriage equality, adoption, and other heteronormative elements into their policy stances. Such an apparently inclusive approach is also being pushed by large parts of the media and the businesses, both of which have to gain from the normalization and commodification of this particular constituency into the consuming masses (all the more because gay and lesbian couples, in contrast to transgender or queer populations, are often viewed as relatively affluent "double-income-no-kids markets" themselves). The more radical view of Gilreath (2011) in her book entitled *End of Straight Supremacy* objects to this adaptation to straight norms and pushes for "substantive equality" abolishing socially constructed binaries and dichotomies altogether (straight/gay, speech/hate, etc.) instead of the now straight-abrogated "formal equality" of heteronormative rights.

In the EU, there still exists a marked difference in the legal recognition of gender and LGBT rights, not only in the degree of protection, but also in the extent to which Brussels must justify any policy initiative with recourse to market liberalization and improvement. In practice, that means that while sexual and gender rights are officially protected in the employment sector through so-called "framework directives" that member states are obliged to adhere to, the more comprehensive horizontal directive protecting LGBT and other individuals in *all* areas of EU competence such as housing, education, access to services etc., has been languishing since 2008 because of the resistance of eight member states (ILGA-Europe, 2013a). ILGA-Europe, together with the Social Platform representing 47 major social INGOs, publicly pressed the case for the broader antidiscrimination directive. Ayoub and Paternotte (2014) show how LGBT advocacy groups have consistently linked EU rights norms and values to their own political agenda, succeeding not only in the liberal-democratic Western European part but also establishing linkages between LGBT-friendly norms and EU integration in Central and Eastern Europe despite the relatively homophobic sociopolitical climate there. However, the primacy of transnational activism distinguishes LGBT advocacy from feminist policy advocacy, which seems as much state oriented as it is transnational. There are two major reasons for this difference: unlike the apex of women's rights activism in the 1960s to 1980s, more recent LGBT rights advocacy operates in a thoroughly globalized social network and media-based environment, which aids in the pursuit of collaborative transnational network activities among civil society groups. Particularly in the EU context, this led to a strong independent as well as EU-supported transnational activism when conducting institutional lobbying or public campaigns. In contrast, the women's movement started out in its earliest configurations as a movement for the right to vote, and as such was/is interested in sending representatives to the political instances such as cabinets, courts and parliaments. It has to be noted, however, that this difference may be due not only to the fact that the LGBTQ community does not have to deal with such substantial discrimination, but that there is more easily detectable visibility in terms of gender than sexuality.

Are particularism, (in)visibility and difference problematic when pursuing LGBT policies?

Particularism, defined here as a unique quality or characteristic that is being expressed and reified on a number of personal, collective or national levels, proves to be an ambiguous strategy for achieving sexual rights. The EU constantly negotiates the demands of particular group or national constituents with its universalist or transversal normative–legal framework. Particularism can be stigmatizing in its stereotyping nature, particularly when cultural homophobic norms are extenuated through "state-sponsored homophobia" (Holzhacker, 2012), as is occurring in many Central and Eastern European countries. Conversely, LGBTQ individuals as a category may be pressured to fit into a heteronormative copy of traditional societal structures, or defamed as an abject sexual "other" when speaking up: "the paradox that you can only get rid of oppressive dichotomies by affirming the subordinate form in order to challenge the hegemonic term is one that continues to haunt the radical agenda" (Weeks, 2013: 7). In the EU, state particularism manifests as a way to lead through progressive domestic implementation the collective group of 28 member states: the degree of "state feminism," for instance, is said to be a decisive factor in how substantive gender representation and equality can be achieved and diffused (Mazur & McBride, 2012). It has also been suggested that EU states historically adhered to a universalist versus differentialist model of sexual inclusion (Banens, 2014) – although this refers more to a state particularism rather than a group particularism. The latter, exemplified by LGBT advocacy claims, may thus mitigate the potentially excluding nature of societal mainstream norms if adopted and supported by (supra)national equality bodies. By extension, EU institutions or agencies such as the EU Fundamental Rights Agency, which aims at the promotion of general human rights in the EU following the incorporation of the Fundamental Rights Charter in the EU's latest Lisbon Treaty in 2009 can support and diffuse those transversal, universalist prescriptions. Hence particularism exposes through the special treatment of these individuals politicized issues related to sexuality and gender that in the past had either been ignored or left in the private realm.

Related to issues of particularism are questions of the deployment of "visibility" of the LGBTQ population. Visibility issues are twofold. On the one hand, it refers to the fact that sexual orientation, unlike race or gender (in most cases, except for transgender or genderqueer individuals), can be hidden and is not an easily detectable identity marker. Policymakers themselves regularly hide their sexual orientation in order to advance their political careers, thus negating political representation. To illustrate the potentially adverse effects of being out, the European parliament's most prominent advocate for LGBTQ rights, Ulrike Lunacek, was the victim of an acid attack at Vienna's pride parade in 2014. In a heteronormative climate such as electoral politics, such pressures create a vacuum in terms of influence and representation. This is more problematic on the national level where popular reelection features more prominently – as opposed to many EU institutions that are unelected and whose policies are further removed from member state scrutiny. The same invisibility exists in the private sector, where about one-third of employees are still closeted, and almost none of the major company executives is out (*The Economist*, 2014). This generalized invisibility prevents the creation of a more tolerant public sphere in which an array of sexual and gender expressions are publicly displayed and subsequently accepted.

On the other hand, within the LGBTQ demographic there exists a familiar hierarchical positioning that relegates, for example, lesbians behind gays in terms of socioeconomic visibility in the wider population, and transgender and bisexuals even behind both categorical sexual dispositions. The latter are less visible in public and often, not even fully accepted within the LGBTQ community. Such divergent experiences and social standings do not easily cluster together, and continue to weaken the standing of LGBTQ populations, particularly as it relates to the creation of transversal-tolerant attitudes and policies encompassing differences not only within the LGBTQ community, but within the larger populace. As the gay and lesbian movement advances in the attainment of marriage or adoption rights, transgender individuals decry being left behind when it comes to more fundamental workplace protection rights or access to healthcare. In this sense, the general pressure for political representation is a real challenge to, for instance, transgender constituents, who often experience disidentification, hypervisibility, transitional temporality, or "passing" in their everyday environments (Sjoberg, 2012). I found this confirmed when conducting interviews with transgender groups that were not participating with other pan-European civil society groups in the EU Fundamental Rights Platform. The consequences of such modi are multifold and can be used to further IR theorizing in terms of moving away from established categories of self and political representation towards more fluid ambiguities, as will be recapitulated in the concluding section.

Thus, is (perceived) difference an important criterion for the differential treatment of gender and/or sexual rights groups? The latter group clearly oscillates between normalization and assimilation, and radical queerness in its self-positioning in society. Similar to the visibility issue, the question of the degree of desired inclusion or "normalization" and remaining difference produces an advocacy setting that is quite different from the gender equality one. Gender equality groups were traditionally more concerned with equal status, and are overall more coherent than contemporary European LGBTQ communities. The latter fluctuate between assimilatory inclusion in all sectors of society, and expressive radical queerness that revolts against traditional societal norms and neoliberal commodification of both consumption and family status. This is pronounced in the current decade, as both political orientations are quite visible and pushed by actors themselves and the sociopolitical environment. It is noticeable that the younger "millenial" generation of LGBT individuals does not necessarily seem to pursue expressively political goals of emancipation, equality, or recognition of being different, but rather promotes an all-inclusive and personalistic stance on gender and sexual orientation issues: for the LGBTQ generation coming of age in Western consolidated democracies, it is not a question of specific social and political expressions, but rather of an open and fluid identification that possibly should not become a political issue and thus overcome some of the "labeling" issues in the LGBT community. Such ambiguity, as much as it is helpful in expressing the diversity of LGBTQ voices internally and to the broader society, is moving away from stated political goals and rather, views acceptance of a wide range of lifestyles and individual expressions as more important (*New York Times*, 2013). This has a potentially detrimental effect for a focused push for more political equality and representation, as it could open up LGBTQ internal or generational schisms and, in the course, dilute the combined force of political campaigns structured in the EU predominantly around equality for gays, lesbians, and, more recently, transgender individuals.

Aside from issues of particularism, visibility and difference, are there other factors that influence how a sex rights regime will be articulated? It seems that organizational-institutional aspects on the claim-receiving end of the institutions are also of significant relevance. The next section details the context in which EU antidiscrimination and gender/sex rights policies are developed.

Are organizational-institutional differences relevant?

Organizational-institutional differences in LGBT advocacy and the EU more generally occur on both the national and supranational levels. As such, the various policy traditions and political cultures in large part determine Brussels' complex multinational, multilevel political environment. For example, a variety of recognized same-sex marriage statuses exist across EU states, ranging from full marriage (in the Netherlands, Denmark, Belgium, Spain, Portugal, Sweden, the Netherlands, Luxembourg, and most of the UK) and registered partnerships to no recognition of such partnerships in many Southern and Eastern European member states. The only way in which a harmonization, no matter if in antidiscrimination or same-sex union equality, in EU member states can occur is through the application of the antidiscrimination framework directive across Europe and through European Court of Justice judgments against member states that are heeded by other ones in order to avoid tensions with Europe's most powerful court.

The institutional constellations within the EU system lend different opportunities to LGBT groups. The preeminent European Court of Justice is viewed as the main provider of equality law when adjudicating issues of same-sex relationships, for example, that then are diffused to varying degrees throughout the EU depending on the extent of national pushback (Kollman, 2009). In the executive and law-proposing EU Commission, which sees itself as the guardian of the EU treaties (including the Fundamental Rights Charter and its Article 21 prohibiting discrimination based on sexual orientation), rights considerations have increased steadily. After the EU's Lisbon Treaty made the Rights Charter legally binding, any new laws are supposed to be reviewed with the help of a "rights impact assessment" to check for possible negative rights implications of new EU laws, which, in effect, mainstreams fundamental rights in all legislation. In terms of advocacy group involvement, the support from the Commission is mixed: while it is vocal on norms, it has few means and little impact on getting states to actually comply with LGBT equality provisions. But the Commission regularly consults formally as well as informally with various rights advocates, elicits their input in online consultations, and materially supports a number of LGBT groups. ILGA-Europe, the largest one, receives core funding since 2000. In the European Parliament (EP), the LGBT intergroup made up of parliamentarians from different parties is very receptive to equality policies and is in close contact with umbrella INGOs based in Brussels, but has even less influence (over member states), and can only assist in making amendments or raising issues in the legislative process when new laws are being discussed. The last major institution in the Union, the nationally dominated European Council, which co-approves legislative proposals with the parliament, remains the bastion of state sovereignty and intergovernmental bargaining, is closed to non-state actors and not receptive to any rights-related "intrusion" into domestic policies. In particular, the more politically and economically powerful countries as well as the newer member states achieve optouts or signify their discontempt and non-agreement, be it because they fear interference into national matters, or because they still need to be socialized into the EU's normative structure. Minor committees (of regions, social) and semi-independent agencies (EU Fundamental Rights Agency, EU Gender Observatory) are largely of auxiliary nature with limited impact on the legal-political provision of rights, although the Rights Agency produced a highly noticed LGBT survey in 2012 (FRA, 2013).

These institutional structures are similar in terms of power when applied to either gender- or LGBT-based provisions. What, if any, differences do these organizational-institutional setting produce when dealing with these somewhat different constituents? While the exertion of legislative EU power institutionally remains the same in both cases, differences in the treatment of LGBT groups become somewhat distinct from gender-based ones in that the national governments still continue to contest sexual orientation antidiscrimination directives on a variety of cultural or instrumental grounds (EU Observer, 2012; ILGA-Europe 2013b). They still guard their own constitutional prerogatives carefully, notably in family law, which often has negative repercussions for transnational LGBT couples residing in a country with restrictive laws. For example, the fact that 11 of the 27 member states do not recognize gay partnerships sealed by family law in other EU states is still largely considered a domestic affair unless contested at the Court. Gender-based antidiscrimination policy has been more or less successfully established with the passing of a gender-mainstreaming policy for all EU policy sectors following the 1997 Amsterdam Treaty. Yet we have not yet seen a similar LGBT mainstreaming. The European Parliament has repeatedly requested a "roadmap" for LGBT rights ranging from antidiscrimination to marriage rights (European Parliament, 2013/2183), but given that its scope goes beyond the horizontal framework directive, it has not found the support of the Commission or the majority of member states. It is difficult to estimate the impact of such roadmaps, which, on the one hand, may lead to a more comprehensive antidiscrimination policy across the EU, but, on the other hand, may represent a particularistic policy instrument that heightens the public, extraordinary visibility of an already politicized demographic (similar to the EU's roadmap for Roma inclusion).

Attempting to theorize these institutional politics, Holzhacker (2012) extends Keck and Sikkink's classic (1998) "boomerang model" of pressure-inducing state–NGO interaction when adding the ricochet process as "powerful trans-border, trans-institutional circulation of information and argumentation between institutions and civil society" (2), which amplifies the pressures when striking multiple institutional actors simultaneously. He makes an interesting case for LGBT groups using the basic civil "right of assembly" to advocate publicly for their policy stances in less friendly states. Holzhacker correctly identifies the ricochet as a multiactor, multilevel involvement process to convince state actors, but it is not quite clear how such a strategy could apply when faced with the EU as a somewhat sovereignty amorphous, supranational governance body. LGBT equality INGOs such as ILGA-Europe are consistently playing a two-level game when they address both EU institutions and member states, and criticizing either one for failure to protect or implement LGBT rights. In fact, ILGA-Europe is expanding its transnational activity focus from

NGOs in 28 EU member states to 42 countries that participated at their last conference, covering non-member states and aspiring candidate countries as well, thus preparing the ground for a pan-European socialization and information exchange.

Following this logic, Santos (2012) examined the strategic moves of South European LGBT movements in pursuing rights equality, and has found that despite the variety of impacts or outputs on the various national levels with regards to the political-legal recognition (successful in Spain and Portugal, not so in Italy), an input-oriented analysis avoids an output-oriented misinterpretation of success on the political-legal level. She terms the novel advocacy form "syncretic activism," which highlights equality goals rather than the ideological content in order to progress and the removal of binaries and insider/outsider boundaries, for example, through the involvement of straight allies. Her findings may prove insightful for IR theorizing in that they go beyond established boundaries and binaries (input/output, straight/gay), but it is doubtful that such movements by themselves can exert sufficient pressure (aka input) if not transformed into longer lasting institutionalized NGOs or advocacy groups. The fact that states continue to have different same-sex partnership regulations is a reminder that the national political level remains relevant.

Lastly, in my own research on the involvement of rights NGOs in the work of the EU Fundamental Rights Agency (Thiel, 2014), I found no significant linkage between gender and LGBT movements, although they tend to support one another's stances, and are now more focused on the EU-favored "structural anti-discrimination" concept. In fact, a particular push by sex equality groups in the agency's civil society platform elicited major pushbacks by more conservative human rights NGOs that felt neglected by the relatively visible LGBT agenda in the EU. And even a women's group representative lamented in an interview that the EU's "equality-for-all" agenda delimits a gender-specific lens. That shows that in recent years a more generalized human rights discourse has become established in Europe that favors a transversal broadening of, albeit, basic rights protection, as opposed to a particularistic focus on specific constituencies. Such broadening is obvious when considering the increase in civil society actor constellations, and the resulting competition of INGOs or states with each other. But it still leaves one with the dilemma of the need for focused sector-specific rights provisions to be balanced with changing LGBTQ internal and more generalized EU human rights ideas that presuppose an "equality-for-all" agenda.

Rights attainment: subordinate to neoliberal market policies?

The preceding sections have hinted at the sometimes competitive, sometimes contradictory claiming of rights differentiated according to the needs of the EU's regional integration project. Among the socially progressive NGOs, LGBT groups compete but also collaborate with women's groups, and among the grouping of LGBT advocates one finds a wide array of civil society actors that pursue everything from heteronormative assimilation to radical rethinking of patriarchal, traditional societal structures. ILGA-Europe tries to combat a hierarchy of rights that as of now prioritizes race and gender antidiscrimination over sexual orientation in EU policy. Within the EU's LGBTQ population, however, gays and lesbians are in a better position to be politically represented in terms of visibility, difference, and significance for the single market project than the largely invisible bisexual or transgender constituents. Watson (2004) highlights the "differentiation of citizenship along the lines of class and gender" (296), and, I would add, along sexual orientation as well. Hence queer political tactics that involve exposing, subverting, and replacing heteronormative policies with more fluid ones often contain an inherent critique of the consumerist-capitalist society, but are not appreciated in a system in which civil society groups have to be viewed as reliable partners if they want an ear with EU institutions (Beger, 2009). The EU's liberalization and competitiveness mantras make transgender populations particularly vulnerable as they do not easily fit into the gender-binary stratified labor market, though their transformative experience can tell us much about, for instance, the experience of women *and* men in the workplace before and after transition. To be fair, large European companies are, on the whole, progressive, sometimes more so than the states they are based in, in an effort to recruit the best and brightest.

In the ideological bent of the EU's single market creation, the market is not necessarily being anymore regulated by governments, but now the state has become embedded in the regionalized market, thus reversing the original postwar structural linkage (Streek, 2000). This has led to a diminished control over economic policies, but also over social and related policies by governments. It also means that through the apparent weakening of a country's sovereignty in the regional market nationalist discourses emerge that decry the EU's interference in economic, but also in LGBT rights–related matters. This is particularly evident in the member states that have more recently joined, some of which decried the creeping "Eurosodomy" of LGBT-friendly norms into the national public spheres (Kulpa & Mizielinska, 2011). Yet governments still have leverage over citizenship policies. By transforming LGBT individuals there into better recognized citizens they can exert a minimal level of control: "In extending adoption and fostering rights to same-sex couples, states widened concepts of the family, that is, potential carers, and as a result reduced the state's burden of care" (Wilson, 2009: 77).

Hulme and Edwards (1995) add another critical perspective on the rise of NGOs under such neoliberal conditions. Convinced that markets and privatized services are more efficient providers of welfare, NGOs are increasingly being funded by states and government agencies outsourced to the private sector (4). This shifts more responsibility onto the shoulders of civil society, while the state, or the EU as a conglomerate of states, retreats and absolves itself from its fundamental role of securing the welfare of its citizens. In practice, many umbrella NGOs and civil society groups are materially supported by the European Commission, but their objectives accordingly need to fall in line with the EU's funding preferences for the reintegration of vulnerable/at-risk individuals into the labor market. Thus, their focus is forcibly shifted from the recognition and combatting of poverty and exclusion to the superordinate goal of increasing the labor participation rate.

Moreover, given the EU-specific origin as a free market, those groups are pressured to prioritize market principles (labor participation, making individuals more competitive), while becoming more dependent on governmental or EU funding and as a result, less independent and without real decision-making power over policy implementation. At the same time, they represent part of the privatizing retreat of governments in social and welfare sectors. LGBT groups are no exceptions to this: groups like ILGA-Europe have to link antidiscrimination activities with more inclusive workplaces and employment if they want to retain funding from major EU lines such as the Progress Program or the European Social Fund. Alternatively, they are increasingly challenged to diversify their funding so as to become less dependent on Brussels. Thus the association of LGBT rights groups with EU funding instruments is a precarious one. The increasing dependency of such groups on neoliberal EU imperatives produces another hierarchy of rights which relegates social inclusion, equal rights and justice to the bottom. More broadly, the EU's erosion of national governance signifies the retreat of the state from its traditional protection of civil welfare, exacerbated by the misled austerity programs prescribed by the EU as a remedy for the Eurocrisis. What is worse, the transnational capitalist class takes advantage of the EU's single market to create further policies that reduce national protections and increases competitive pressures on the general population and in particular, on the more vulnerable ones.

In a larger IPE context, the cooptation of rights advocacy NGOs by economic stakeholders and political institutions leads to a hollowing out of the former's legitimacy and radical agenda. Moreover, the supranational regionalization of the single market weakens the regulatory power of the state *vis-à-vis* economic actors. And the portrayal of economic policy as a technocratic, rather than political affair serves to shield market-based antidiscrimination policy from political accountability and cultural critique (Duggan, 2004). Such dominance of neoliberal thinking thus restricts alternative, critical views on the fact that rights are accorded only partially (at the workplace) in the absence of universal and broader human and social rights, and the NGOs' implicit reliance on the Union. The feminist contribution to IR highlights the uneven, gendered power relations, but a critical IPE that merges concerns with structural injustice with the thoughtful critique of queer theory's view on state economy relations, civil society, consumption and globalization is sorely needed. Is it acceptable to empower neoliberally minded institutions above the state if they provide more narrow but possibly far-reaching rights that are accrued by virtue of the market (and indirectly, purchasing power)? Such commodification of rights in itself is problematic, yet cannot be politicized in a system in which economic policy is protected by its supposed non-political nature reminiscent of Foucault's power–knowledge linkage.

Conclusion: challenging rights- and market-based hierarchies

The working out of different characteristics of the two groups under observation, gender and LGBT, should not be viewed as eliminating the intersectional connections that can result in multiple discriminations for individuals belonging to both categories. Given limited material and informational resources, the problem of treating both groups as separate, or in a hierarchical manner, becomes obvious. As Elman (2007) states, "without a greater willingness to confront contexts where gender converges and/or collides with other identities, those tasked with implementing equality will continue to wonder how to balance the needs of women with everyone else" (161). Applied to the EU context, those subtle differences in terms of policy reception by EU institutions may thus be amplified, and can have adverse effects on the impact of claim making and agenda setting of the various groups, such as European Women's Lobby, or ILGA-Europe, which have to adhere to the mandate given by their chapter members and have in practice little interaction with each other (aside from irregular exchanges and a common agreement on fighting structural discrimination).

More importantly, the EU's neoliberal orientation means that equality provisions, in whatever form perceived, are largely evaluated on market-based terms. This puts women in a higher hierarchical status followed by gay men, because they represent a larger constituency and are easier to classify than the increasingly diverse LGBTQ community. The Eurocrisis resulted in EU funding for social inclusion that prioritizes the young or long-time unemployed (some of which may be LGBTQ). Queer theory reminds us that such power structures and reifications need to be challenged on both essentializing and marketization grounds (Yekani et al., 2013). It also signifies that a substantive engagement with and reflection of normativity is needed, in the way neoliberal heteronormativity is desired by EU stakeholders and accordingly (re)produced or challenged by gender-/sex-based rights groups. The same can be said about the assumptions regarding the well-earning-white-gay-double-income-no-kids consumer elite. Thus, the equal treatment of the LGBTQ community may not be realizable, after all, as it is differentiated according to consumption patterns and its alignment with EU policy goals. A queer perspective is important for a critical reflection on the politically expedient normalization of non-traditional sexualities, although, in practice, such groups' critical or corrective function is underutilized in an effort to gain political support as an EU ally.

It appears, from a synoptic review of the preceding analyses, that a qualitatively different LGBTQ movement may take shape that values expressions of internal diversity and the advocacy of more generalized tolerance more than the pursuit of strategic political goals. This may have a positive impact on antidiscrimination more generally, but detracts from a concerted effort for LGBT rights. Sexual rights as such are not well recognized in the EU as a focus on neoliberal antidiscrimination policies prescribes a particularistic approach towards affected minorities that highlights their contribution to the economy, while trying to balance normatively a transversal "equality for all" agenda. Similarly to the feminist movement that gained diversity and emphasized intersectionality, the LGBTQ movement has attempted to become more inclusive internally but also became more amorphous with the rising influence of the millenial generation that tends to display more personal-individualistic and sexually ambiguous views. Hence, with time, transversal attitudes may give shape to transversal politics, aiming to expand notions of generalized sexual rights that should be accorded in a more universal and at the same time, individualistic manner. A move away from identity (sexual orientation or gender-based) conceptualizations of sexuality in the pursuit of sexual rights and overall social justice opens up a window for broader coalition building with other social or straight allies. NGOs such as ILGA-Europe, for instance, have started to build coalitions with eight major umbrella organizations when addressing the EU institutions.

In terms of novel ways of IR theorizing that could be deduced from this research, the gradual inclusion of the LGBTQ movement and "its" (if "it" exists as a collective whole as such) position on claiming equality – or maybe rather, individuality and expressive freedom – highlights the depoliticizing effect of the advancement of such rights in the Western neoliberal democracies, i.e., the retreat from political activism in view of an apparent inclusion and progress on rights claims as opposed to the vocal claims of representatives from more oppressive societies. It is hard to predict at this point to what degree openness in more traditional but liberal societies such as the U.S., Spain, Argentina, or Mexico that granted significant equal rights to LGBT groups will affect the diffusion of sexual expression rights globally. If sexual rights are to follow the relative success of women's rights, the current same-sex rights wave across the (Western) world, led by liberal democracies and post-authoritarian systems, may present a global opportunity window for global advocacy of those across the globe, but may also lead in course to a higher degree of internal (homonational) and external (homocolonial) contestation.

Just like "gender" or "LGBT" are increasingly contested positional-representative categories, IR/IPE concepts (neoliberalism, regulatory markets, universal human rights) are often perceived as uncontestable providers of stability. But non-conforming strands of theorizing challenge us to reach new critical inquiries that go beyond deconstructing and relativizing, as much of queer theory has done thus far. In practice, it appears that the LGBTQ community in the EU slowly takes a different shape towards a more individualized, but also less cohesive constituency; one that experiences simultaneously a wave of positive and negative attention by governments and intergovernmental organizations. The transnational strength of LGBTQ advocates, embedded in the neoliberal regional and global market and the "human-rights industrial complex" (Puar, 2013) changes the way states and civil society adapt to governance, operate and regulate commodified minority affairs, though a critical interrogation of such processes through non-traditional IR is still in its infancy.

Notes

1 In the following, I use LGBTQ for movements or communities that include, albeit unevenly, all those individuals. I reserve LGBT for the political stakeholders involved in EU advocacy politics, recognizing that internal differences in terms of claims and representation exist in this group category.

2 The Council of Europe (unrelated to the EU) maintains the European Court of Human Rights, which also provided LGBT friendly judgments in the past. However, these correct national laws and actions and thus lack the EU-wide application provided by the EU's Court of Justice.

Suggested further reading

Ayoub P and Paternotte D (2014) *LGBT Activism and the Making of Europe: A Rainbow Europe?* New York: Palgrave.
Beger N (2009) *Tensions in the Struggle for Sexual Minority Rights in Europe: Que(E)Rying Political Practices.* New York: Palgrave.
Downing L and Gillett R (eds.) (2011) *Queer in Europe.* Farnham: Ashgate.
Kulpa R and Mizielinska J (2011) *Decentering Western Sexualities: Central and Eastern European Perspectives.* Farnham: Ashgate.
Scholten P (2012) Gender and sexual politics: a central issue for European studies. *Perspectives on Europe* 42(1).

Bibliography

Ayoub P and Paternotte D (2014) *LGBT Activism and the Making of Europe: A Rainbow Europe?* New York: Palgrave.
Banens M (2014) *Same Sex Unions in Europe, Council for European Studies Commentary,* May 8. http://councilforeuropeanstudies.org/critcom/same-sex-unions-in-europe-some-observa tions-on-european-diversity/
Beger N (2009) *Tensions in the Struggle for Sexual Minority Rights in Europe: Que(E)Rying Political Practices.* New York: Palgrave.
Binnie J (2014) Neoliberalism, class and LGBTQ politics in Poland. *International Journal of Political Cultural Sociology* 27: 241–57.
Duggan L (2004) *The Twilight of Equality? Neoliberalism, Cultural Politics, and the Attack on Democracy.* New York: Beacon.
Economist (2014) *Schumpeter: The Corporate Closet.* May 31. New York: Alacra Store. http://news.alacrastore.com/economist/Schumpeter-The-corporate-closet-EN_EN_MAIN_2014 0531T000000_0089
Elman A (2007) *Sexual Equality in an Integrated Europe.* New York: Palgrave.
EU Observer (2012) LGBT Roadmap. http://euobserver.com/lgbti/116590
European Parliament, Resolution on the EU Roadmap against Homophobia and Discrimination (2014). http//www.europarl.europa.eu/sides/getDoc.do?type=TA&reference=P7-TA-2014-0062& language=EN&ring=A7-2014-0009
Fundamental Rights Agency (2013) LGBT Survey. http://fra.europa.eu/en/press-release/2013/fear-isolation-and-discrimination-common-europes-lgbt-community
Gilreath S (2011) *The End of Straight Supremacy.* New York: Cambridge University Press.
Holzhacker R (2012) State-sponsored homophobia and the denial of the right of assembly in Central and Eastern Europe. *Law and Policy* 35: 1–28.
Hulme D and Edwards M (1995) *NGOs, States and Donors: Too Close for Comfort?* New York: Palgrave.
ILGA-Europe (2013a) 5th anniversary of the horizontal framework directive. http://www.ilga-europe.org/media_library/euro_letter/2013/july/equality_and_non_discrimination/happy_5th_anniversary_of_the_equal_treatment_directive_proposal
——(2013b) ILGA Rainbow Map Europe Report on Legislation and Policies. http://www.ilga-europe.org/home/publications/reports_and_other_materials/rainbow_europe
Kamenou N (2011) Queer in Cyprus. In: Kulpa R & Joanna M (eds.) *Decentering Western Sexualities: Central and Eastern European Perspectives.* Farnham: Ashgate.
Kantola J (2010) *Gender and the European Union.* Basingstoke: Palgrave Macmillan.
Keck M E and Sikkink K (1998) *Activists Beyond Borders: Advocacy Networks in International Politics.* Ithaca, NY: Cornell University Press.
Kollman K (2009) European institutions, transnational networks and national same-sex unions policy: when soft law hits harder. *Contemporary Politics* 15(1): 37–53.
Mazur A and McBride D (2012) State feminism in Europe. *Perspectives on Europe* 42(1): 26–32.

New York Times (2013) Generation LGBTQIA. January 10. http://www.nytimes.com/2013/01/10/fashion/generation-lgbtqia.html?pagewanted=all&_r=0

Paternotte D and Ayoub P (2012) Building Europe. ILGA and LGBT activism in Central and Eastern Europe. *Perspectives on Politics* Special Issue 42(1).

Puar J (2013) Rethinking homonationalism. *International Journal for Middle East Studies* 45: 336–39.

Rahman M (2014) *Homosexualities, Muslim Cultures and Modernity*. New York: Palgrave.

Santos A (2012) *Social Movements and Sexual Citizenship in Southern Europe*. Basingstoke: Palgrave.

Scharpf F (2002) The European Social Model: Coping with the Challenge of Diversity. Max Plank Institute Working Paper No. 02/8.

Sjoberg L (2012) Towards trans-gendering international relations? *International Political Sociology* 6(4): 337–54.

Stein M (2012) *Rethinking the Gay and Lesbian Movement*. New York: Routledge.

Streek W (2000) Competitive solidarity – rethinking the European social model. In: Hinrichs K, Kitschelt H, & Wiesenthal H (eds.) *Kontingenz und Krise*. Frankfurt: Campus.

Swiebel J (2009) LGBT human rights: the search for an international strategy. *Contemporary Politics* 15(1): 19–35.

Thiel M (2013) Caught between "solidarity" and retrenchment: European civil society and human/social rights attainment in the EU. *Journal of Human Rights*: 24–42.

——(2014) European civil society and the EU Fundamental Rights Agency: creating legitimacy through civil society inclusion? *Journal of European Integration* 36(5): 435–51.

Tremblay M, Paternotte D, and Johnson C (2011) *The Lesbian and Gay Movement and the State. Comparative Insights into a Transformed Relationship*. New York: Ashgate.

Waites M (2009) Critique of "sexual orientation" and "gender identity" in human rights discourse: global queer politics beyond the Yogyakarta Principles. *Contemporary Politics* 15(1): 137–56.

Watson P (2004) Rethinking transition: globalism, gender and class In: Scott J W & Keats D (eds.) *Going Public: Feminism and the Shifting Boundaries of the Public Sphere*. Urbana: University of Illinois Press.

Weeks J (2013) *Making Sexual History*. New York: Wiley & Sons.

Wilson A (2009) *Why Europe is Lesbian and Gay Friendly (and the US Never Will Be)*. New York: SUNY Press.

Woodward A (2012) Gender and EU politics. *Perspectives on Europe* 42(1): 44–49.

Yekani E, Kilian E, and Michaelis B (2013) *Queer Futures. Reconsidering Ethics, Activism and the Political*. Farnham: Ashgate.

Yuval-Davis N (1999) What is transversal politics? *Soundings* 12: 94–99.

5

SEXUAL DIFFUSIONS AND CONCEPTUAL CONFUSIONS

Muslim homophobia and Muslim homosexualities in the context of modernity

Momin Rahman

Introduction

Born Free and Equal is a 2012 report from the United Nations Human Rights Commissioner, which argues that LGBT[1] people are indisputably covered by human rights principles and recommends that UN member states move to both decriminalize homosexuality and protect LGBT people from violence directed towards them. The European Union (EU) remains the only IGO to incorporate sexual orientation within its rights architecture (see Thiel, this volume) but the UN report nonetheless represents a significant step in legitimizing queer rights in the global context. Taken with the increasing public visibility of LGBTIQ identities globally and associated policy advances in rights, particularly since the 1990s (Hildebrandt, 2014), it seems plausible that we are on the threshold of establishing the international normalization of LGBT rights. There are, of course, obstacles to this process, most obviously in the resistance of some states to decriminalizing same-sex acts (Hildebrandt, 2014) and the emergence of political homophobia as a transnational phenomenon that allies governing elites with nationalist and/or religious social movements (Weiss & Bosia, 2013). Religious groups within states that have LGBTIQ rights have also been active in campaigning against these advances, both from within the dominant established religion, as in the case of Christians in the USA (Rayside & Wilcox, 2011) and from minority faiths associated with immigrant ethnic groups (Mepschen et al., 2010). Muslim majority nations, Muslim IGOs and Muslim minority immigrant populations have all figured prominently in this resistance. This chapter focuses on Muslim homophobia to illustrate some key conceptual issues that underpin the current expansion of LGBTIQ rights internationally. In doing so, I argue that there are assumptions behind the expansion of queer rights and identities that are derived from their emergence in Western societies during the modern era. Above all, there is an underlying sense that sexual politics will gradually diffuse from Western cultures to the rest of the world as the benefits of Western modernity are expanded globally. I suggest, in contrast, that these assumptions produce conceptual confusions when attempting to chart the course of a globalized LGBTIQ politics.

I frame my critique as a series of conceptual confusions, and I suggest that the conceptual *clarifications* that are required to more accurately assess contemporary Muslim sexual diversity must begin with an intersectional approach to understanding identities and experiences. I begin with a brief summary of the extent of Muslim homophobia and then consider how this is explained through a lack of modernization. Queer rights are identified with modernizing societies and hence Muslim homophobia is equated with a stubborn traditionalism of Muslim cultures that positions them outside of modernity. I argue, however, that the equation of LGBTIQ with modernity is based on a number of conceits about Western societies that generalize the Western experience of modernity to all societies. I suggest that current conceptualizations of LGBTIQ identity and equality derive from a partial, rather than universal, model of queer politics. I then consider whether postcolonial analysis provides a useful alternative conceptualization in the contemporary era. Focusing on the work of Joseph Massad, I suggest that there are dangers of reinstating a Euro-centric view of modernity in postcolonial analyses that see international queer rights campaigns primarily as neocolonialist politics. In contrast, we need to acknowledge both the global intersecting sociological and political formations of sexuality across cultures of East and West, and the legitimacy that certain postcolonial states derive from deploying homophobia as a nationalist tool, exemplified by, but not limited to, Muslim cultures. I discuss how we might begin to reconceptualize LGBTIQ identities and equality in ways that challenge both the conceits of the West and the resistance of the East. In conclusion, I think through what aspects of this analysis are relevant for wider examples of the internationalization of LGBTIQ politics.

Muslim homophobia and the modernization thesis

The annual report from the International Lesbian, Gay, Bisexual, Trans and Intersex Association (ILGA) shows that 31 out of a total 47 Muslim majority countries criminalize homosexual acts, although eight of these only criminalize male/male sex (Itaborahy & Zhu, 2013). The report confirms that homosexual acts are illegal in 76 countries out of 192 worldwide, and so Muslim nations constitute almost half of the nations that criminalize same-sex acts. All of the five states in which homosexuality is punishable by death are also Muslim majority nations.[2] When we turn to attitudinal surveys, the picture of Muslim homophobia is equally bleak. Becker's (2010) analysis of the World Values Survey (WVS)[3] remains one of the few comparisons that demonstrate a lower average level of acceptance of homosexuality in Muslim cultures. Given the limited number of Muslim countries included, however, he makes the point that these results may not be generalizable. Adamczyk and Pitt (2009) also point out that there is limited evidence on attitudes to homosexuality in both the WVS and other surveys.[4]

There is similarly limited evidence on Muslim minority populations but what exists does indicate a higher than average resistance to homosexuality. A survey of Muslims in the USA showed that 61% thought that homosexuality should be discouraged compared with 38% who thought the same in the general population (Pew, 2007). A survey on Canadian Muslim attitudes to homosexuality found that only 10% of Muslims expressed strong agreement with same-sex marriage (legal in Canada) while 58% expressed strong disagreement with this right (Rahman & Hussain, 2011). A cross-national Gallup survey (2009) found that none of the 500 British Muslims interviewed showed any acceptance of homosexuality (compared with 58% of the general public); only 19% in Germany showed acceptance (compared with 68% of the general public) and only 35% of French Muslims showed acceptance in comparison with 68% of the general population.

The preceding is only a brief sketch of the extent of Muslim antipathy to homosexuality and there are both methodological issues with the existing quantitative evidence and limitations in the scale of available qualitative evidence on attitudes and beliefs.[5] Nonetheless, what evidence we have does indicate Muslim majority nations and Muslim populations tend to be resistant to homosexual rights and identities. This resistance is explained by an assumption regarding the lack of modernization on the part of Muslim states and populations, which makes them unwilling to accept homosexuality. Processes that symbolize modernization like economic development, democratization, and secularization are understood as the foundational basis for the social equality of LGBTIQ. For example, Becker confirms the modernization thesis on tolerance and acceptance of non-normative identities. The thesis argues that economic development leads to wider acceptance of issues of "self-expression," whereas less developed countries emphasize patterns of economic survival that correlate with less tolerant attitudes (Inglehart & Baker, 2000; Inglehart & Welzel, 2005). Adamczyk and Pitt's analysis on the "self-expression" versus "survival" thesis concludes that if Muslims appear to be the least tolerant of homosexuality they share similar levels of disapproval with Protestants – particularly when the "survivalist" culture of their nation is predominant (2009: 349). In light of the available quantitative evidence, and the limited supporting qualitative evidence (Rahman, 2014), the modernization thesis seems useful in explaining Muslim antipathy to homosexuality because the evidence is cross-culturally consistent: men are less tolerant than women, higher levels of class and education produce more tolerance, broader social and gender equality seem to be important contextual factors.

What concerns me is that, within this frame, the "solution" to Muslim antipathy to sexual diversity becomes focused on modernizing "progress." There is therefore an inevitable assumption that the teleological diffusion of socioeconomic conditions, democratic institutions and associated cultural values would permit the acceptance of homosexuality. These assumptions reduce modernity from a global historical social formation to a specific set of processes that are both derived from Western experiences of modernity and are seen to have reached a critical threshold in the West. This model informs much contemporary research on queer Muslim experience (Yip, 2004, 2005, 2008, 2009) as well as broad theoretical arguments about globalized social change around sexuality (Weeks, 2007).

Conceptual confusions in the conceits of LGBTIQ equality as modernization

The equation of LGBTIQ with modernization is based on these conceits about Western societies that purport to generalize the Western experience of modernity to all societies. This means that we have to question current Western conceptualizations of sexual identity and equality in LGBTIQ politics since they derive from a partial, rather than universal, model of queer identity and politics. The modernization thesis is a problematic "solution" to Muslim homophobia because it assumes all modernization processes equate to a Western outcome of gendered binaries and sexual identities, rather than a potentially different outcome which is produced through cross-cultural intersections between West and East or, in IR terms, between the core and the non-core. Western patterns of development cannot be replicated in the East, as if it merely needed to "catch up" to the Western threshold of modernization. First, the foundational components of socioeconomic wealth, democratic governance, and secularization must be understood in their national or regional context in terms of how they impact gender and sexual organization. Analysis from *Western* societies shows important complexities and variations within each of these categories when accounting for attitudes to homosexuality (Gerhards, 2010) and the development of sexual diversity identities and politics (Adam et al., 1999), and so we must also adopt a more complex approach to non-Western societies. As evidence just cited suggests, Muslims are similar to other highly religious groups in the West. In addition, not all Muslims exhibit the same religiosity, calling for a nuanced assessment of the impact of the "Islamic" variable as an ethnocultural identity (Meer, 2010).

Second, the conditions for LGBTIQ politics in the non-core today are significantly different than those found in the period of gay liberation in the West. We cannot sustain the assumption that sexual diversity will emerge in the same way as it has in the West. The discourse of LGBTIQ rights promoted by intergovernmental organizations with the support of Western countries politicizes the international context in which queer politics unfold. Similarly, LGBTIQ visibility is now global through popular cultural technologies such as the internet, broadcast media, and political campaigns that internationalize queer human rights. The recent campaigns against Russia's anti-gay laws in the lead up to the 2014 Olympics and Uganda's criminalization of homosexuality are just the most recent examples of how LGBTIQ rights have become part of international politics. None of these conditions existed in the formative period of Western gay liberation or for most of the recent period that saw the formalization of queer citizenship (Hildebrandt, 2014). Muslim reactions to same-sex identities and homosexuality must be understood in a contemporary context that is markedly international, and thus fundamentally different from Western gay liberation that was nationally focused.

Third, it is important to consider this internationalization of the gay rights discourse in the context of global Islamophobia. Gay rights are increasingly instrumentalized within a discourse of Western civilizational superiority that underpins Islamophobia (Puar, 2007; Mepschen et al. 2010; Rahman, 2014). We have to approach the formation of Muslim homophobia *within* the context of Islamophobia rather than reduce it to a preexisting component of a pre-modern, monolithic Islamic culture. Can we logically claim that Muslim societies and Muslim populations have to simply "catch up" with Western modernization in order to be accepting of sexual diversity? Muslim antipathy to homosexuality is a complex combination of factors. It may become further embedded in Muslim identities as a consequence of the contemporary "exemplary" positioning of LGBTIQ rights as central tenets of Western modernity (Mepschen et al., 2010). Moreover, public queer politics has become one of "natural" sexual *minority* politics, leaving the dominant heterosexual matrix untouched. We should be aware that the context of current human rights strategies – both in national and international contexts – is based on Western experiences of coming out and the consequent constructions of gender and sexuality. These culturally specific essentialist formations are reinforced by the political strategies that purport to provide universal routes to sexual liberation but do not challenge the naturalized dominance of heterosexuality that remains a foundational cause of homophobia.

This is not to deny that rights discourses and strategies based on identity politics have been successful in many contexts because they provide the basis to both represent experiences of oppression and for collective political participation. We need, however, to acknowledge the successes of LGBTIQ politics in their political and sociological context, rather than uncritically reinstate a progress narrative of modernization that somehow implies the sexual liberation of a pre-political identity group of subjects has occurred in the West and now simply needs to be extended to others around the world. Gay liberation has been part of Western experiences of modernity because it has emerged through Western forms of political and sociological subjectification. This conceit of sexual equality as modernization is based on a eurocentric view of modernity, whereby its Western formation is understood as the exemplary model that other parts of the world will inevitably follow (Bhambra, 2007).

Counter-intuitive confusions in the characterization of "homosexualization" as neocolonialism

Cross-cultural research on sexuality has challenged one of the conceptual confusions in the modernization thesis – that of a universal, essential sexual identity. We might be tempted, therefore, to make a claim for culturally specific versions of gender and sexual identity as the basis for regional or national versions of queer rights that challenge the various conceits of LGBTIQ equality as modernity. Murray and Roscoe suggest, however, that "'homosexualization,' the social forces and historical events that produce modern Western homosexual identity, is spreading throughout the world" (1997: 55) and consequently that Muslim ways of knowing and being sexual are under threat. Joseph Massad is more specifically interested in who is responsible. He identifies the International Lesbian and Gay Association (ILGA) and International Gay and Lesbian Human Rights Commission (IGLHRC) as key players in imposing Western sexual formations (2007), particularly through their emphasis on a human rights discourse foregrounded in development policies since the 1990s (Springborg, 2009).[6] Massad's criticism of the "Gay International" can be seen as inflating the successes of the internationalization of queer rights since this institutionalization has not been uniformly successful, either nationally or internationally (Sweibel, 2009; Waites, 2009).[7] Nonetheless, he rightly questions the teleology of a putative international gay liberation because the liberal human rights discourse defaults to an essentialist understanding of sexual identity. Its internationalization provides a route for Western conceptualizations of sexuality under the shell of an apparently universal technology of equality. There are, however, certain assumptions operating in his postcolonial analysis that are indicative of further conceptual confusions around sexual identities, colonialism, and modernity.

In Muslim cultures, the historical diversity of sexual behaviors was connected to pre-Islamic local influences that were not uniformly transformed by the advent of Islam, whether the religion was chosen or imposed through imperialism (Roscoe, 1997). In both the pre-Islamic and Islamic periods, evidence suggests that sexuality was not seen as identity in the modern Western sense. European imperialism played a significant role in transforming traditional Muslim homoeroticism and gender binaries by creating an epistemological cultural shift in understanding diverse sexual behaviors as indicative of binary sexual identities thus creating the modern sense of homosexuals as a "type" of person (Murray & Roscoe, 1997; Massad, 2007). Colonial discourses on homosexuality also served to construct the "home" nations as morally superior, reinforcing the gender hierarchies and sexual moralities that were being consolidated during the imperial industrial eras by characterizing Eastern and native homoeroticism as depraved and contrasting this with superior Western morality (McClintock, 1995; Murray & Roscoe, 1997; Morgenson, 2010). The historical emergence of homosexuality and homophobia through colonialism does not, however, simply disappear in postcolonial times. Instead, it is furthered with the deployment of more rigid gender/sexual moralities as part of national liberation strategies and national resistance to Western cultural influence in postcolonial times. This occurs from Algeria and Palestine (Abdulhadi, 2010) to India, where the anti-sodomy law imposed by the British in 1861 was retained by post-independence political elites as a defense of traditional Indian culture (Vanita & Kidwai, 2000; Bhaskaran, 2002). In another example, Singapore defended keeping colonial anti-sodomy laws on the basis of national and Asian "values" (Chan, 2009), a discourse repeated across Southeast Asia (Peletz, 2006; Blackwood, 2007).

I have agreed with those like Massad who criticize the current political formations of gay politics as conceits of Western modernity. I resist, however, the argument that the antidote to Western impositions can be culturally exclusive and "authentic" non-Western traditions of gender and sexual organization. I do not think that we can explain "homosexualization" as a process that is a one-dimensional continuation of colonialism in contemporary times. The significance of contemporary LGBTIQ identity cannot be reduced to its neocolonialist politics; rather politics in the form of liberal democratic individualist rights strategies is one component of the way in which queer identity was constructed. There is a wider basis to the emergence of homosexual identity that includes bureaucratization and social control; urbanization and the creation of homosocial leisure spaces; the reorganization of gender divisions and ideologies based on wage labor/domestic binaries; the impact of legally free wage labor in industrial societies on notions of individuality; and the medicalization of sexual identity (Greenberg, 1988; Weeks, 1989; Seidman, 1996). Modern states have had the ability to deploy homophobia because "homosexualization" creates a stigmatized other as the target, but technologies of oppression are part of a wider sociological development of regulation in modernity. Political homophobia may therefore have emerged in Western modernity and then been exported, but we cannot argue that it is limited to the West in the current era because modern statehood has developed globally along with homosexualization. Homophobia has thus become a widespread phenomenon in postcolonial states and increasingly, in transnational movements (Weiss & Bosia, 2013). For example, Awwad's analysis of the *Queen Boat* affair in Cairo provides a complex rendering of the Egyptian state's repression of sexual license. Prostitution was identified with servicing the British colonizers producing a movement towards regulation and more conservative morality in postcolonial politics. This later converged with the state's attempt to preempt the rise of conservative transnational Islamism by increasing sexual regulation (2010). We cannot seriously contemplate that modern sources of social control, regulation, and socioeconomic ordering are exclusively Western when we know that contemporary states have many, if not all, of these aspects at their disposal and are happy to use them against LGBTIQ populations.

Even if we begin with the proposition that Western epistemologies have dominated national cultures of gender and the sexual since colonial times and now dominate the international arena, that analysis cannot fully explain the investment in these epistemologies by national cultures that are often seeking to distinguish themselves from Western neoimperialism. In postcolonial times, the continued and sometimes expanded regulation of homosexuality suggests a continuing connection in how sexuality can be conceptualized by a ruling national elite (whether exclusively as a government or more widely in elite public culture) to promote its own governing legitimacy (Lennox & Waites, 2013; Weiss & Bosia, 2013). That fact alone suggests that we cannot simply see modern constructions of sexuality as wholly Western in contemporary times, even if the technologies that brought them to bear are understood as emanating from the West.

In terms of the consequences for international politics, many others have criticized the potential cultural imperialism of queer human rights discourses but they have also simultaneously recognized that the translation of anti-essentialist, culturally variable understandings of sexual identities into viable political frameworks is extremely difficult because there is an inevitable institutional momentum to talk in terms of human rights that are "attached" to a specific identity group, seen as the reflection of natural, essentialist, identities (Waites, 2009; Budhiraja et al., 2010). As Waites points out, the tension between recognizing cultural variability in sexual identities and organization and the Western-derived concepts that dominate political strategies "is the context in which it is necessary to develop a strategy for engaging with these concepts, appraising costs and benefits for political movements" (2009: 152). Massad's rejection of queer rights and identities as Western imperialism is a symptom of conceptualizations that ultimately replay cultural exclusivity between Western and Eastern social constructions of sexuality. The characterization of queer rights as a battle between Arab formations and Western ones indicates a theoretical assumption about the "ownership" of modernity that equates modernity with colonialism and LGBTIQ identities as part of this view of "modernity as colonialism."

My concern is that both modernization ideas and postcolonial arguments like Massad's share the mistaken assumption of modernity's direction and "ownership" by reducing sexuality to a reflex of Western processes, whether that is seen positively (Western modernization is the only route for queer equality) or negatively (as neocolonialism). Massad's thesis is not explicitly framed by an assumption of divergence in modernity, but he nonetheless assumes a cultural exclusivity between West and East with different social formations of sexuality that can be read as implicit multiple modernities of the sexual. While we must resist conceits universalizing Western versions of LGBTIQ identities and politics, we fall prey to further confusions if we only see contemporary queer identities within a neocolonialist frame. Such frame repeats a mutual exclusivity between the social constructions of sexuality that potentially reinstates a eurocentric worldview by de-emphasizing local and/or national cultures of sexuality. Indeed, the evidence we have on contemporary Muslim LGBTIQ politics and identities indicates that a more interconnected appreciation of the sexual is needed, and that the construction of the sexual in this interconnected modernity cannot be reduced to a neocolonialist conceptualization. I turn to this evidence next to elaborate how we might overcome the preceding sets of conceptual confusions.

Contemporary intersectional sexual modernity

For Bhambra, the assumption that modernity emerged in the West and is now being followed by other regions is a mistaken understanding. Modernity and its consequences have always been globally interconnected. Her argument is thus a critique of both classical sociological theory and some postcolonial approaches, particularly those that put forward the idea of multiple modernities in order to de-emphasize Western social formations as the only possible outcome of modernization. Bhambra argues that the multiple modernities thesis unwittingly replays the prioritization of the West when it suggests that non-Western countries are *following* modernization patterns, albeit in different way (Bhambra, 2007: 70). In the realm of the sexual, I have drawn on this analysis to argue that we need to reject both modernization arguments and those that imply multiple modernities, whereby non-Western cultures are framed as fundamentally distinct from the West but both following and/or resisting Western formations. In place of these conceptualizations, I suggest that we can use Bhambra's formulation of "connected histories" to think through both the historical era of Western sexual formations and their colonial impositions and, crucially, the contemporary postcolonial era of continued connections in sexual modernity. Others have already established the historical relevance of sexuality to this argument by demonstrating that modern sexual discourses developed in a dialectic of respectability/otherness applied at "home" to different classes and in settler colonization of native peoples, and abroad in the colonial encounter (McClintock, 1995; Morgenson, 2010). What I am suggesting is that we extend this appreciation of connection around sexuality into contemporary times, rejecting a simple polarity in sexual cultures from either the Western exceptionalist or postcolonial sides of the debate.

The emergent body of work on contemporary Muslim homoeroticism, both in Muslim majority nations and among Muslim immigrant minorities, suggests a complex intersection of factors in how sexuality is developing (Abraham, 2010; Habib, 2010; Khan, 2010). For example, Mahdavi's recent ethnographic research in Iran throws light on the lived experience of young people in the Islamic Republic, arguing that a sexual revolution has occurred since around 2000 whereby young people see discussions of sexuality in terms of a broader social movement of change that challenges the restrictions of Islamic law under the Iranian regime. While her research is focused more on the changes in young heterosexual culture and discourse, there is some evidence that homosexual organizing was also part of this shift, and that that dialectical discourse of homosexuality and Islam was a self-conscious part of such organizing:

> Maybe we used to see being gay as a Western thing, but it seemed that being gay was seen as being Western by the regime too, and it was a threat to them, so we decided, yes, let's go for a sexual and social movement that is Western, sexual and the regime hates! Yes, let's do that! (Mahdavi, 2012: 37)

Western conceptualizations of both politics and identities can be an important resource for local developments of queer identities yet they are not necessarily a blueprint for how sexual diversity will develop in non-Western cultures. In her detailed ethnographic research on Indonesia, Blackwood (2010) demonstrates that lesbians incorporate Western discourses into national ones to make sense of their identities and create communities that are influenced by Western gay identity discourses but adapt them in the creation of locally distinct identities. While Western "queer knowledge" is used as a resource for modelling activism and in creating a sense of shared identity, international politics of identity are translated to adapt to local realities, and Indonesian homosexual men and women experience them differently according to national and regional context, depending on class and gender.

Boellstorff's anthropological studies on transvestites and gay men in Indonesia support this framing of localized experiences of transnational sexualities. His work challenges the teleological model of expansionist globalization of sexuality. He directs our attention to the strategies that "gay" Muslim men use to inhabit the "incommensurability" of being gay and Indonesian and Muslim as part of their everyday life (Boellstorff, 2005, 2007). Recent research on same-sex behavior among men in Turkey also suggests that Western versions of gay identity are becoming more common, although they remain a minority and indeed co-exist with the more common gender variant understanding of homosexuality in Turkish culture (Bereket & Adam, 2006, 2008).

These brief and limited examples suggest an ontological construction distinct from the West for queer Muslim identities and queer Muslim liberation. This is not one that is exclusively Eastern or consistent across Muslim cultures. The ontology of contemporary homosexual identities is being formed in intersection with the increasingly globalized discourse of Western gay political identity and localized histories of gender identity and, crucial to our concerns, the contemporary reactions of Muslim cultures to both traditional and Western forms of homosexuality in times of global Islamophobia. Research on LGBTIQ Muslims living in the West is even more recent than the scholarship on Muslim cultures and homosexuality (Saed, 2005; Siraj, 2006; Yip, 2009; Abraham, 2010; Al-Sayyad, 2010; Rahman, 2014). Research shows that Western versions of gay identity are indeed used as resources by LGBTIQ Muslims in the West but this does not mean that they are inevitably adopting the teleological subject position that prioritizes gay identity over other forms of social belonging. In particular, the context of Islamophobia within both gay culture and wider society seems to create a desire to keep some form of ethnic identification despite the experiences of Muslim antipathy to homosexuality.

Same-sex behaviors do exist in Muslim cultures but not necessarily in the same way as they do in the West. However, as the context for the development of individual identities, these provide both political resources *and* provoke post-colonial state and cultural group resistance. They are therefore neither exclusively "progressive" bequests nor "negative" impacts of the West, and therefore cannot be accurately characterized either as timelag modernization processes or neocolonialist impositions on discrete non-Western modernities. Rather, I suggest an acknowledgement that sexual diversity in Muslim majority countries exists as a historically *new* set of developmental intersections. Furthermore, LGBTIQ Muslims in the West stand at the intersections of an apparently incompatible framing of Muslims versus LGBTIQ equality that *disrupt* these assumptions.

The possibilities of Muslim sexual diversity and the improbabilities of queer IR

Given this epistemological bent, it is no surprise to see how mainstream IR theory finds it difficult to grasp sexual diversity, whether conceptually or politically.

Cynthia Weber's recent article argues that the disciplinary inheritance of IR makes it appear as if there is no queer international theory developing, despite the fact that many scholars are engaged in such research (Weber, 2014). Weber suggests that IR needs a clearly defined object of study and that queer international politics fails to conform to these traditions of IR, thus delegitimizing queer IR, or what Weber describes as global queer studies. Two of the "failures" are that the broad scope of research that is focused on sexuality is interdisciplinary and these studies also combine both "high" and "low" politics. In the study of sexuality, neither of these is avoidable. Sexuality as an identity that people inhabit as a "fact" of politics is unremarkable and does not matter much; what matters is the social significance of sexual identities and how they come to be used as the basis for discrimination and oppression. Such an anti-essentialist perspective is necessarily controversial in mainstream positivist IR but without it, we are reduced to talking about queer politics in the way that the WVS or Islamophobic discourses do. This prevents a wider understanding of cultural difference in how sexualities are configured and come to be the basis of social significance, either in positive or negative ways.

The contemporary deployment of queer politics as the vanguard of Western modernity in its battle with Muslim cultures is not explicable through a positivist frame that only measures attitudes and legal outcomes. Indeed, on the basis of attitudes and laws, one could argue queer politics would be the *least* likely contender for use as a consistent and credible criterion of Western exceptionalism. Sexuality studies must be interdisciplinary because sexual identities are socially constructed through intersecting hierarchies of knowledge and identity that then become meaningful across the realm of politics *through* this construction. For example, my argument criticizing the conceits of see LGBTIQ equality as modernization draws on classical social theory, democratic theory, postcolonial theory, intersectionality theories, sexuality and race studies, and qualitative empirical studies of Muslim homoeroticism to build its case. If we are to care about oppression, moreover, sexuality studies must be focused on the everyday experiences of that oppression and so we must traverse the social realm, from high-level analytical frameworks to the lived experience of groups of individuals who suffer stigma.

The dominant privileged majority need not care about oppression of the socially constructed minority. This is probably the underlying reason for the lack of mainstream acceptance of LGBTIQ issues, but it seems to me as a sociologist that IR is also repeating the historical resistance found in many other disciplines, including my own. This reluctance can only be challenged by the consequences of "presence" – committed individual scholars who not only research these issues, but conceptualize them in a way that resonates with established frameworks and, as Weber points out, the increasing presence of queer scholars is gradually having this effect. This happened in sociology through the impact of women's studies, feminism, and lesbian and gay scholarship and it may be that IR is "lagging behind" these disciplines that have become more open to epistemological and theoretical diversity through the presence of those who adopted different frameworks to put new issues on the disciplinary agenda. I am not sure that I agree with Weber's characterization of a "global queer studies" as a definable body of interdisciplinary work. I am also hesitant to embrace the development of a queer international theory because it seems to me that sexuality studies is conceptually and politically *more advanced* than IR and so may not benefit from being framed through an IR lens that could potentially demand narrow (positivist?) epistemological and methodological frames in order to be seen as "credible." Indeed, Weber raises the danger of future "gentrification" of sexuality studies by IR, resulting in its permanent ghettoization and deradicalization. Of course, for those students and scholars located within IR programs and careers, the legitimacy of queer studies is undeniably important in an institutional context. However, from an outsider's perspective, I wonder whether this concern with legitimization is looking at the issue the wrong way. Perhaps it is IR that needs conceptual and epistemological "modernization," not issues of sexual diversity that need political or intellectual legitimization.

Conclusion

I have argued that we need to reject explanations of LGBTIQ identities and equality that universalize their Western version through the modernization thesis. Moreover, we should reject postcolonial assumptions of divergent modernities because this perspective reinforces the partial view of LGBTIQ identities as exclusively Western. In contrast, I suggest an approach that is both open to the connected colonial histories of sexual regulation and identities and the contemporary intersections in Muslim experiences of sexual diversity. Issues around Muslim homoeroticism and Muslim homophobia illustrate that what we are dealing with in contemporary LGBTIQ politics is emphatically *not* the diffusion of Western outcomes of equality and routes to that particular liberation, but historically distinct circumstances that require a precise intersectional appreciation of how the sexual is being constructed in contemporary modernity. This intersectional perspective demands a relativist epistemological approach to research in both methodology and theoretical concepts that has wider implications for studying the current putative threshold of international legitimization of queer rights. The Muslim example demands that we take a critical view of empirical "facts" and derivative theories, resisting the equation of quantifiable modernization processes with a universal theory of LGBTIQ political progress. Moreover, the very basis of LGBTIQ identity categories must be understood as culturally specific and open to adaption in non-Western cultures, so that we can imagine Muslim sexual diversity as a formation in its own right, forged at the intersection of a variety of individual sociological, historical, and political contexts and hierarchies rather than assume that it is merely a less advanced version of Western LGBTIQ identities.

Notes

1 LGBT is used in the report although I use LGBTIQ in common with contributions throughout this volume. I use queer synonymously with the acknowledgement that this is predominantly found in Western cultures.

2 These are Iran, Mauritania, Saudi Arabia, Sudan, and Yemen.
3 The World Values Survey is an international network of social scientists who analyze national data on attitudes, currently from 80 countries (see: http://www.worldvalues survey.org/).
4 Beckers' analysis is based on a comparison of datasets from 1981 to 2003, which included only 11 Muslim majority nations, and the fifth round of surveys (2005–8) that included only seven Muslim countries. Beckers points out that, in the fourth wave, only seven countries had acceptance levels above the mean of 5.5 on a scale of 1–10. In this context, the seven Muslim countries displayed much lower levels of acceptance at a mean level of acceptance at 1.9.
5 For example, in her research on heterosexual Muslims in Scotland, Siraj concludes that their attitudes to homosexuality are influenced mainly by religiosity, with educational levels, age, and gender showing no discernible effect, although the vast majority of her respondents were highly educated (2006). In their comparative study of adolescents in Canada and Belgium, Hooghe et al. (2010) found that Muslims were less accepting of gay rights activism than other religious groupings, and more religiosity indicating less tolerance. For a fuller discussion, see Rahman, 2014, Chapter Three.
6 Human rights increasingly became part of the shift to neoliberal practices in economic development by dominant organizations such as the IMF and World Bank in the 1990s (Springborg, 2009). The main aim was to secure property rights and efficient market systems through "good governance," but this permitted an increasing use of human rights as both goal and criteria for assessing "development" in poorer countries.
7 In the West, the EU has been more receptive to queer rights than the UN (Swiebel, 2009), but with significant national differences (Kollman, 2009; Gerhards, 2010). Canada leads LGBTIQ policy, but the U.S. remains conflicted (Rayside, 2008; Rayside and Wilcox, 2011).

Suggested further reading

Massad J (2007) *Desiring Arabs*. Chicago, IL: University of Chicago Press.
Murray S and Roscoe W (eds.) (1997) *Islamic Homosexualities: Culture, History, and Literature*. New York: New York University Press.
Puar J K (2007) *Terrorist Assemblages: Homonationalism in Queer Times*. Durham, NC/London: Duke University Press.
Rahman M (2014) *Homosexualities, Muslim Cultures and Modernity*. Basingstoke: Palgrave Macmillan.
Weeks J (2007) *The World We Have Won: The Remaking of Erotic and Intimate Life*. New York: Routledge.

Bibliography

Abdulhadi R (2010) Sexualities and the social order in Arab and Muslim communities. In: Habib S (ed.) *Islam and Homosexuality, Vols 1 and 2*. Santa Barbara, CA: Praeger.
Adam B, Duyvendak J W, and Krouwel A (eds.) (1999) *The Global Emergence of Gay and Lesbian Politics: National Imprints of a Worldwide Movement*. Philadelphia, PA: Temple University Press.
Adamczyk A and Pitt C (2009) Shaping attitudes about homosexuality: the role of religion and cultural context. *Social Science Research* 38: 338–51.
Al-Sayyad A A (2010) "You're what?": Engaging narratives from diasporic Muslim women on identity and gay liberation. In: Habib S (ed.) *Islam and Homosexuality, Vols 1 and 2*. Santa Barbara, CA: Praeger.
Altman D (1993[1971]) *Homosexual Oppression and Liberation*. New York: New York University Press.

——(2001) *Global Sex*. Chicago, IL/London: University of Chicago Press.

Awwad J (2010) The postcolonial predicament of gay rights in the *Queen Boat* affair. *Communication and Critical/Cultural Studies* 7(3): 318–66.

Beckers T (2010) Islam and the acceptance of homosexuality: the shortage of socioeconomic well-being and responsive democracy. In Habib S (ed.) *Islam and Homosexuality*. Santa Barbara, CA: Praeger.

Bereket T and Adam B (2006) The emergence of gay identities in contemporary Turkey. *Sexualities* 9(2): 131–51.

——(2008) Navigating Islam and same-sex liasions among men in Turkey. *Journal of Homosexuality* 55(2): 204–22.

Bhambra G (2007) *Rethinking Modernity: Postcolonialism and the Sociological Imagination*. Basingstoke: Palgrave Macmillan.

Bhaskaran S (2002) The politics of penetration: Section 377 of the Indian Penal Code. In: Vanita R (ed.) *Queering India: Same-Sex Love and Eroticism in Indian Culture and Society*. New York: Routledge.

Blackwood E (2007) Regulation of sexuality in Indonesian discourse: normative gender, criminal law and shifting strategies of control. *Culture, Health and Sexuality* 9(3): 293–307.

——(2010) *Falling into the Lesbi World: Desire and Difference in Indonesia*. Honolulu: University of Hawaii Press.

Boellstorff T (2005) *The Gay Archipelago: Sexuality and Nation in Indonesia*. Princeton, NJ: Princeton University Press.

——(2007) *A Coincidence of Desires: Anthropology, Queer Studies, Indonesia*. Durham, NC: Duke University Press.

Budhiraja S, Fried S T, and Teixeira A (2010) Spelling it out: from alphabet soup to sexual rights and gender justice. In: Lind A (ed.) *Development, Sexual Rights and Global Governance*. New York: Routledge.

Chan P C W (2009) Shared values of Singapore: sexual minority rights as Singaporean value. *International Journal of Human Rights* 13(1–2): 279–305.

Gallup (2009) *Gallup Coexist Index, 2009: A Global Study of Interfaith Relations*. http://www.abudhabigallupcenter.com/144575/Gallup-Coexist-Index-2009.aspx

Gerhards J (2010) Non-discrimination towards homosexuality: the European Union's policy and citizens' attitudes towards homosexuality in 27 European countries. *International Sociology* 25(1): 5–28.

Greenberg D F (1988) *The Construction of Homosexuality*. Chicago, IL: University of Chicago Press.

Habib S (2010) Introduction. In: Habib S (ed.) *Islam and Homosexuality, Vols 1 and 2*. Santa Barbara, CA: Praeger.

Hildebrandt A (2014) Routes to decriminalization: a comparative analysis of the legalization of same-sex sexual acts. *Sexualities* 17(1–2): 230–53.

Hooghe M, Dejaeghere Y, Claes E, and Quintelier E (2010) "Yes, but suppose everyone turned gay?": The structure of attitudes toward gay and Lesbian rights among Islamic youth in Belgium. *Journal of LGBT Youth* 7(1): 49–71.

Inglehart R and Baker W (2000) Modernization, cultural change and the persistence of traditional values. *American Sociological Review* 65(1):19–51.

Inglehart R and Welzel C (2005) *Modernization, Cultural Change and Democracy*. New York: Cambridge University Press.

Itaborahy L P and Zhu J (2013) State-sponsored homophobia, a world survey of laws: criminalization, protection and recognition of same-sex love. http://ilga.org/ilga/en/article/1161

Jackson S and Rees A (2007) The appalling appeal of nature: the popular influence of evolutionary psychology as a problem for sociology. *Sociology* 41(5): 917–30.

Khan B (2010) Longing, not belonging, and living in fear. In: Habib S (ed.) *Islam and Homosexuality, Vols 1 and 2*. Santa Barbara, CA: Praeger.

Kollman K (2009) European institutions, transnational networks and national same-sex unions policy: when soft law hits harder. *Contemporary Politics* 15(1): 37–53.

Lennox C and Waites M (2013) Human rights, sexual orientation and gender identity in the Commonwealth: from history and law to developing activism and transnational dialogues. In: Lennox C & Waites M (eds.) *Human Rights, Sexual Orientation and Gender Identity in the Commonwealth: Struggles for Decriminalisation and Change.* London: School of Advanced Study.

McClintock A (1995) *Imperial Leather: Race, Gender and Sexuality in the Colonial Context.* London: Routledge.

Mahdavi P (2012) "The personal is political and the political is personal": sexuality, politics and social movements in modern Iran. In: Aggelton P, Boyce P, Moore, H L, & Parker R (eds.) *Understanding Global Sexualities: New Frontiers.* London: Routledge.

Massad J (2007) *Desiring Arabs.* Chicago, IL: University of Chicago Press.

Meer N (2010) *Citizenship, Identity and the Politics of Multiculturalism: The Rise of Muslim Consciousness.* Basingstoke: Palgrave Macmillan.

Mepschen P, Duyvendak J W, and Tonkens E (2010) Sexual politics, orientalism and multicultural citizenship in the Netherlands. *Sociology,* 44(5): 962–80.

Morgenson S L (2010) Settler homonationalism: theorizing settler colonialism within queer modernities. *GLQ* 16(1–2): 105–31.

Murray S (1997) Male actresses in Islamic parts of Indonesia and the southern Philippines. In: Murray S & Roscoe W (eds.) *Islamic Homosexualities: Culture, History, and Literature.* New York: New York University Press.

——(1997b) The will not to know: Islamic accommodations of male homosexualities. In: Murray S & Roscoe W (eds.) *Islamic Homosexualities: Culture, History, and Literature.* New York: New York University Press.

Peletz M G (2006) Transgenderism and gender pluralism in Southeast Asia since early modern times. *Current Anthropology* 47(2): 309–40.

Pew Research Center (2007) Muslim Americans: Middle Class and Mostly Mainstream. http://religions.pewforum.org/affiliations

Puar J K (2007) *Terrorist Assemblages: Homonationalism in Queer Times.* Durham, NC/London: Duke University Press.

Rahman M (2014) *Homosexualities, Muslim Cultures and Modernity.* Basingstoke: Palgrave Macmillan.

Rahman M and Hussain A H (2011) Muslims and sexual diversity in North America. In: Rayside D & Wilcox C (eds.) *Faith, Politics and Sexual Diversity in Canada and the United States.* Vancouver: UBC Press.

Rahman M and Jackson S (2010) *Gender and Sexuality: Sociological Approaches.* Cambridge: Polity Press.

Rayside D (2008) *Queer Inclusions: Continental Divisions: Public Recognition of Sexual Diversity in Canada and the United States.* Toronto: University of Toronto Press.

Rayside D and Wilcox C (2011) Introduction: the difference that a border makes: the political intersection of sexuality and religion in Canada and the United States. In: Rayside D & Wilcox C (eds.) *Faith, Politics and Sexual Diversity in Canada and the United States.* Vancouver: UBC Press.

Roscoe W (1997) Precursors of Islamic male homosexualities. In: Murray S & Roscoe W (eds.) *Islamic Homosexualities: Culture, History and Literature.* New York: New York University Press.

Saed K (2005) On the edge of belonging. In: Abdul-Ghafur S (ed.) *Living Islam Out Loud.* Boston, MA: Beacon Press.

Seidman S (1996) Introduction. In: Seidman S (ed.) *Queer Theory/Sociology.* Cambridge, MA: Blackwell.

Siraj A (2006) On being homosexual and Muslim: conflicts and challenges. In: Ouzgane L (ed.) *Islamic Masculinities.* London: Zed Books.

——(2009) The construction of the homosexual "Other" by British Muslim heterosexuals. *Contemporary Islam* 3(1): 47–57.

Springborg R (2009) Conclusion: not Washington, Beijing nor Mecca: the limitations of development models. In: Springborg R (ed.) *Development Models in Muslim Contexts; Chinese, "Islamic" and Neo-Liberal Alternatives.* Edinburgh: Edinburgh University Press.

Swiebel J (2009) Lesbian, gay, bisexual and transgender human rights: the search for an international strategy. *Contemporary Politics* 15(1): 19–35.

United Nations Office of the High Commissioner for Human Rights (2012) Born Free and Equal: Sexual Orientation and Gender Identity in International Human Rights Law. http://www.ohchr.org/EN/Issues/Discrimination/Pages/LGBT.aspx

Vanita R and Kidwai S (2000) Introduction. In: Vanita R & Kidwai S (eds.) *Same-Sex Love in India: Readings from Literature and History*. London: St. Martin's Press.

Waites M (2009) Critique of "sexual orientation" and "gender identity" in human rights discourse: global queer politics beyond the Yogyakarta Principles. *Contemporary Politics* 15(1): 152–53.

Weber C (2014) Why is there no queer international theory? *European Journal of International Relations* April 3: 1–25.

Weeks J (1989) *Sex Politics and Society*, 2nd edn. London: Longman.

——(2007) *The World We Have Won: The Remaking of Erotic and Intimate Life*. New York: Routledge.

Weiss M L and Bosia M J (2013) Political homophobia in comparative perspective. In: Weiss M L & Bosia M J (eds.) *Global Homophobia: States, Movements and the Politics of Oppression*. Chicago, IL: University of Illinois Press.

Yip A K-T (2004) Embracing Allah and sexuality? South Asian non-heterosexual Muslims in Britain. In: Jacobsen K A & Kumar P P (eds.) *South Asians in the Diaspora*. Leiden: Brill.

——(2005) Religion and the politics of spirituality/sexuality: reflections on researching British Lesbian, gay, and bisexual Christians and Muslims. *Fieldwork in Religion* 1(3): 271–89.

——(2008) The quest for intimate/sexual citizenship: lived experiences of Lesbian and bisexual Muslim women. *Contemporary Islam* 2(2): 99–117.

——(2009) Introduction to the special issue on Islam and sexuality. *Contemporary Islam* 3(1).

6

PERIPHERAL PRIDES

Amazon perspectives on LGBT politics

Manuela Lavinas Picq

Introduction

In December 2011 Benjamin Constant held its first gay pride celebration. Tikuna lesbians and Peruvian drag queens gathered in a flamboyant parade sprawling through the small Amazon town. Benjamin Constant sits at the triple border between Brazil, Peru, and Colombia, where the Amazon and Javari rivers meet, near the region with most Indigenous groups in voluntary isolation in Latin America.[1] According to participants, the parade would have been larger had Cavallococha, a Peruvian old rubber boom town upriver, not been holding its popular annual drag queen contest that same day. How did Indigenous peoples come to participate in a parade for gay rights in one of the most isolated regions of the Amazon? What may appear as anecdotal raises less trivial questions. Mainstream studies of international relations (IR) dismiss the Amazon as irrelevant to political modernity. Yet lesbian, gay, bisexual, and transsexual (LGBT)[2] perspectives reveal a vibrant cosmopolitanism at the peripheries of world politics. Informed by empirical research in Amazonia, this chapter explores the contributions of LGBT approaches for thinking IR critically.

Amazonia offers all forms of sexual diversity. Lady Gaga's "Born this way" plays on the BlackBerries of young gays, transvestites watch the Sunday soccer by Catholic priests, and lesbian couples raise their children in Tikuna Indigenous communities. Whether such expressions of sexuality are stirred up by global trends or embedded in local culture, they are daily business across Amazon societies. The adoption of LGBT discourses indicates the influence of international frameworks in Amazonia. It also reflects that such sexual practices preexisted the arrival of Western codification. Amazonians have engaged in diverse sexualities long before globalization gave them the political language (and songs) to say so.

This analysis contests two interrelated premises: the perception that the Amazon is largely "non-modern" and the assumption that sexual identity is primarily a product of Western modernity. The Amazon tends to be understood as an apolitical Eden; inhabited by historically isolated peoples who resist international forces (Slater, 2002; Hutchins and Wilson, 2010). Still treated as "a land without history," the region is validated for its natural exuberance rather than appreciated as a historical place of dynamic political change (Raffles, 2002; Adams et al., 2006; Da Cunha, 2006). Amazonia is imagined as wild, not modern. Sexual diversity, in contrast, has become a bastion of modernity, a perception Momin Rahman questions in the prior chapter. The reshaping of sexual life is discussed in conjunction with globalization while queer is a site of cosmopolitanism (Binnie, 2004). Debates about same-sex marriage are tackled in relation to global flows, while homosexual liberation signals a modern progress implicitly associated with the Western secular state (Cady & Fessenden, 2013; Rahman, 2014). Overall, LGBT politics and Amazonia are wor(l)ds apart that hardly fit together in the social sciences.

The evidence of sexual diversity in Amazonia challenges assumptions about modernity. First, it sheds light on global dynamics of gender in peripheries where they tend to be overlooked. To look at the Amazon through gay lenses illuminates global dynamics of gender where we tend to overlook them. LGBT politics are everywhere, all along the Amazon, pointing the extent to which the "local" and the "global" are permanently interacting with and redefining each other. Second, a look at gender identities shatters flattening generalizations about the Amazon as pre-modern. Gay pride activities depart from the imagination of an atemporal and homogenous Amazon to reveal instead a diverse, complex society that partakes in global politics. Cynthia Enloe once pointed out that our surprises reveal our assumptions. The surprise of finding gay prides in isolated corners of the Amazon is embedded in the assumption that *those* places are not part of *our* political modernity. Such gaze is doubly displaced for perceiving the Amazon as a one-dimensional periphery and reading gay prides as signifying Western modernity.

This chapter seeks not to explain the emergence of LGBT movements in the Amazon as an effect of globalization or to prove that the region is entering global modernity (it has long been embedded in world dynamics, not least with the nineteenth-century rubber boom). Rather, it takes a theoretical interest in LGBT lives and experiences to destabilize conventional ideas of where the international is to be found, question what political modernity is made of, and why neither can be taken to signify a Western political core. My point is not that (sexual) modernity reached the Amazon; it is that modernity has always been present in political peripheries that tend to be defined by its supposed absence. This empirical research demonstrates that the difference between an invented core versus its imagined periphery is more tenuous than often assumed.

LGBT lenses are part of various critical approaches that have been radically transforming the study of international relations (IR). Feminist research accused the discipline of perpetuating masculine hegemonies, made feminist sense of war, and proposed new methodologies to do feminist IR (Ackerly et al., 2006; Enloe, 2010). Scholars of race and coloniality made visible how white supremacy is constitutive of the modern world system (and how imperialist assumptions inform most theoretical constructs (Hobson, 2012). Most recently, an emerging literature out of and about the non-core decried the inability of IR theories to travel outside the U.S. and beyond the West (Tickner & Blaney, 2013). Recognizing the importance of feminist and postcolonial critiques, my research argues that LGBT lives and experiences too are strategic sites for challenging disciplinary canons. If race and sex are inextricable, as anthropologists have argued, IR scholarship must foment dialogues between LGBT perspectives and postcolonial thought.[3] In that effort, Ann Tickner analyzed feminism and race as distinct yet complementary positions of marginality that are crucial sites for producing alternative forms of knowledge in IR (Tickner, 2011). Similarly to feminist insights, LGBT approaches debunk conceptual assumptions of IR from the periphery, and their intersections with postcolonial studies permit to rethink the nation-state from truly alternative perspectives. The question then becomes whether sexuality is just another feminist gaze, or whether it contributes a light of its own to break free from IR's disciplinary straightjackets. I propose Amazonia as a case study in the South from where to fuel dialogues between sexuality studies and postcolonial approaches in IR theory.

My analysis discusses the significance of LGBT approaches to rethink IR in three steps. First, I explore celebration of sexual identity in the Amazon, from gay prides to drag queen contests. Second, I posit sexual diversity as a site of Amazonian modernity, dismissing imaginaries of the region as detached from Western understandings of cosmopolitanism. Third, I question whether LGBT perspectives contribute new gazes or whether they are merely an expansion of the critical perspectives developed by feminist research in IR.

Amazon prides

Benjamin Constant is a quintessential Amazon town. Accessible only by river, it sits at Brazil's border with Peru and Colombia. This crossroads is the furthest away from the Brazilian state, the furthest away from the Colombian state, and the furthest away from the Peruvian state. In theory, there are three countries bordering the intersection of two rivers. In practice, the rivers are the spinal cord than integrates daily exchanges crosses borders more often and in more varied ways that can be accounted for. With over 30,000 people, Benjamin Constant is as ethnically diverse as it is complex. The town overlooks the embouchure of the Javari River Valley, which delineates the border between Brazil and Peru, and which is home to the most territories of Indigenous peoples living in voluntary isolation, like the Matís.[4] Underneath a colorful market with abundant local fruits and fish, a deprived econ-omy, high migration, and a rather religious community influenced by missionaries of all kinds, Benjamin Constant also boasts a thriving gay community.

The local branch of Brazil's Federal University of the Amazon (UFAM) orga-nized the town's first LGBT forum in December 2011 thanks to the leadership of anthropology professor Flávia Cunha and her dynamic group of students. After a daylong event that discussed LGBT rights to education, security, health, and work, over 60 participants gathered to parade a large rainbow flag through town.

Transvestites dancing to the gay anthem "I will survive" in sexy glittering outfits opened the march alongside anthropology students, followed by a lively crowd chanting slogans against homophobia. Mothers carried young children on honking motorbikes, grandparents mixed with Indigenous lesbians, soccer players paraded alongside sex workers. The worst reactions the event generated were a few confused looks and awkward smiles, but no signs of violence. Instead, the contagious enthusiasm enticed bystanders to join in a lively group of perhaps 100 people as the parade made its way to the port. Transportation difficulties prevented more people from participating. A Tikuna Indigenous group from the Brazilian town of Feijoal, a good 4 hours away on boat, got stuck on its way upriver. The crowd was not larger also because of a competing event: many people were attending the annual Country Drag Queen Contest in the old rubber town of Cavallococha, Peru. Jackie, the town's recurrent Carnival Queen, had won last year's contest and expectations were high for a repeat.

The local LGBT scene has been blossoming steadily for over a decade. In 2002 the town already had its first indoor soccer gay team. The members, some of whom came out of the closet at the occasion, were booed the first time they walked onto the court dressed up as nurses. But they brought such joy to the game (and tied the match) that people came back to watch them regularly. They eventually became as popular as the regular teams. Activists claim that what really brought LGBT peoples to the public eye was the carnival bloc "As Marias," whose queen Jackie was elected the overarching queen of all carnival blocs in town. Diverse sexualities exist well beyond gay pride celebrations. There are Tikuna lesbians like Josiane, who lives in the outskirts of Benjamin Constant with her female partner and shares parenting responsibilities with her ex-husband. There is even Silvana, a transvestite from Atalaia do Norte where Brazil melts into Peru. She lives as a woman with her husband yet every morning she puts on her masculine self to go teach math. At school, students and parents treat Silvana as a man, off and on the streets, they salute her as a lady. Transvestites hang out with the rest of town in the main square of Islandia, a Peruvian town built on stilts on the Javari River, watching the town's volleyball across from the Catholic church on Sunday afternoons.

The experience of Benjamin Constant echoes a much larger Amazon trend. In 2012 Manaus (Brazil) celebrated its 16th gay pride event and Iquitos (Peru) the tenth. Over 10 smaller towns along the Amazon River have already held such celebrations. In Brazil, Mancapurú held more than six gay prides; Itaquatiara, Rio Preto da Eva, and Presidente Figueiredo each held more than two celebrations. Tabatinga, the military town across the river from Benjamin Constant, is past its fifth successful gathering. The list goes on, and there is much more than gay prides as well with towns like Cavallococha, upriver in Peru, hosting gay pride celebrations as well as its internationally acclaimed drag queen contest. Manaus's gay volleyball league is over 10 years old, and hosts nationally acclaimed players coming from São Paulo and Bogotá. Not all LGBT communities in Amazonia have articulated a distinct political discourse, preferring instead to embody their demands in the celebration of beauty and differentiated gender identities. There are innumerable ways – and places – in which to practice politics. The absence of a public political agenda should not obscure the political dimension of the daily practices of its members.

LGBT market dynamics are stepping up as well. Iquitos, once a booming Peruvian rubber town has now a gay scene of its own, with a web page called "Gay Ikitos" promoting rainforest adventure travel for openly gay men.[5] Over a week's journey down the Amazon River, the city of Manaus brought together LGBT activists with entrepreneurs in the fashion and tourism industries to promote gay-friendly tourism – a marketing strategy sponsored by the Brazilian airline company TAM. Amazon towns are not yet at the level of Bariloche, Argentina, where the gay-friendly scene includes a six-star ski hotel. There is nevertheless a growing interest for LGBT initiatives beyond an active nightlife. Policy planning around LGBT issues is about expanding local economies to global market dynamics. Efforts to create a gay guide for Manaus are one more indicator of a broad strategy to strengthen gay-friendly markets.

Governmental policies to secure LGBT rights are spreading too, despite their limited operational capacity at the furthest peripheries of the state. When the LGBT Amazonense Forum gathered 24 NGOs to organize Manaus's first March Against Homophobia in May 2011, the state Secretariat of Public Security followed up by signing a cooperation agreement to fight homophobia. The Ministry of Justice of the state of Amazonas is developing monitoring tools to strengthen antidiscrimination laws and is offering workshops for teachers and police forces on gender and sexual diversity. Implementation is insufficient, as is often the case with human rights. Brazil's National Secretariat on Human Rights counts with only one center against homophobic violence per state. Local activists ask for much more, proposing the government creates one center for each municipality.

Policy is perceived as insufficient in part because violence against LGBT individuals runs high. One of the contradictions of the Amazon, like in most of Latin America, is that underneath a promising pink factor, crimes against sexually deviant individuals abound. Trans and homosexuals are cruelly assassinated by people who "just hate gays" (Mott, 2003). The assassination of the Amazon gay singer Omar Faria, brutally strangled and stabbed in September 2011, showed the signs of mutilation that often mark homophobic violence. The public persona of Faria provoked enough outcry for Manaus's government to discuss security alternatives with civil society activists during a municipal conference on LGBT rights. According to Francisco Nery Furtado,[6] the coordinator of Benjamin Constant's LGBT forum and a leading regional activist, every two weeks a homosexual is assassinated in Manaus – with no responsible criminals yet identified as of 2012. Although government discourse constantly reiterates a commitment to address, resolve, and punish homophobic crimes, in practice, they are often treated with impunity. The Amazon is no exception to world trends: crimes against LGBT people are particularly macabre and rarely punished (Report on Homophobia, 2011).[7] More often than not, homophobia creates impediments to access the legal and political rights of citizenship. Trans individuals are not only vulnerable to extreme violence but also subject to daily forms of discrimination. Transphobia has dramatic consequences on transvestites' physical wellbeing. Many are constrained to work in beauty salons and in the sex industry, with professional choices often dictated by limited educational opportunities and burdened by violence. The body politics of being a transvestite are ever present, even when the act is performed without political intentions.

The celebration of sexual diversity that exists today in the Amazon echoes the larger consolidation of LGBT across Latin America. Despite a reputation for machismo, the region has taken center stage in the global LGBT scene (Corrales, 2012). Many countries passed progressive legislation to expand homosexual civil rights, from the legalization of sex change in identity documents in Ecuador to same-sex marriage in Argentina. Immediately after Brazil abolished references to gender in the constitutional clause on marriage in September 2011, close to 2,000 homosexual couples received a social pension from the state.[8] The largest gay pride in the world gathers 3 million people in São Paulo once a year, and Rio de Janeiro was awarded the title of hottest gay destination in the world for two consecutive years after being elected best global destination city for gay travelers in 2009.

LGBT politics in the Amazon are inevitably interwoven in this larger picture. In that sense, they are local manifestations of international politics. Amazonian expressions of varied sexualities have gained impetus and visibility through the globalization of LGBT discourse as part of human rights. Yet if local demands reflect international norms, they are also intrinsically locally grown. There is nothing foreign about sexual diversity in the Amazon, even if it invokes the legitimacy of international norms. The region's sexual diversity is neither a novel phenomenon nor a global import. Indigenous queerness, in its own contextual realities, predates the international LGBT framework. What the global framework permits, instead, is a specific political conceptualization, together with the recognition of civil and economic rights attached to LGBTQ identities. The first gay pride demonstration in Benjamin Constant may invoke international discourse to open public venues to integrate sexual identities in political agendas, at once expanding the rights of LGBT citizens and facilitating alternatives to exit the closet. Yet it does not create new sexualities. The multiplicity of sexualities that exists today in the Amazon was always there, before the globalization of LGBT rights. What was missing, perhaps, was the outsider's capacity to see it. Through sexuality and equipped with LGBT language, the outside eye may be more inclined to discern complexity, even modernity, within the Amazon.

Sexually modern Amazons

Few things epitomize modernity better than gay pride celebrations. They are associated with urban, cosmopolitan phenomena in capitals such as New York and São Paulo. They evoke global centers of modernity, represent the cutting edge of international human rights norms, progressive politics, and cultural development. LGBT politics at large have become indicators of modernity par excellence, and by extension the antithesis of the traditional, religious or conservative. In many ways, homosexual rights have become a site of the modern secular state, echoing the consolidation of legal rights as much as European universalism. So much so that queer politics are often caught up in eurocentric conceptions. Homosexual rights are used to situate Muslim cultures outside modernity and assert the superiority of Western civilization (Rahman, Chapter 5). The Amazon is the last place that comes to mind when conceptualizing LGBT politics because it is a non-site of modernity.

As other spaces conceptualized as "natural," such as the Arctic or the Himalayas, Amazonia epitomizes the absence of political modernity. It symbolizes nature at its purest, and is invoked as one of the most biologically diverse regions on Earth to be "preserved" from the influences of global modernity. As such, it tends to be perceived as an apolitical Eden isolated from world politics and homogeneously pre-modern. The region is perceived as scarcely inhabited by peoples without history who roam (presumably naked) a wild habitat uncontaminated by global dynamics. Like their forests, un-modern Indigenous peoples are imagined in semi- or total isolation to be preserved from contact with modern, globalized, and urban societies. They are relegated to some romantic, apolitical past, and carefully preserved as part of nature. Amazonia is not an object of study of international relations because the region is not considered part of world politics. IR scholars, unlike anthropologists exploring Indigenous societies or biologists studying rare plants, have therefore no business there. When the political realm reaches the Amazon, it tends to be from ecological perspectives that analyze how external powers use (and abuse) its natural resources. Political ecologists tackle issues related to natural resources, such as conflicts over oil exploitation or water management through the Amazon Basin Co-operation Treaty (Braga et al., 2011; Vasquez, 2014). As Hecht and Cockburn made clear in their title, political approaches concerned with the "fate of the forest" reinforce the idea of a passive region prey to international geopolitics (Hecht & Cockburn, 2001; Becker, 2005).

It does not matter how many times Amazonian history is told and retold. The region seems to be endlessly treated as a land without history. Eurocentric gazes have continuously identified Amazonia as their quintessential *other*, conceptualizing it as a uniform, unified entity, a frontier of civilization that resists external forces of modernization. Time and again it is imagined as isolated from world politics. It does not matter that Lincoln planned to send freed slaves to Amazonia in 1862, or that Henry Ford tried (and failed) to build an industrial town on a plot of rainforest twice the size of Delaware (Lincoln, 1862; Grandin, 2009). Selective processes of history making also forget to tell that without Amazon rubber there would have been no car revolution in the first place or that the Allies tapped it to win the Second World War after Japan occupied Southeast Asia in 1942 (Wilkinson, 2009). The conceptualization of Amazonia as a vast empty Indigenous land ignores immigration inflows like the 20,000 workers from over 50 nationalities to build the Madeira-Mamoré railroad in the early 1900s (Foot Hardman, 1988), the establishment of a solid Japanese immigration around the jute economy in 1930 (Brasil de Sá, 2010), or today's influx of Haitian workers. This invented Eden impedes us to see the Amazon as the headquarters of today's global drug trafficking industry (Hecht, 2012).[9]

Historians are debunking various mythologies about the Amazon to unveil a different story. The wildest of all natural places on Earth is also economically dynamic and politically modern (Zárate, 2008; Harris, 2011). In the seventeenth century its rivers were already a stage for the construction of European sovereignty (Benton, 2009). The idea of an apolitical Amazon does not withstand serious historical inquiry. It appears to be less the result of its de facto marginality than of the silences created by hegemonic processes of knowledge production. In a way, the disregard for the Amazon in IR is similar to the omission of centuries of slave trade. Just like the Haitian Revolution failed to be recognized as a critical juncture in the history of state making and world politics, the Amazon is denied any semblance of political modernity.[10] This, of course, lies in the eyes of a beholder who stands in the Western core and looks at the periphery with an intrinsic exoticism that denies it any political role. In that sense, the invisibility of the Amazon in IR scholarship is, like that of Africa, symptomatic of a fragmented knowledge produced through silences and omissions.

What is valid for Amazonia is valid for all things "Amazonian," or the "natural other." Indigenous peoples represent the non-modern, and as such are not expected to participate in sexual modernity. The reality is that Indigenous peoples are intrinsically part of expressions of sexual identity beyond Amazonia. Indigenous queerness is tangible even where it lacks formal organizing or when it is not conceptualized under the LGBT codification. The documentary "Tibira is gay" reveals the complex variety of sexual identities in Indigenous communities in rural regions hard to access. Indigenous expressions of queerness can be found across the Americas. In Oaxaca, the city of Juchitán, described as one of the purest Indigenous communities in Mexico, is also famously accepting of homosexuality. Indigenous men who openly dress in traditional Zapoteca female attire are called "muxes" and recognized as a third sex (Mirandé, 2014). In the U.S., Native Americans refer to sexual variation through the concept of Two Spirits, and at least three tribes have formally recognized marriage equality for same-sex couples. According to Julieta Paredes, an Aymara Lesbian activist in Bolivia, her Indigenous language comprises up to nine different gender categories. Intergovernmental institutions recognize the significance of Indigenous queerness. On March 16, 2013, the Inter-American Commission on Human Rights of the Organization of American States heard the testimonies of elected officials at a panel "Situation of the Human Rights of Lesbian, Gay, Bisexual, Transgender and Intersex Indigenous Persons in the Americas."

LGBT activists in the triple border area of Benjamin Constant claim that sexual identities are as fluid as national borders. Often, people who openly assume non-heterosexual sexualities identify as transvestites. This is the case of Silvana, the transvestite cited earlier who regains a male identity in her work life. Her double sexual identity, man during the day at work and woman in her private life, permits Silvana not only to keep her job but to be accepted by the community. Transvestites walk the streets, have beauty salons, and hang out Sundays by the church in the Peruvian towns of Islandia and Santa Rosa, across the river from Benjamin Constant. An activist suggests that it may be easier to adopt transvestite identities, keeping the couple as a heterosexual enterprise, than to challenge established gender norms by engaging in homosexual relationships. What is certain is that transvestites are more visible in this triple border of Amazonia than in the streets of New York.

There is a profound gap between what is (un)told about the Amazon and the international interactions at play on the ground. LGBT perspectives debunk the myth of an Amazon isolated in some imagined periphery disentangled from global modernity. The analysis of gay pride celebrations tells the story of how the isolated natural Eden is, in fact, a stage of Western modernity. The Amazon is indeed a region that has remained beyond stateness. This is in part related to a geography that resists colonization efforts, thus a space favorable to evade the state, as much as because state institutions did not necessarily make sense in local context. Sexual approaches to the Amazon show not only that the region is surprisingly modern, but also that the conventional association of political modernity with stateness is, at best, flawed.

World politics are conceptualized as a state system. While it would be erroneous to locate Amazonia outside the state, state-centric approaches are insufficient in understanding Amazon experiences. James C. Scott (2009) analyzed the Zomia, the uplands of Southeast Asia, as a region having successfully evaded state coercion for centuries. He posited the peoples of Zomia as runaway, fugitive communities who managed for millennia to flee oppressive state-making projects – and the slavery, taxes, and epidemics they often entail. Amazonia entails similar historical experiences, most notably being a place where African diasporas took refuge to escape slavery. *Quilombos*, the Brazilian term referring to autonomous cities of runaway slaves or maroon communities, abound across Amazonia, and the Brazilian state has been granting land rights on the basis of ethnicity and ancestrality to *quilombolas* communities for the past decade (Hecht & Mann, 2012). Amazonia is not outside the state system or disconnected from the global political economy, yet its political autonomy has a Zomia flavor.

Amazon complexities are difficult to grasp from state-centric perspectives. The region is crossed by many national borders (Brazil, Bolivia, Peru, Ecuador, Colombia, Venezuela, Guyana, Suriname) and the scramble for the Amazon was at the core of Latin American efforts of nation making in the early 1900s.[11] Yet people organize along ecological patterns and transnational economic flows rather than around states. It is a social organism of its own, autonomous yet in constant dialogue with the international community of states. It makes no sense to study the Amazon from the conceptual confinements of the nation-state. However, it makes no sense either to leave it out of stateness, the primary object of study in IR. Surprisingly, however, IR fails to account for the salience of Amazonia, even though the region is inherently entangled in world politics. Pierre Clastres argued that Indigenous peoples in the region are not unsophisticated societies that failed to invent polities of their own but sedentary groups that abandoned their socioeconomic settlements in response to the symbiotic process of conquest and state formation (Clastres, 1982). Historians suggested that Indigenous slash-and-burn lifestyles in today's Amazon are in part the result of a century of extremely violent slavery for the production of rubber for export to industrialized countries. Indigenous autonomy and fragmentation is in that sense a political stance, just like the tribalism of the Berbers in the Moroccan Atlas, and political fragmentation a rejection of coercive forms of government.[12] The Indigenous/Tribal populations should not be thought as disentangled from modern processes of state formation but as their direct by-product. This perspective is reiterated by the LGBT analysis developed in this chapter.

The state, to echo Dipesh Chakrabarty, is inescapable yet deeply inadequate to make political sense of Amazonia (Chakrabarty, 2000). The Westphalian core is conceptualized as the present, dislocating non-core spaces to atemporal dimensions, subaltern temporalities. The Amazon is the home of peoples without history who stand outside the temporality of the state (Wolf, 1982). John Agnew pointed out that the study of modernity is characterized by binary language distinguishing the past and the present in geographical spaces, contrasting the advanced and the backwards, the developed and the developing countries (Agnew, 2003). The non-West is defined not only as that which is located outside of the modern (Anglo-European) political core but also as that which is constantly catching up, lagging behind on the civilizational path. Temporal displacement reveals that modern nation-states create not only political subjects but with it a certain developmental time too, a sort of temporal imperialism (Fabian, 2002). In that sense, the Amazon was invented as pre-modern and located in a non-Western time–space that is irrevocably behind on the civilizational timeline and structurally peripheral in space.

The problem with a state-centric approach is that it relegates Amazonia to the past. The Amazon, just like the Arctic and the Himalayas, is theorized as a place of nature in contrast to stateness, and as such relegated to an atemporal place beyond history making. It is situated before politics. John Locke's *Second Treatise of Government* back in 1690 articulates the native with the past: "In the beginning, all the world was America." This Western practice of temporalizing difference still permeates knowledge production today (Hindess, 2007). It is this combination of out of space/out of time that permits the conception of the non-core as an apolitical space. It lies "outside" state temporality, beyond the unfolding of world politics. LGBT approaches are useful because they locate Amazonia into the present. They relate the pre-modern Amazon to the Western core. As this periphery is rediscovered as a site of political modernity, LGBT perspectives permit to rethink the mostly unquestioned association between stateness and modernity. The question, then, becomes whether they also bring Amazonia into the state. They at least open our imagination to the possibility of a political modernity detached from stateness.

LGBT experiences: introducing new critical gazes?

A theoretical interest in LGBT lives and experiences in Amazonia does more than reveal modernity in unexpected places. It suggests that the modern core and the un-modern periphery are indissociable parts of one coin. In other words, they are relational categories. The core does not exist without the periphery and the idea of a wild Amazon only acquires meaning as a category relational to a supposedly civilized West. State modernity is the result of a North–South collaboration, a "world-historical production" (Comaroff & Comaroff, 2012). Modernity separated worlds that are, in fact, intimately linked, with political economies deeply intertwined. The state as we know it emerges out of its encounters with peripheries. Frantz Fanon stated it differently when he said, "Europe is literally the creation of the Third World" (Fanon, 2013). Places like Amazonia are co-constitutive of the state modernity.

This research echoes a growing body of literature that has been contesting IR's disciplinary straightjacket. Routledge's series *Worlding Beyond the West* questions processes of knowledge production that reinforce core–periphery dynamics in IR (Tickner & Blaney, 2013). Scholars seek to undermine the methodological inflexibility that confines IR, whether it is by recognizing the role of personal narratives or probing IR's methodological claims to science (Inayatullah, 2011; Jackson, 2011). This study advances LGBT insights to debates in critical theory. The Amazon is an opportune periphery from where to analyze how the international is practiced in the non-core. It is also a place where epistemological breakthroughs are possible when trying to rethink stateness. Further, an Amazon-based approach to IR permits to tackle IR's entrenched coloniality (Shaw, 2008; Shilliam, 2010).

Feminist research was groundbreaking for introducing the idea of positionality to global politics, and its impact in renovating IR's themes and epistemologies should not be undermined. Feminist IR expanded conventional understandings of what constitutes the international, contested core IR epistemologies such as security, and introduced new research methodologies (Tickner, 1997; Enloe, 2005; Ackerly et al., 2006). Beyond showing how gender matters, feminist gazes revealed other invisibilities, such as racist, colonial traits of the discipline. Together with postcolonial approaches, feminist insights permitted to establish the interaction of sexuality and race in the making of the modern nation-states. The sexual dimension of colonialism, in particular, has been analyzed in depth by a fast expanding body of literature. Colonial history showed how modernity implanted a new sexual order of "homo/hetero," identifying the interdependence of nation, race, gender, and sexuality.[13] Bringing together historical and ethnographic cases, Scott Morgensen argued that U.S. queer projects became non-Native and normatively white by comparatively examining the historical activism and critical theory of Native queer and Two-Spirit people (Morgensen, 2011).

Is it possible to think IR differently from within, or does it require moving outside it? Is it necessary to move to Zomia or Amazon lands to understand modernity as detached from the state? Feminists have tackled the question of the gatekeeper in depth. In fact, one of J. Ann Tickner's recent articles, "You may never understand," expresses the lingering difficulties encountered by feminist scholars trying to shift IR epistemologies (Tickner, 2011b). After breaking epistemological walls and expanding the legitimate content of world politics in theory and practice, many critical scholars have started to wonder whether their efforts can significantly renovate conventional ways of understanding IR or if we will need to kill the discipline, as Robbie Shilliam once claimed.

Feminist and postcolonial perspectives in IR have long challenged the Westphalian limits of their discipline. So why invoke the distant peripheries of the Amazon to reinvent the wheel in critical theory? Do sexual identities in the Amazon provide simply an expansion of existing approaches or do they actually contribute new insights from the intersections of conceptual and geographical margins? There are various possible theoretical implications of redefining the geography of modernity through LGBT lenses. As LGBT approaches bring the Amazon into modernity, they force IR to reconsider its obsession with state sovereignty. The question then becomes whether other approaches can also see the Amazon as modern. LGBT perspectives, as significant they may be, owe much to the pioneering work of feminist projects. Yet if feminist scholars paved the way, does it mean that LGBT insights operate within the same continuum of the feminist critique? Or do they offer a gaze of their own for doing IR?

Feminist and LGBT approaches think IR from similar positions of sexual marginality. Both perspectives share a commitment to redefining conceptual foundations of IR away from familiar gender-neutral, patriarchal narratives. Both denounce hierarchies based on sexual difference as well as the invisibilization of such inequalities by patriarchal practices. They both seek to problematize theoretical assumptions founded on hegemonic masculinities. Each contests claims of universal knowledge based largely on the questions of privileged men. Each seeks to bring sexual difference as fundamental to the understanding of global politics.

Yet LGBT lenses may enable a different gaze to read modernity. Feminist research has unmasked many mistaken assumptions about the Amazon but not the modernity of Amazon diverse sexual practices. A gender gaze would perhaps challenge certain hegemonies, but not necessarily unveil how the international discourses of LGBT rights have smoothly entered local, Indigenous communities across the Amazon region. The study of Amazon's sexual modernity not only dismantles the gender binary in a way feminist approaches have been timid to do, but immediately displaces the temporal imperialism that keeps the region in the shade of global politics. As this research was unfolding, I kept wondering whether there was a way in which LGBT(IQ) perspectives permitted a rereading of the modern state beyond feminist lenses. The question, then, is whether LGBT approaches are to be dissociated from feminist ones in any significant manner. Are these distinct approaches tackling sexuality with the same conceptual outcome? Or is there something that LGBT eyes can see better than feminist ones?

Laura Sjoberg has explicitly raised the question of what specific insights transtheorizing might contribute to the study of world politics (Sjoberg, 2012). She analyzes to what extent trans and feminist theorizing can be combined to diversify the content and epistemology of IR and unlock understandings of gender per se. One of her arguments is that thinking in terms of sexes, instead of gender, permits to embrace concepts of diversity and leave behind the traditional gender dichotomy. This permits to replace linearity by diversity, which, in turn, can make space for a creative body politics. Sexing politics, thus, has a considerably distinct undertone than gendering politics, as has been so often suggested (Tickner, 2001). But if transtheory can influence feminist interpretations of what gender is, could it also significantly interpret post-/decolonial interpretations of what modernity is? If LGBT perspectives can foment a transtheory that brings diversity to debates on modernity, moving away from linear dichotomies like with gender, perhaps it may shed light on truly alternative ways of rethinking international politics beyond the center and the periphery. Perhaps it can even permit truly diverse ways of rereading concepts of stateness and IR's obsession with sovereignty.

Such considerations become particularly interesting in the Amazon because of its sustained yet distinct experience of stateness. Leaving the Amazon at the margins of the study of world politics is not only a wasted opportunity to see alternative forms of the international at play. The consequence is worse than outright academic obscurantism. It makes evident IR's inability to face any politics different from what it has defined for itself.

Conclusion

This study engages an ethnographic study of LGBT dynamics in Amazonia to suggest alternative cartographies of political modernity. It debunks misconceptions of natural spaces in the non-core disconnected from world politics by portraying a cosmopolitan region embedded in sexual modernity. It hopes to contribute a voice from unusual peripheries to expand the horizons of non-core thought while contesting the disciplinary imperialism of state centrism. LGBT research can expand the borders of what constitutes legitimate IR, and where it is located. In my analysis, LGBT approaches contribute unique insights to understand Amazonia as a relevant site for thinking alternative forms of the international. The region gains salience in IR because (and despite) of a politics that escapes conventional approaches.

Telling stories of Amazonian sexualities sheds light on a small fragment of the multitude of vibrant realities taking place in the non-core. This research responds to scholarly calls to account for alternative practices of the international beyond the dominant core, while at the same time reaching beyond the increasingly evident inadequacies of the European nation-state to understand the world we live in. In doing so, it seeks to challenge existing critical theory to push IR even further from its self-imposed confinements. My hope is that LGBT perspectives be engaged to revamp IR theorizing in unexpectedly revolutionary ways that open up IR's collective imagination.

Notes

1 This chapter capitalizes the word Indigenous because, according to the *Chicago Manual of Style* (8.41, 15th edition), names of ethnic and national groups are to be capitalized, including adjectives associated with these names.

2 I favor the LGBT acronym for two main reasons: first, it was the exact acronym used by activists in the Amazon; second, the word queer is associated with the Anglo-American experience and is contested across Latin America as a politically charged concept.

3 For debates on race and sex, see Peter Wade, *Sex and Race in Latin America* (New York: Pluto Press 2009); Ann McClintock, *Race, Gender, and Sexuality in the Colonial Contest* (New York: Routledge 1995).

4 The Brazilian government regulates access to the Javari River Valley, with river patrols that only let through boats with ministerial authorization. There has been much debate

about uncontacted tribes across the Amazon having had prior contact with mainstream societies. Scholars and practitioners increasingly prefer to refer to them as groups in voluntary isolation.

5 For more information, see Ikitos web page: http://www.ikitos.com/tourism/gay.htm
6 Interview with the author, January 2012.
7 United Nations Report on Homophobia, 2011.
8 Since 2001 the Brazilian government provides benefits to homosexual partners, such as pension in case of death (http://www.ggb.org.br/Inss20%casais20%gays20%recebem20% beneficios20% 2011). The Ministry for Social Security released new benefits for same-sex couples, which the government estimates to be over 60,000.
9 Susanna Hecht reinterprets the survey exploration of Euclides da Cunha at the turn of the twentieth century to show an Amazon at the center of the international economics and politics of his time.
10 For the invisibility of Haiti in the history of political thought, see Susan Buck-Morss, *Hegel, Haiti, and Universal History* (Pittsburgh: University of Pittsburgh Press 2009).
11 For geopolitical borders of Amazonia today, see Beatriz Garcia, *The Amazon from an International Law Perspective* (Cambridge: Cambridge University Press 2012).
12 In *Saints of the Atlas*, Ernst Gellner argues that the marginality of Berber tribes is a political stance, a deliberate resistance of coercive government and an aware withdrawing from political authority (in Scott 2009: 30).
13 In the Philippines, *baklà* (men attracted to men) are considered a third gender. See Garcia (2008) for an analysis of baklà's effeminate identity.

Suggested further reading

Corrêa S and Parker R (2014) *Sexuality and Politics: Regional Dialogues from the Global South.* Rio de Janeiro: Sexuality Policy Watch.
Driskill O (2011) *Queer Indigenous Studies: Critical Interventions in Theory, Politics, and Literature.* Tucson: University of Arizona Press.
Hecht S (2012) *The Scramble for the Amazon and the "Lost Paradise" of Euclides da Cunha.* Chicago, IL: University of Chicago Press.
Tickner A B and Blaney D (2013) *Claiming the International.* New York: Routledge.
Trávez D F, Catellanos S, and Viteri M A (2014) *Resentir lo queer en America Latina: diálogos desde/con el Sur.* Barcelona: EGALES.

Bibliography

Ackerly B, Stern M, and True J (2006) *Feminist Methodologies for International Relations.* Cambridge: Cambridge University Press.
Adams C, Murrieta R, and Neves W (eds.) (2006) *Sociedades caboclas amazônicas: modernidade e invisibilidade.* São Paulo: Annablume.
Agnew J (2003) *Geopolitics.* New York: Routledge.
Becker B (2005) Geopolítica da Amazônia. *Estudos Avançados* 19(53): 71–88.
Benton L (2009) *A Search for Sovereignty: Law and Geography in European Empires, 1400–1900.* Cambridge: Cambridge University Press.
Binnie J (2004) *The Globalization of Sexuality.* London: Sage.
Braga B, Varella P, and Gonçalves H (2011) Transboundary water management of the Amazon Basin. *Water Resources Development* 27(3): 477–96.
Brasil de Sá M (2010) *A Imigração Japonesa no Amazonas a Luz da Teoria das Relações Internacionais.* Manaus: FAPEAM.
Buck-Morss S (2009) *Hegel, Haiti, and Universal History.* Pittsburgh: University of Pittsburgh Press.
Cady L and Fessenden T (2013) *Religion, the Secular, and the Politics of Sexual Difference.* New York: Columbia University Press.

Chakrabarty D (2000) *Provincializing Europe: Postcolonial Thought and Historical Difference.* Princeton, NJ: Princeton University Press.

Clastres P (1982) *Society Against the State.* Brooklyn, NY: Zone Books.

Comaroff J and Comaroff L (2012) *Theory from the South: Or How Euro-America is Evolving Towards Africa.* Boulder, CO: Paradigm Publishers.

Corrales J (2012) LGBT rights in the Americas. *Americas Quarterly* Spring: 88–94.

Da Cunha E (2006) *Amazonia: Land Without History.* Oxford: Oxford University Press.

Enloe C (2005) Masculinity as a foreign policy issue. *Foreign Policy In Focus* October 11. http://fpif.org/masculinity_as_foreign_policy_issue/

——(2010) *Nimo's War, Emma's War: Making Feminist Sense of the Iraq War.* Berkeley: University of California Press.

Fabian J (2002) *Time and the Other: How Anthropology Makes its Other.* New York: Columbia University Press.

Fanon F (2013) *The Wretched of the Earth.* In: Zimmerman A, Africa in imperial and transnational history: a multi-sited historiography and the necessity of theory. *Journal of African History* 45(3): 333.

Foot Hardman F (1988) *Trem-Fantasma: A ferrovia Madeira-Mamoré e a modernidade na selva.* São Paulo: Companhia das Letras.

Garcia B (2012) *The Amazon from an International Law Perspective.* Cambridge: Cambridge University Press.

Garcia, J N C (2008) *Philippine Gay Culture: Binabae to Baklà, Siahis to MSM,* 2nd edn. Quezon City: University of the Philippines Press.

Grandin G (2009) *Fordlandia: The Rise and Fall of Henry Ford's Forgotten Jungle City.* New York: Metropolis Books.

Harris M (2011) *Rebellions on the Amazon.* Cambridge: Cambridge University Press.

Hecht S (2012) *The Scramble for the Amazon and the "Lost Paradise" of Euclides da Cunha.* Chicago, IL: University of Chicago Press.

Hecht S and Cockburn A (2001) *The Fate of the Forest: Developers, Destroyers, and Defenders of the Amazon.* Chicago, IL: University of Chicago Press.

Hecht S and Mann C (2012) Where slaves ruled. *National Geographic* April.

Hindess B (2007) The past is another culture. *International Political Sociology* 1: 325–38.

Hobson J (2012) *The Eurocentric Conception of World Politics: Western International Theory 1760–2010.* Cambridge: Cambridge University Press.

Hutchins F and Wilson P (2010) *Editing Eden: A Reconsideration of Identity, Politics, and Place in Amazonia.* Lincoln: University of Nebraska Press.

Inayatullah N (2011) *Autobiographical International Relations: I, IR.* New York: Routledge.

Jackson P (2011) *The Conduct of Inquiry in International Relations: Philosophy of Science and its Implications for the Study of World Politics.* New York: Routledge.

Lincoln A (1862) Negro colonization: Brazil proposed by our minister. *New York Times,* December 28, 1862.

McClintock A (1995) *Race, Gender, and Sexuality in the Colonial Contest.* New York: Routledge.

Mirandé A (2014) *Transgender Identity and Acceptance in a Global Era: The Muxes of Juchitán in Joseph Gelfer, Masculinities in a Global Era.* New York: Springer.

Morgensen S (2011) *Spaces between Us: Queer Settler Colonialism and Indigenous Decolonization.* Minneapolis: University of Minnesota Press.

Mott L (2003) *Matei porque odeio Gay.* Salvador: Editora Grupo Gay da Bahia.

Raffles H (2002) *In Amazonia: A Natural History.* Princeton, NJ: Princeton University Press.

Rahman M (2014) *Homosexualities, Muslim Cultures and Modernity.* New York: Palgrave.

Scott J C (2009) *The Art of Not Being Governed: An Anarchist History of Upland Southeast Asia.* New Haven, CT: Yale University Press.

Shaw K (2008) *Indigeneity and Political Theory: Sovereignty and the Limits of the Political.* New York: Routledge.

Shilliam R (2010) *International Relations and Non-Western Thought: Imperialism, Colonialism, and Investigations of Global Modernity.* New York: Routledge.

Sjoberg L (2012) Towards trans-gendering international relations? *International Political Sociology* 6: 337–254.

Slater C (2002) *Entangled Edens: Visions of the Amazon.* Berkeley: University of California Press.

Tickner A B and Blaney D (2013) *Claiming the International.* New York: Routledge.

Tickner J A (1997) You just don't understand: troubled engagements between feminists and IR theorists. *International Studies Quarterly* 41(4): 611–32.

——(2001) *Gendering World Politics.* New York: Columbia University Press.

——(2011a) Retelling IR's foundational stories: some feminist and postcolonial perspectives. *Global Change, Peace & Security* 23(1): 5–13.

——(2011b) You may never understand: prospects for feminist futures in international relations. *Australian Feminist Law Journal* 32: 9–20.

United Nations Report on Homophobia (2011).

Vasquez P (2014) *Oil Sparks in the Amazon: Local Conflicts, Indigenous Populations, and Natural Resources.* Athens: University of Georgia Press.

Wade P (2009) *Sex and Race in Latin America.* New York: Pluto Press.

Wilkinson X (2009) *Tapping the Amazon for Victory: Brazil's "Battle for Rubber" of World War II.* Unpublished PhD dissertation.

Wolf E (1982) *Europe and the Peoples Without History.* Berkeley: University of California Press.

Zárate C (2008) *Silvícolas, Siringueros y Agentes Estatales: el surgimiento de una sociedad transfronteriza en la Amazonia de Brasil, Perú y Colombia 1880–1932.* Leticia: Universidad Nacional de Colombia.

7

BETWEEN THE UNIVERSAL AND THE PARTICULAR

The politics of recognition of LGBT rights in Turkey

Mehmet Sinan Birdal

Introduction

LGBT rights have recently been put, however contentiously, on the agenda of international law and human rights. In 2006 a group of human rights experts convened at Gadkah Mada University in Yogyakarta, Indonesia, to draft a set of principles related to sexual orientation and gender identity. In the introduction to what is now known as the Yogyakarta Principles, the co-chairpeople of the meeting explained that "the international response to human rights violations based on sexual orientation and gender identity has been fragmented and inconsistent. To address these deficiencies a consistent understanding of the comprehensive regime of international human rights law and its application to issues of sexual orientation and gender identity is necessary" (International Commission of Jurists, 2007: 6–7). Two years later the French and Dutch representatives at the United Nations proposed a resolution in support of LGBT rights backed by the European Union. The Organization of the Islamic Conference, in turn, supported a statement arguing that the proposal "threatened to undermine the international framework of human rights by trying to normalize pedophilia, among other acts" (United Nations General Assembly, 2008; MacFarquhar, 2010). As of now, 94 states have signed the statement.

Interestingly, both sides of the debate make references to universalizing and particularizing narratives simultaneously to justify their arguments. Those who oppose the international recognition of LGBT rights base their arguments on a universalistic narrative emphasizing national sovereignty and non-interference while also pointing out the prevalence of homophobia in many societies as an indication of its universal grasp. Opponents also resort to a particularistic narrative highlighting national or local culture. By way of contrast, proponents of the recognition of LGBT rights argue in return that LGBT rights are human rights and that the global prevalence of homophobia is partly due to the colonial diffusion of sexual norms. Reporting debates at the UN General Assembly, the *New York Times* signals that "although laws against homosexuality are concentrated in the Middle East, Asia, and Africa, more than one speaker addressing a separate conference on the declaration noted that the laws stemmed as much from the British colonial past as from religion or tradition" (MacFarquhar, 2010). The diffusion of international norms about sexuality as well as their embeddedness in local cultures will likely remain contentious topics.

I argue that though the recognition of international LGBT rights remains an important resource for local LGBT movements across the globe, the main challenge for them lies in building political alliances with local actors. What these alliances will be built on and what concrete results they will yield are far from predictable and require careful contextual analysis. In this chapter, I analyze the central role of debates about LGBT rights for the identity construction of Turkey's Justice and Development Party (AKP). The growing LGBT movement and its role in the Gezi protests of 2013 present an interesting case for ongoing theoretical debates about the universality and particularity of LGBT rights in the context of postcolonial theories. I suggest that Gezi protests bear important clues about how the LGBT movement can go beyond a politics of recognition and represent universality in its particularity.

The LGBT movement and the politics of Turkish identity

Turkey refrained from the vote on LGBT rights at the UN General Assembly leading to protests by LGBT organizations. Current debates about homosexuality in Turkish politics indicate that heteronormativity is playing a key role as Turkey negotiates its identity in the process of reasserting itself as a key regional actor upholding international norms, applying for membership in the EU, and drafting a new constitution. Turkey's particularity cannot be reduced to culture and identity, but needs to be situated in the global capitalist division of labor. Being a member of NATO for over half a century, a country in the Customs Union with the EU for 20 years and a candidate for the EU membership, Turkey is far more integrated with the center of global capitalism than any other country with an overwhelming Muslim majority. This makes Turkey also a unique case in the development of Islamism and the LGBT movement. The consequences of neoliberal reforms and export-oriented development strategy, imposed by the coup of 1980, created a rising class of small and middle-size Anatolian businessman, who became the backbone of Islamism in the 1990s. However, the rise of conservative capitalists also led to a transformation of Islamism in the course of the 1990s. Thus, Turkey's Islamists tamed their anticapitalism and facilitated the absorption of their constituency into global capitalism (Tuğal, 2009). The political result of this social transformation was the rise of the Justice and Development Party (AKP) as the dominant actor in Turkish politics. AKP's formulation of "conservative democracy" and its attempt to transform Turkish politics in its own image has been accompanied by a reinvention of Turkish identity, democracy, and citizenship. It is in this context that the rise of the LGBT movement in Turkey took place.[1]

The AKP, in power since November 3, 2002, articulated a political discourse combining conservatism with liberalism. The same time period also attested the consolidation of the LGBT movement in Turkey. The demands of the LGBT community significantly challenge the AKP's conservative–liberal synthesis, revealing the faultline between a liberal narrative based on universal human rights and democracy, and a conservative narrative based on particular values. Since their party's foundation, AKP's leaders were eager to dispel any affiliation with Islamism and instead promoted themselves as "conservative democrats." This new identity was also promoted as a model for the larger Middle East and provided a justification for a more assertive Turkish foreign policy.

The AKP employs the rhetorical devices of a populist subaltern nationalism to consolidate the party's rule in Turkey. Its success lies in its execution of neoliberal reforms with a populist rhetoric, which interpellates a democratic populist subject. Like other populist movements, the AKP claims to represent the wise yet silent majority against its enemies: technocratic and degenerate elites, powerful minorities, organized interest groups, and complex political institutions (Taggart, 2000; Laclau, 2007). Thus, AKP's populist discourse employs two strategies: emphasizing the distinctiveness and particularity of certain social demands; and claiming the sameness and equality of the demands. Laclau identifies the former strategy based on othering as the "logic of difference," and the latter resting on a common identity as the "equivalential logic" (Laclau, 2007: 96). Both logics facilitate the construction of the populist subject, which signifies the people and its enemies. The most significant aspect of AKP's strategy was to forge a coalition of both winners and losers of neoliberalism: the rising Anatolian bourgeoisie and the urban poor (Öniş, 2006; Tuğal, 2007; Hale & Özbudun, 2010). The AKP's ability to legitimize neoliberal reforms, which necessitates the centralization and concentration of political authority to implement policies dismantling a social regime, lies at the core of its political success.

Yalçın Akdoğan, advisor to the AKP's leader Recep Tayyip Erdoğan, provides a semi-official definition of "conservative democracy." In Akdoğan's view, modern conservatism and liberalism share a commitment to free market, but in distinction to liberalism, conservatism also seeks the restoration of authority in the social field (Akdoğan, 2004: 38–45). Conservative democracy invokes the principles of participatory democracy as respect for, and recognition of difference as well as consensus based on mutual tolerance (Akdoğan, 2004: 65–66). Mutual tolerance, however, is predicated on adherence to so-called "national values," a central pillar of Turkish conservatism (Akdoğan, 2004: 70–71). Westernization needs to be a selective process in order to prevent social degeneration (Akdoğan, 2004: 53). This reliance on a set of substantive values is the crux of conservative democracy's incompatibility with liberal democracy. In Akdoğan's narrative, the liberal dichotomy between civil society and the state is replaced by a yearning for the fusion of the state and the nation:

> The reconsolidation of the democratic regime is the fundamental precondition for the peaceful coexistence of social differences, for the fusion of the

state and the nation to occur and for the restoration of the corroding system. (Akdoğan, 2004: 67)

Socialization through family, school, and community is the most important mechanism procuring the fusion of the public good with national values, and merging the state with the nation (Akdoğan, 2004). Thus, Akdoğan warns against separatist, destabilizing, and marginal demands:

> Human rights should not be regarded as "separatist" and destabilizing "marginalizing" demands, but to the contrary as a meta-value aggregating the will of individuals and groups to live together and thereby, creating a general consensus and domestic peace. (Akdoğan, 2004: 75)

By constructing the AKP as the agent representing the people and defending the national values against the elites and degenerates, conservative democracy becomes a hegemonic, rather than deliberative project. Conservative democracy resorts to an "invention of tradition," characterized by a constant tension between the need to respond to novel situations and attempting to construe certain parts of social life as unchanging (Hobsbawm, 1997: 2). Topics such as family, school, and community are symbolic aspects of the conservative democratic invention of tradition registering sexual deviance as a sign of the degeneration of the nation.

Conservative democracy raises the question of who gets to decide which demand is separatist, destabilizing, and marginal. Since underprivileged groups are subject to misrecognition, their demands for recognition of equal moral and social status is usually construed as separatist, destabilizing, and marginal. Thus, assessing whether a certain demand for recognition warrants the protection of law and human rights based on their compatibility to a vaguely defined "general consensus and domestic peace" can likely reproduce misrecognition. The conservative discourses on LGBT claims present significant evidence of how such a majoritarian conception of human rights and democracy provides a basis for discrimination, misrecognition, and humiliation. An analysis of these discourses reveals how homosexuality has been associated with crime, disease, and sin.[2]

LGBT struggles in discussions about a new constitution reveal the exclusionary practices of conservative democracy. LGBT organizations shared their constitutional demands with civil society activists and politicians. Their reports emphasized that constitutional references to "general morality," "public order," and "manners" serve as legitimating concepts of discrimination against LGBTs (Sosyal Politikalar, Cinsiyet Kimliği ve Cinsel Yönelim Çalışmaları Derneği (SPoD) Çalışma Grubu, 2012: 5). Such general clauses allow the state to conceal a discriminatory administrative practice or an exclusionary political order in the form of a legal decision of a judge (Neumann, 1937: 581). Thus, the elements of a substantive Turkish identity, which form the core of the AKP's populist discourse, function as legitimating concepts to exclude LGBTs from the protection of the law.

The AKP's distinction between economic and political modernization and the preservation of family and culture follows the same logic identified by Partha Chatterjee with regard to postcolonial nationalism (Chatterjee, 1999: 38, 52). It acknowledges the need to adopt Western institutions in the domain of economy, statecraft, science, and technology, but preserves the domain of culture, religion, and family as a foundation for national identity construction. In current Turkish politics, the discourses on LGBT individuals are articulated within the context of the AKP's attempt to redefine Turkish identity using both a universalist liberal discourse with an emphasis on democratic procedure and a particularistic conservative discourse with an emphasis on invented traditions. Thus, after a period of liberal democratic reforms the AKP turned increasingly to a conservative discourse casting aside its appeal to liberal democracy. At the peak of this process, when the AKP leader Erdoğan was preparing for a change from a parliamentary to a presidential system consolidating his populist personal rule, a small protest in Gezi Park in the center of Istanbul ignited a series of massive street movements. The protests cut across the extant ideological and political cleavages and thus, posed a serious risk for Erdoğan's populist binaries of people versus elites. Furthermore, they increased the visibility and the legitimacy of the LGBT movement to an unprecedented extent, and thus provided an opportunity for the movement to engage with various actors across class and identity divisions, to move beyond identity politics and, thus, to have an effect on national politics.

LGBT politics after Gezi: can the LGBT movement represent the people?

Like the AKP, the LGBT movement also resorts to both universalizing and particularizing discourses. On the one hand, it refers to universal human rights, democratic norms, and civil liberties; on the other hand, it presents a particular minority identity demanding to be recognized. In this context, it is politically highly significant to pose the question whether the LGBT movement can subvert the logic of this identity construction. I assert that as long as the LGBT movement reiterates the postcolonial master narrative about modernity and authenticity, it will inevitably be bound by current political cleavages reproducing neoliberal hegemony. In the current context of Turkish politics, increasingly polarized by AKP's populism, the LGBT movement runs the risk of becoming subordinated to the conservative–secularist polarization rather than allying itself with other progressive social movements to create an antihegemonic alternative. I contend that such a trajectory will increasingly constrain the emancipatory potential and the unity of the movement and reduce it to an instrument of a vicious culture war. Thus, I propose a radical democratic strategy of building and strengthening alliances with antisystemic social movements, which will allow the LGBT movement to represent the people. This strategic shift, however, requires a change in the movement's approach to rights-based politics and the politics of recognition, which are modeled after the LGBT movements in the West.

The possibility of a counterhegemonic intervention appeared in the Gezi protests of May and June of 2013. These protests increased the visibility of LGBTs to an unprecedented extent and opened new venues for future alliances and the consolidation of old ones. The protests were based on a certain understanding of human and civil rights, such as the right to assemble, the right to association, the right to protest, free speech, and the right to privacy and the freedom of conducting one's own life, i.e., choosing one's own lifestyle. At the same time, they were expressions of discontents with the neoliberal working regime, city planning and governance based on rent distribution and the discontent of the so-called white-collar precariat about job security. As such, they were part of a global wave of revolts that broke out between 2009 and 2013 in Greece, Iceland, Western Europe, the U.S., Tunisia, Egypt, Spain, and, finally, Brazil and Turkey.[3]

Massive protests broke out on May 28, 2013, as the police raided the tents of a handful of urban activists occupying Gezi Park, adjacent to Taksim Square, to prevent the construction of a shopping mall on the park. Inspired by the Occupy movements in the West, these activists have been protesting various projects, which were part of the so-called urban transformation imposed by the AKP government and the AKP municipality.[4] Urban transformation involves the appropriation of public land that is handed over to construction companies, often politically aligned with the AKP government, which build expensive residences or shopping malls. It constitutes the backbone of the AKP's growth strategy and reflects the restructuring of the urban space as a means of social control. While projects in various parts of the city could be sold to existing inhabitants through rent distribution (with the promise of new, better, and more expensive homes), the projects around Taksim and Beyoğlu, the cultural heart of Istanbul, provoked a series of protests. The gentrification of this area was designed to turn it into a tourism spot filled with expensive coffee shops, bars, restaurants, galleries, hotels, and shopping malls. The destruction of a historical movie theater and the closing of a historical pastry shop also led to criticism about how urban transformation is destroying the cultural fabric of the city and turning it into a gigantic open-air shopping area. This destruction was also regarded as the AKP's attempt to stamp its conservative identity on the city. Municipal regulations restricting the coffee shops, restaurants, and bars to provide service outdoors and regulations of the sale of alcohol coinciding with Erdoğan's move to constrain access to abortion and his public talks recommending each family to raise at least three children were perceived as the footsteps of a creeping authoritarianism. Since Erdoğan's populist discourse increasingly polarized society to achieve his goal of establishing a presidential system, larger and diverse social groups grew wary of the AKP. In this context, the brutal attack against Gezi occupiers who stopped the construction machines led to an unprecedented gathering of hundreds of thousands of people. On the night of May 31, clashes between the police and the protestors reached a high point and continued on the next day. On June 1, as the police withdrew, the protestors occupied the entire Taksim and Beyoğlu area, erected barricades and turned Gezi Park into a commune with a free kitchen, a playing ground for children, a vegetable garden, a library, a veterinarian, and a first aid clinic.

Thousands started to stay overnight in tents and organized discussion forums, workshops, music concerts, art performances, and yoga classes. Although the park commune was dispersed by a police attack on June 15, the protesters turned to local parks to gather and established neighborhood forums and social media networks, and continued to launch street protests on certain occasions.

Gezi protests brought together diverse social movements: soccer fans, feminists, ecologists, securalist-nationalists, Kurds, Armenians, anticapitalist Muslims, LGBT groups, communists, anarchists, liberals, libertarians, artists, students, white-collar middle classes, and some worker unions. They came together in a common opposition to AKP's neoliberal populism. The peaceful communal life of individuals belonging to diverse and often conflicting identities posed a real threat to AKP's social disciplining project based on "national values." The peaceful coexistence of these identities made the AKP's ideological stance appear like a polarizing rather than a unifying force in Turkish society. This was very problematic for a party claiming to represent the people as a totality and damaged the AKP's image both domestically and internationally.

AKP's main strategy against Gezi protests was to launch a campaign calling its constituents to the defense of the charismatic leader they identified with. Against a possible crack among the party ranks and social base Erdoğan insisted on the indispensability of his leadership. International conspiracy theories and fabricated news stories mobilized the AKP base around an imminent threat and forced factions within the AKP coalition to choose their sides either with or against Erdoğan (Birdal & Tarhan, 2013). Erdoğan's response framed the protests as part of the culture war reactivating the political cleavage along a secularist versus religious axis. Had he manipulated the public discourse to frame Gezi as an attempt of the old secularist/nationalist elite to go back to the military-dominated 1990s, he could have persuaded the Kurds and the liberals to stay away from the protests (Birdal, 2013e).

LGBT visibility was crucial in dispelling the AKP's framing of the protests as a conspiracy to bring back military rule. LGBTs stood at the forefront of the Gezi movements. During the protests they invented new slogans subverting gender roles and using femininity as a form of protest, which have also been adopted by non-LGBT protesters.[5] People who had not been activists prior to Gezi gathered in the camping ground of what they named the LGBT bloc. Acting as a collective, the bloc was not dominated by any existing LGBT organizations. Inside the park, young LGBTs went around with rainbow flags and shouted slogans. LGBT visibility continued to increase after the police raid on Gezi Park commune. Despite the ensuing police brutality in the aftermath of June 15, the Istanbul pride march of June 30 became the most crowded and most cheerful in all the march's 20-year history. According to media reports, the march was attended by 50,000 people shouting LGBT slogans of Gezi. With thousands of Gezi protesters of all social and political backgrounds attending, this march signified the rise of the LGBT movement from a suppressed sexual minority to being a symbol of liberty and equality.

The beautification projects, which spread throughout Turkey after June 15 in an attempt of the citizens to reclaim public space from the government, also provide an interesting example of LGBT's rise to a universal symbol of Gezi. In late August, a retired engineer and his son-in-law decided to carry out a beautification project with no political aim by painting the staircase in their neighborhood around Taksim in rainbow colors (Erçiçek, 2013). The next morning when the AKP-governed municipality painted them back to gray, the rainbow stairs became an instant phenomenon in the social media. As the news and images circulated under the hashtag #resiststaircase, protestors all over Turkey started posting pictures of their beautification projects: staircases, sidewalks, streets, crosswalks, rails, speed bumps in rainbow colors. Rainbow colors, associated with the LGBT, now represented not only the resistance but also the attempt of a mobilized citizenry to reclaim the urban public sphere.

The post-Gezi political context presents both opportunities and risks for the LGBT movement, urging it to reevaluate its strategy and tactical maneuvering space. In a piece I wrote with Mehmet Tarhan during the Gezi protests on an invitation by the major LGBT organization KAOSGL, we predicted that the political debates within the LGBT community would increase and welcomed the expression of diverse political attitudes as a factor increasing the dynamism of the movement. We argued that this process is the inevitable result of the massification of the movement and it would help the movement to reach out to larger segments of the society and force the political actors in Turkey to be more responsive to LGBT demands. Although concerns about the unity of the movement are understandable, they are both unnecessary and undemocratic. We contended that the movement could rely on its tradition of pluralism and cooperation practices and even make a contribution to Turkish politics in this regard. Otherwise, the existing associations and organizations would be either ineffective or split up within an increasingly political LGBT movement in the context of a culture war (Birdal & Tarhan, 2013).

The tension between the two opposition parties, which are seeking to incorporate LGBT demands in the political platform, raises important challenges. The Peoples' Democracy Party (HDP), the alliance of the socialist left with the Kurdish liberation movement and the Republican People's Party (CHP), the center-left, secularist, nationalist main opposition party, which founded the Republic, compete over LGBT constituencies. When it emerged in the 1990s the LGBT movement in Turkey bore leftist and anarchist characteristics and drew support from feminists, anarchists, and ecologists. These initial allies helped the movement to establish links with socialists. Crucial support came from the Kurdish movement, which has been undergoing a major ideological change since the capture and the incarceration of its leader Abdullah Öcalan in 1999 by the Turkish government. Starting from the mid-2000s with the help of the women's movement, the socialists, and the Kurdish movement, the LGBTs gained recognition, visibility, and a political space to advance their agenda. Connections with legal Kurdish parties proved essential for the participation of LGBT associations in the parliamentary debates on the new constitution. Although no new constitution came out of this process, the effort itself allowed the associations to make new contacts in the political establishment, especially the CHP. Against the AKP's populist rhetoric framing the CHP as an elitist and statist actor, trying to prevent the nation's will from coming to power and reestablish the tutelage of the judicial, civil and military bureaucracy, the so-called the "New CHP" has been trying to replace the party's emphasis on secularism with an emphasis on personal liberty and respect for difference and pluralism. However, nationalism remained an issue preventing the CHP from cooperating with the Kurdish movement (Uysal, 2011).

The relations of the LGBT movement with political parties took a different turn after the Gezi protests. Its ability to represent Gezi made the LGBT movement an attractive ally in the lead-up to local elections in March 2014. CHP's decision to ally itself with the ultra-nationalist National Movement Party (MHP) played into Erdoğan's hands and reproduced the established secular vs. Islamist cleavage. The fear that Erdoğan's victory would increase political repression and the nationalist distance toward the Kurdish movement among the secularists replicated the same cleavage within the LGBT movement. The charge against the HDP of secretly agreeing with Erdoğan in return for concession in the peace negotiations between the government and the Kurdish leader Öcalan further consolidated this divide. Thus, the polarization between the CHP and the HDP, the two main political allies of the LGBT movement, increased the tensions within the movement and Gezi protestors at large. In the elections both the CHP and the HDP had LGBTs run for municipal offices and competed for LGBT votes. For both parties the LGBT candidates were signifiers of Gezi representing the promise of a democratic Turkey.

In the lead-up to the presidential elections of July 2014, tensions subsided, as the CHP-MHP candidate remained silent over LGBT issues while the HDP candidate specifically emphasized that he intended to fight against homophobia and transphobia in this opening campaign speech. Still, the LGBT community remains split between the CHP and the HDP over who can secure democracy against the increasingly authoritarian AKP. The political conjuncture requires the LGBT movement to lead a discussion about its long-term goals and strategies as opposed to short-term electoral gains, in order to maintain its unity and diversity. Gezi protests have been a historical mark in the recognition of LGBT visibility. In its aftermath, the LGBT movement is still in the process of formulating what to do with such visibility. In this context, it is important to remember Joseph Massad's criticism against the "Gay International." Rather than replicating Western LGBT movements, the historical trajectory of the movement in Turkey presents a unique opportunity to transform itself into a universal radical democratic subject that immediately entered the electoral realm in Turkey in the aftermath of Gezi.

The quest for LGBT rights: between the universal and the particular

Gezi protests provide the vocabulary and the grammar of a new radical discourse, which can subvert the prevailing postcolonial narrative and break the antagonism between the secular and the Islamist modes of authoritarianism. The LGBT movement, with its internal diversity and pluralism and its political connections with major political actors in Turkey, has become a subject that can represent universal interests of the people in its particularity. This possible outcome would not only radically change Turkish politics, but also the way we think about LGBT movements in the non-West. The Turkish case highlights the significance of strategy in building political alliances with other social movements and political parties in advancing LGBT rights. Extant political cleavages have a divisive effect on the movement, while Gezi has opened new opportunities for the movement to have a transformative effect on political cleavages.

The debate over universality and particularity, identity and difference, hegemony and subalternity lies at the core of the controversy over the international diffusion of LGBT rights. On the one hand, there are the defenders of universal human rights as the foundation for making legitimate claims to justice and recognition. In their view, establishing a formal procedure for adjudicating political claims is sufficient to assert the universality of human rights. Jürgen Habermas presents a sophisticated account of this view by arguing that a particular claim has to be able to generate consensus and therefore, has to present itself as a reasonable, justifiable, and criticizable discourse representing generalizable interests (Habermas, 1973: 150–52). On the other hand, critics assert that formal procedure always masks particular hegemonic interest since there is no universal rationality outside substantive power struggles. Chantal Mouffe and Ernesto Laclau criticize Habermas' consensus-oriented approach for neglected the antagonistic nature of politics. Mouffe emphasizes that the struggle for legitimacy is always a political struggle over the definition of the public good (Mouffe, 2005). In a democracy, Laclau argues, "the people" or the popular identity is constructed by a hegemonic discourse, which simultaneously connects popular demands through a universalist equivalential logic and distinguishes them from non-popular or antipopular demands through a particularistic logic of difference (Laclau, 2007). Although Habermas' approach can be useful in revealing how far AKP's conservative democracy lies from formal liberal democracy, Mouffe and Laclau's approach is more useful in analyzing the populist hegemony of the AKP and devising strategies against it. A major challenge for LGBT strategies is to shield against conservative charges that LGBT claims for recognition run against national values.

How can the LGBTs defend themselves against accusations of human rights imperialism in Turkey? For Judith Butler, the answer to this question lies in "cultural translation." She states that "without translation, the only way the assertion of universality can cross a border is through colonial and expansionist logic" (Butler, 2000: 35). Rather than the diffusion of a universal discourse ethics enabling consensus, Butler uses the metaphor of translation, but she still cherishes the possibility of lesbian and gay international rights. In her view, international LGBT rights have the capacity to redefine what the definition of human in different cultural contexts is (Massad, 2007: 37, citing Judith Butler, 2004: 37). In response, Joseph Massad launches a serious critique against the notion of international LGBT rights, claiming that it reproduces the Orientalism of the global human rights discourse and the imperialist/colonial logic imbedded in it. Massad argues that he is "sympathetic to the political project of an all-encompassing utopian inclusivity," but "less sanguine about its feasibility and more worried about its cruelty" (Massad, 2007: 42). International LGBT organizations, which Massad dubs the "Gay International," produce LGBT identities and discourses where they did not exist previously (Massad, 2007: 174). This discourse elicits either support or opposition to a universally defined gayness and thus, not only produces gayness, but also the opposition to gayness. This opposition turns against various sexual and social practices, which have not been defined as gay prior to Western intervention.

Massad points out that the Gay International's campaigns in the early 1980s coincided with the rise of Islamism, the Iranian Revolution, and the outbreak of AIDS (Massad, 2007: 177). In this context, the Islamist critique of Western interventionism also responded to the Gay International's diffusion of LGBT identities. The Gay International's use of the same organizations that are being used by US imperialism increased the sense that gay identity was a penetration of Western culture and thus, perceived as a threat to Islamism's quest for social regeneration. Thus, Islamist discourses about sexual deviance increased in the 1990s as a response to the Gay International's practices. Interpreting the raids on gays and their persecution in Egypt, Massad claims that "'it is not the same-sex practices that are being repressed by the Egyptian police but rather the sociopolitical identification of these practices with the Western identity of gayness and the publicness that these gay-identified men seek" (Massad, 2007: 183). Rather than posing a challenge to each other both the Gay International (and its Western assimilationist allies consisting mainly of middle and upper-middle classes exposed to Western culture in the diaspora or in the homeland) and the Islamists operate with the same Western sexual epistemology and together reproduce the hegemonic sexual practices, identities and desires (Massad, 2007: 48–50).

I argue that in his attempt to reveal the Western-centrism of universal LGBT rights Massad also denies the reality of existing of LGBT and queer identities, their struggles and their transformative capacity in their homeland. More importantly, he does not tackle the question of what kind of strategies are available to sizeable LGBT-identifying communities in a country such as Turkey. Although Massad restricts his analysis to Arabs, his argument about the Gay International's role in diffusing LGBT identities would also be valid for Turkey. Turkey presents an interesting case: despite the Ottoman society's affinity with the Arabic cultural attitude towards the diversity of sexual practices, Turkey is much more integrated with global capitalism than any other country in the region. Although Turkey's LGBT activists are to a large extent middle class members exposed to Western education and cooperate with the Gay International, their ranks also include members of the lower middle class and the urban poor. Beyond the activists, the larger LGBT community encompasses all kinds of people from different class, ethnic, religious, and educational backgrounds. Recent years also witnessed the spread of activist groups in the provincial towns of Anatolia. There are currently over 10 legal associations and over 20 university campus groups operating in

Turkey. Multiple factors facilitate the diffusion of LGBT communities and activism, which cannot be reduced to Massad's Gay International.

There are several problems with Massad's argument that make it hard to apply to Turkey's case. First, although Massad points out the functions of human rights universalism for U.S. imperialism and the role of Westernized middle classes in their diffusion, he never questions what made universalism, imperialism, and Westernized middle classes possible, i.e., global capitalism. Neither the emergence of the Gay International nor the diffusion of sexual desires and identities can be understood without a proper understanding of the dynamics of the global movement of capital and its social and political consequences. Focusing on the effects of tourism, cultural products, and human rights campaigns, Massad neglects why these phenomena are part and parcel of the movement of capital in the non-West. Not only the Gay International, but various venues of searching for sex, through associations, clubs, and internet sites; the changing definitions and modes of attractiveness, beauty, fashion, sexual and other bodily practices *in toto* are diffusing through the investment of capital. Where the Gay International cannot reach, the movement of capital will.

The contemporary resurgence of Islamism can also be explained as a symptom of global capitalism. The neoliberal restructuring of global capital drained the various resources of Middle Eastern states, whose state-led capitalism was legitimized by generation of employment and distribution of rent. The adaptation of these authoritarian states was impossible without losing their legitimacy. Islamist solidarity networks responded to the social demands of a population, which was increasingly impoverished and was becoming insecure in an age of global capital mobility (Rosefsky Wickham, 2002; Henry & Springborg, 2005). Both the rise of Islamism and the diffusion of LGBT identities have been part of the reorganization of global capitalism since the late 1960s (Castells, 1998). The social protests of 2009–13 signal that the world system is going through a crisis of governability. Sociologist Cihan Tuğal, who studies the protests comparatively, points out that as the U.S. is turning away from productive to financially driven growth, production is shifting to non-Western regions. The rise of non-Western emerging powers as engines of world growth leads to a shift from consent-based models to increasingly coercion-based models of hegemony generating revolts against anti-authoritarian and anti-war protests. Turkey, as other Middle Eastern regional powers, perceives a power gap and engages in complex political alliances to enhance its regional influence. Analogous to the U.S., imperial overreach simultaneously intensifies domestic coercion. Thus, the recent Gezi protests can be read as reactions not only to AKP's increasing authoritarianism, but also against the "Turkish model," which has been marketed by the U.S. to the Middle East as a blueprint for success (Tuğal, 2013: 163–65). The comparative study of latest global protest movement offers important insights into the contemporary development of the world system and the anti-systemic social movements against it. As the recent rise of ISIL following the breakup of authoritarian regimes in Iraq and Syria demonstrates, the analysis of contemporary global politics and security threats requires a proper understanding of social movements.

Conclusion

My analysis in this chapter illustrates how a protest can open up new opportunities for alliances for a social movement in order to advance its agenda. However, social movements do not operate in a vacuum, but within historically and socially constructed political cleavages. How they navigate the political landscape and whether they are divided along the cleavages or attempt to redefine them is a question of strategy, which cannot be answered a priori. The next step in this research agenda is to locate this analysis in the broader regional and global context. Debates in the UN and in academic circles suggest that questions about the universality and particularity of LGBT rights are intimately bound up with imperialism, hegemony, subalternity, and national identity construction. Several research programs are relevant for pursuing this research agenda. Research on transnational advocacy networks goes beyond the state level to explain the strategies employed by social movements across state borders (Keck & Sikkink, 1998). Research on norms points out legitimation, prominence and the intrinsic characteristics of the norm as factors determining the influence and thus, the diffusion of a norm (Finnemore & Sikkink, 1999). The concept of state socialization provides an analytical tool to gauge the extent of the diffusion of LGBT rights through international forums such as the UN (Checkel, 2005; Goodman & Jinks, 2013). Whether the emerging powers will adhere to the norms of the liberal world order, including LGBT rights, or challenge them remains an important question to be addressed by the literature (Xiaoyu, 2012). My analysis of the LGBT movement in Turkey suggests that the antisystemic movements unleashed by global capitalism are going to be key factors in the future shaping of a normative world order. In this regard, the goals, values, and strategies available to LGBT movements across the globe will be related to the location of their country of origin within the world system. The world system theory, by combining an analysis of both the world economy and interstate system, is crucial in analyzing the dynamics of social movements within the contemporary world order (Arrighi et al., 1989).

The analysis of the role of the LGBT movement in Turkey's Gezi protests demonstrates that, similar to Chatterjee's conception of postcolonial nationalism, the diffusion of LGBT identities through global capitalism can create antisystemic LGBT identities and not merely agents of Gay International, as Massad suggests. This requires the cultural translation of universal LGBT rights into the public discourse of domestic politics by presenting LGBT demands as universal demands of the people. The success of the LGBT movement in Gezi protests reveals that the persuasiveness of such cultural translation is dependent on prudence in political alliances rather than merely discursive competence.

Notes

1 The following discussion is based on Birdal, 2013a, 2013b, 2013c.
2 For a discussion of conservative discourses on the LGBT, see Birdal, 2013b.
3 For a sociological analysis of Gezi protests in the context of worldwide protests from 2009 to 2013, see Tuğal, 2013.

4 For an early account of the protests, see Birdal, 2013d.
5 The slogan #direnayol (which translates as #resistayol – ayol is an exclamation commonly associated with women, feminine gay men, and transsexuals) was both graffitied on the street and circulated widely in the social media. Another slogan, which was widely used after Gezi, goes "Where are you my love? Here I am," followed by repeated shouts "ay, ay, ay, ay" (a feminine exclamation).

Suggested further reading

Akça I, Bekmen A, and Özden B A (eds.) (2013) *Turkey Reframed: Constituting Neoliberal Hegemony*. London: Pluto Press.
Amar P (2013) *The Security Archipelago: Human-Security States, Sexuality Politics and the End of Neoliberalism*. Durham, NC: Duke University Press.
Birdal M S (2013) Queering conservative democracy. *Turkish Policy Quarterly* 11(4): 119–29.
Özkırımlı U (2014) *The Making of a Protest Movement: #occupygezi*. London: Palgrave.
Tuğal C (2013) "Resistance everywhere": the Gezi Revolt in global perspective. *New Perspectives on Turkey* 49: 157–72.

Bibliography

Akdoğan Y (2004) *AK Parti ve Muhafazakar Demokrasi* [AK Party and Conservative Democracy]. Istanbul: Alfa Yayınları.
——(2006) The meaning of conservative democratic political identity. In: Yavuz M H (ed.) *The Emergence of a New Turkey: Democracy and the AK Parti*. Salt Lake City: University of Utah Press.
Arrighi G, Hopkins T K, and Wallerstein I (1989) *Antisystemic Movements*. London: Verso.
Birdal M S (2013a) Queering conservative democracy. *Turkish Policy Quarterly* 11(4): 119–29.
——(2013b) Neden LGBT Tarihi? Türkiye'de Siyaset ve LGBTfobi. [Why LGBT history? Politics and LGBTphobia in Turkey]. In Bilmez B (ed.) *Cumhuriyetin Tartışmalı Konuları* [Controversial Issues of the Republic]. Istanbul: Tarih Vakfı Yurt Yayınları, 159–90.
——(2013c) The Davutoğlu Doctrine: the populist construction of the strategic subject. In: Akça I, Bekmen A, & Özden B A (eds.) *Turkey Reframed: Constituting Neoliberal Hegemony*. London: Pluto Press.
——(2013d) Generation Y on the rise in Turkey. *Ahram Online*. http://english.ahram.org.eg/NewsContentPrint/4/0/73677/Opinion/0/Generation-Y-on-the-rise-in-Turkey.aspx
——(2013e) Zayıf halka nerede? [Where is the weak link?] *Evrensel*. http://everywhere taksim.net/tr/evrensel-zayif-halka-nerede
——(2014) Gezi'den soma'ya: bir Toplumsal protestonun Serencamı [From Gezi to Soma: the aftermath of a social protest]. *Evrensel Kültür* 270: 69–71.
Birdal M S and Tarhan M (2013) Gezi sonrası üzerine [On post-Gezi]. *KAOSGL* 132: 18–21.
Butler J (2000) Restaging the universal: hegemony and the limits of formalism. In: *Contingency, Hegemony, Universality: Contemporary Dialogues on the Left*. London: Verso.
——(2004) *Undoing Gender*. New York: Routledge.
Callinicos A (1999) *Social Theory: A Historical Introduction*. Cambridge: Polity Press.
Castells M (1998) *The Information Age, Vol. II: The Power of Identity*. Oxford: Blackwell.
Chatterjee P (1999) *The Partha Chatterjee Omnibus: Nationalist Thought and the Colonial World*. New Delhi: Oxford University Press.
Checkel J T (2005) International institutions and socialization in Europe: introduction and framework. *International Organization* 59(4): 801–26.
Erçiçek S (2013) Bir gecede gri bir gecede renkli ldu [It became gray overnight it became colorful overnight]. *Hürriye*. http://www.hurriyet.com.tr/gundem/24616754.asp
Finnemore M and Sikkink K (1999) International norm dynamics and political change. In: Katzenstein P J, Keohane R O, & Krasner S (eds.) *Exploration and Contestation in the Study of World Politics*. Cambridge, MA: MIT Press.

Goodman R and Jinks D (2013) *Socializing States: Promoting Human Rights through International Law*. Oxford: Oxford University Press.

Habermas J (1973) *Legitimationsprobleme im Spätkapitalismus*. Frankfurt am Main: Suhrkamp.

Hale W and Özbudun E (2010) *Islamism, Democracy and Liberalism in Turkey*. London: Routledge.

Henry C M and Springborg R (2005) *Globalization and the Politics of Development in the Middle East*. Cambridge: Cambridge University Press.

Hobsbawm E (1997) Introduction: inventing traditions. In: Hobsbawm E & Ranger T (eds.) *The Invention of Tradition*. Cambridge: Cambridge University Press.

International Commission of Jurists (2007) Yogyakarta Principles – Principles on the Application of International Human Rights Law in Relation to Sexual Orientation and Gender Identity. http://www.unhcr.org/refworld/docid/48244e602.html

Keck M E and Sikkink K (1998) Activists beyond borders: advocacy networks in international politics. Ithaca, NY: Cornell University Press.

Laclau E (2007) *On Populist Reason*. London: Verso.

MacFarquhar N (2010) In a first, gay rights are pressed at the U.N. *New York Times*, December 18. http://www.nytimes.com/2008/12/19/world/19nations.html?_r=0

Massad J A (2007) *Desiring Arabs*. Chicago, IL: Chicago University Press.

Mouffe C (2005) *The Return of the Political*. London: Verso.

Neumann F (1937) Die Funktionswandel des Gesetzes im Recht der bürgerlichen Gesellschaft [The change in the function of law in bourgeois society]. *Zeitschrift für Sozialforschung* 6: 542–96.

Öniş Z (2006) The political economy of Turkey's Justice and Development Party. In: Yavuz M H (ed.) *The Emergence of a New Turkey: Democracy and the AK Parti*. Salt Lake City: University of Utah Press.

Rosefsky Wickham C (2002) *Mobilizing Islam: Religion, Activism and Political Change*. New York: Columbia University Press.

Sosyal Politikalar, Cinsiyet Kimliği ve Cinsel Yönelim Çalışmaları Derneği (SPoD) Çalışma Grubu [The Working Group of the Association for Social Policies, Gender Identity and Sexual Orientation] (2012) LGBT Yurttaşların Yeni Anayasaya Yönelik Talepleri [The Demands of LGBT Citizens from the New Constitution].

Taggart P (2000) *Populism*. Buckingham/Philadelphia, PA: Open University Press

Tuğal C (2007) NATO's Islamists: hegemony and Americanization in Turkey. *New Left Review* 44: 5–34.

——(2009) *Passive Revolution: Absorbing the Islamic Challenge to Capitalism*. Stanford, CA: Stanford University Press.

——(2013) "Resistance everywhere": the Gezi Revolt in global perspective. *New Perspectives on Turkey* 49: 157–72.

United Nations General Assembly (2008) General Assembly Adopts 52 Resolutions, 6 Decisions Recommended by Third Committee on Wide Range of Human Rights, Social, Humanitarian Issues. http://www.un.org/News/Press/docs/2008/ga10801.doc.htm

——(2011) Discriminatory Laws and Practices and Acts of Violence Against Individuals Based on Their Sexual Orientation and Gender Identity: Report of the United Nations High Commissioner for Human Rights. http://www2.ohchr.org/english/bodies/hrcouncil/docs/19session/A.HRC.19.41_en.pdf

United Nations Office of the High Commissioner for Human Rights (2011) Council Establishes Mandate on Côte d'Ivoire, Adopts Protocol to Child Rights Treaty, Requests Study on Discrimination and Sexual Orientation. http://www.ohchr.org/EN/NewsEvents/Pages/DisplayNews.aspx?NewsID=11167&LangID=E

Uysal A (2011) Continuity and rupture: the "new CHP" or "what has changed in the CHP?" *Insight Turkey* 13(4): 129–46.

Xiaoyu P (2012) Socialization as a two way process: emerging powers and the diffusion of international norms. *Chinese Journal of International Politics* 5: 341–67.

8

QUEERING SECURITY STUDIES IN NORTHERN IRELAND

Problem, practice, and practitioner

Sandra McEvoy

In many conflict and postconflict societies, victory often comes to those that remain vigilant, cautious, and attentive. When I arrived to Belfast in 2006, 8 years after the signing of the Good Friday Agreement (GFA), Northern Ireland was still in the process of making sense of peace and struggling with its past. Some citizens engaged with outsiders to their communities very cautiously and used a sophisticated process of "telling," or recording of subtle cues that might reveal the religious background or community affiliation of those they encountered. A street name, a song someone would hum, or the name of a pub visited with friends, was enough to confirm or deny suspicions.[1] As a queer scholar, I too was trying to make sense of the social and political environment of the city. I wondered, could this aptitude, one that had become so engrained in the Northern Irish, enable the Loyalist[2] community I was working with to "tell" my sexuality? Would the "telling" of my lesbian identity make me so much of an outsider that I would not be accepted? What would the community think?[3]

In the midst of this personal and professional minefield, my focus remained on exploring Loyalist women's participation in/support for paramilitary organizations in Northern Ireland during the country's 30-year conflict.[4] Over the next 7 months, I interviewed 30 women from working-class areas of Northern Ireland seeking to understand their participation in/support for such groups with a specific interest in the ways in which their participation was gendered and what this participation could mean for men and masculinity (McEvoy, 2009). It is from these extended encounters with Loyalist communities that I began to question how queer and LGBT perspectives might inform the practice and theory of security studies.

Introduction

Lesbian, gay, bisexual and transgender (LGBT) and queer theory[5] perspectives have become valuable analytical lenses that scholars from across international relations

(IR) and its subdisciplines have come to appreciate.[6] LGBT perspectives and examinations of sexuality and gender identity are finding a place in international law, policy, and human rights agendas (Kollman & Waites, 2009). In so doing, LGBT and queer theory have injected vibrancy for new theorizing, notably into what can seem like the stale discipline of IR. Kollman and Waites argue that the 2006 Declaration of Montreal and the 2007 Yogyakarta Principles on the Application of International Human Rights Law in Relation to Sexual Orientation and Gender Identity "symbolize a significant acceleration and intensification of international struggles by LGBT movements" (Kollman & Waites, 2009: 1). While the momentum to codify protections for the LGBT community is exciting and should be celebrated, IR scholars, specifically those in security studies, have begun to ask what contributions LGBT and queer approaches can make to the field. An appetite is growing for more analysis that can benefit the discipline, but the question remains: How do we get there?

The aim of this chapter is to offer a critical reflection on contemporary security studies by making explicit some of the ways in which LGBT approaches and queer theory can contribute to the mainstream concept of security. To do so, I will first identify some of the key limitations of mainstream security studies, drawing primarily from insights from feminist theories of IR. My intent in highlighting these entry points is to create a basic context for the second section of the chapter, in which I suggest some of the ways in which LGBT and queer perspectives can contribute to our thinking on contemporary security issues in IR. I will demonstrate how these approaches have clarified my own thinking about security studies as a lesbian researcher working with Loyalist women paramilitaries in postconflict Northern Ireland. The opportunity to examine how these approaches are negotiated on the ground in a postconflict setting offers important insights to the study of security, especially related to conflict. It is my hope that this interplay of theoretical examination and practical application will encourage more inclusive conversations between IR and LGBT and queer theory in a way that generates both practical and methodological benefits.

Sketching and critiquing security studies

In 1998 Evans and Newnham argued that security studies was one of the most "buoyant areas of IR scholarship," asserting that its "highly eclectic" nature would, in itself, ensure its future viability (496). While I appreciate Evans and Newnham's excitement about the future of security studies, I am more skeptical about the "buoyancy" they described. That is to say, simply because the field has room for growth does not suggest that it has yet matured. In the 16 years since their description of the "highly eclectic" nature of security studies and the "opening of new economic/environmental agendas" (496), the field seems largely inattentive to move beyond a narrow focus on the state and military–security.

Unfortunately, much of the field continues to privilege approaches that place the nation-state at the center of the security debate. This is surprising given how state centric models failed to explain the rapid fracturing of states in the post-Cold War period. More recently, the international community has observed several states become politically unstable as a result of the threat posed by widespread protests, militant groups, terror networks, and the increasing use of private military contractors. Moreover, rapidly shifting global and regional alliances are being reshuffled, compromising the integrity of states, and breaching borders that were previously considered secure and fixed.[7]

Also problematic for the field of security studies is the tendency to regard too many issues as security issues, such that its purpose and intentions are becoming imprecise. In her 2012 review of the concept of international security, U.S. feminist and IR scholar Nicole Detraz (2012) asserts that issues as varied as cybersecurity, tensions between states, insurgent groups and social security are now part of security studies. Detraz suggests that the list has become so problematically long that security has become "an idea with multiple meanings" (1).[8] In fact, it is a very small leap from considering a more broad range of *issues* that the field is concerned with to identifying elements within these issues as security *threats*. Not only are more governments and power brokers designating issues as security threats but by doing so, the reach of the state is extended into areas never before thought important in our dialogues about security. Drawing on Weaver (1995), Detraz offers a warning that "expanding the notion of security may actually serve to strengthen the hold the state assesses over more areas. [Weaver's] logic is that since security issues have traditionally been seen as the purview of the state, identifying threats other than military ones as security threats will give the state greater control over more issues" (10). I extend Detraz's argument to suggest that the appetite of the field to include an ever broader list of issues as security concerns makes it eerily mirror the old adage about the duck: "If it looks like a security issue, and sounds like a security issue, it probably is a security issue."[9] Just 4 years following the citizen-led rebellions known as the "Arab Spring" in Northern Africa and the Middle East, it seems as important as ever to be vigilant about the ways in which the state justifies its reach in the name of security (Khorrami, 2011).

It is not only the reach and influence of the state that feminist scholars of IR have critiqued. Dating back to the late 1980s, feminist IR scholars' primary critique of security studies was that the field and the discourses surrounding it were highly gendered. Feminists exposed that the values, beliefs and norms commonly associated to security "privileged perceived masculine values such as rationality and autonomy over perceived feminine values such as emotions and dependence" (Basu, in Tickner & Sjoberg, 2011: 98).[10] More than just a bias against women, feminist scholars argued that conventional definitions of security flatly dismissed the kind of violence waged against vulnerable groups and omitted its underlying nature. Tickner (2010), one of the foremothers of the field, asserts the importance of making this distinction:

> Security is not just about the security of states but also of individuals and groups; it is about violence of all forms, including structural violence and violence we are committing against our natural environment (577).

In the approximately 25 years since Enloe's (1990) and Tickner's (1992) path-breaking work (widely considered the birth of feminist IR), observers of security studies have noted an increase in the use of race, class, gender, and, increasingly, able-bodiness as lenses of analysis in the field. In some way, we might say that because of the work of feminist IR over this period we may have even become a little complacent believing that while feminist IR has certainly not transformed the entire field, we also find mainstream IR more thoughtful and committed to incorporating alternative lenses of analysis than we might have ever thought possible.

LGBT and queer contributions to security studies: identifying entry points

Tickner (2004) asserts that one of the greatest limitations of "typical IR theory" is that it does not account for the identity of victims and/or populations targeted by war. As we now know, victims' multiple identities are central considerations in the ways that wars are waged and sustained – especially ethnonationalist conflicts. Tickner further claims that mainstream IR, together with its "rationalist explanations," fails to sufficiently consider such issues highlighting additional limitations of the field. Undoubtedly, the sexual identity of LGBT communities is an identity vector that is frequently overlooked by security studies, however, the attention paid to LGBT communities by North American scholars is not unproblematic. Rahul Rao (in Steans 2013) cautions that LGBT rights have become a Western foreign policy priority such that Western governments use the mistreatment of LGBT individuals as an indication of how "uncivilized" portions of the Third World can be and how dangerous the Third World is (unlike modern states in the West). As such, "LGBT rights have become a marker of modernity, resulting in the creation of new global hierarchies – what John Binnie calls a 'new racism' in international politics" (135). In a similar vein, in this volume, Momin Rahman emphasizes the danger in uncritically advocating for the expansion of Western notions of queer rights as a "solution" to a lack of modernity often associated with Muslim cultures. He states:

> The modernization thesis is a problematic "solution" to Muslim homophobia because it assumes all modernization processes equate to a Western outcome of gendered binaries and sexual identities, rather than a potentially different outcome which is produced through cross-cultural intersections between West and East or, in IR terms, between the core and the non-core. (Rahman, this volume: 95)

Rahman illustrates that while the West has historically been preoccupied with "modernizing" communities of the East for a range of ills, its approach does not adequately adapt to the sociohistorical context within the countries it seeks to redeem. Returning to Rao, he draws on Gayatri Spivak's 1998 research on colonial feminisms, to remind us of the disturbing tendency of "white men saving brown women from brown men" (1998: 287). Rao argues that this sentiment is echoed in contemporary instances of "white homosexuals saving brown homosexuals from brown homophobes" (Rao, 2010: 145). In this formulation, sexual liberation becomes the means through which imperialism represents itself as the establisher of good society, "championing women and queers as objects of protection from their racial and national kind. By the same token, marginal metropolitan groups some-times seek full citizenship at home through participation in imperialism abroad" (Rao, 2014: 5). Rao's powerful analysis pinpoints a terrifying, almost morbid relationship that develops between liberation and imperialism. And, it is one that would likely go unnoticed without the insights from LGBT studies. Even more worrisome is the insidious nature of a "championing" that appeals so perfectly to the liberator spirit of the West while simultaneously warranting violations of state sovereignty and the development of invasive foreign policies.

Drawing on queer theory, Brettschneider (2011) investigates the differentials in law and practice regarding LGBTQ and non-LGBTQ people seeking to adopt children in the United States. She asserts that queer theory exposes one of the central operating assumptions of Western thinking – its use of the concept of "natural" as a mode to "camouflage areas of politics in need of critical examina-tion" (23). From this basis, Brettschneider uncovers a powerful mechanism: deli-neating "'nature' as a sphere outside of or prior to politics and relegating various phenomena to this sphere, political theorists can overlook important power relationships" (23).

When that which is deemed natural is heterosexual (and by default, homosexuality deemed "unnatural"), I suggest that scholars of security studies should pay careful attention. In the field of security studies, Laura Sjoberg (2014) has been paying close attention to that which is considered natural and normal, especially related to transgendered people during times of war. Sjoberg argues that understanding gender perceptions and norms are crucial to the ways states wage war. In fact, it is through traditional, naturally informed gender norms that we can best understand the "traditional logics of war." Sjoberg states:

> [W]hen men behave *like men are expected to* and women behave *like women are expected to*, and no people except men and women are visible, then wars and conflicts function as they are supposed to – with ideal-typical masculine just warriors" claiming to fight on behalf of ideal-type feminine "beautiful souls".
> (Sjoberg, 2014: 88)

Sjoberg's examination of the disruption of gendered scripts most often associated to war and conflict is instructive in our thinking about the importance of LGBT and queer perspectives in our scholarship of security studies. That is, Sjoberg solidifies the notion that when bodies do not act the way that they are supposed to, these bodies become "signifiers of danger" (88) and that when such bodies "transgress" the boundaries of coherence and continuity" they are, "by definition ... deviant, inappropriate, and threatening" (89). Sjoberg is right to bring to our attention the dangers of such a rationale and reminds us that powerful states have used military force to impose their own conception of what is "natural" and "beneficial." One might immediately think of Nazi Germany's use of military force to imprison and murder gays and lesbians during the Second World War.

Taken together, Brettschneider, Rao, Rahman, and Sjoberg help identify the theoretical gaps present in mainstream security studies thinking, namely, that violations of (particularly) Western notions of how "natural" bodies (read, straight) are supposed to behave are incoherent, suspicious, and therefore dangerous to the state. Queer and LGBT perspectives argue for a more broadminded approach to understanding security and insecurity. This approach asserts that that bodies (sexed, raced, classed, or otherwise) are not in and of themselves security risks.

Negotiating complex postconflict fields

My first extended period of fieldwork in Northern Ireland began in early January 2006 and ended in late July of that same year. Over approximately 7 months I conducted open-ended, semi-structured interviews with 30 women who self-identified as former members or supporters of Loyalist paramilitary organizations (LPOs) during the conflict. My primary research goals were to establish the existence of women in LPOs and to understand the experiences and motivations for participation from the perspectives of the women themselves. Critically important to gaining access to the Loyalist paramilitary community were my family background and familiarity with the city. As a first-generation Northern Irish-American with parents and grandparents from Loyalist areas of Belfast, I had the right kinds of "credentials" for men and women to consider talking to me about their experiences. By the time I began my project I had visited Northern Ireland many times and felt very comfortable in the city. I recall feeling incredibly lucky that these factors could help pave the way for me to talk with a population of women that have been somewhat overlooked by scholars for over 40 years.[11]

Should you mention you are gay? Human security and the researcher

As I implemented my interview protocol, I took seriously the ways that my own cultural and political identity could impact the study. Although I grew up in peaceful 1970s southern California, my family regularly received distressing reports about Republican violence from family members still living in Belfast. This early bias required that I take even more seriously my obligation to reflect on how my own Northern Irish background, rooted in Loyalism and Unionism, might affect the ways I made meaning of women's testimony about the use of violence against Republicans.

It was within this context that I became vigilant about concealing my sexuality. I worried that revealing this information to members of the Loyalist community might pose several problems for me. One concern was the dangers it may pose to my ability to gain access to some of the more conservative sections of the Loyalist community.[12] Despite years of research experience on the conflict, I did not really have any sense of the ways the Loyalist community conceived of the LGBT population. I also worried that if potential interviewees knew that I was a lesbian they might question whether I could understand their important, often very personal, stories about their relationships with men during the Troubles. As months passed, my efforts to make the community feel comfortable with me appeared to be paying off. Four months into the project, I had become what Kanuha (2000) refers to as an "insider–outsider" to the Loyalist community where I was conducting research "within the cultural context of one's own people," and relying on my familiarity to them to enhance the research project. Despite this status, a concern remained that I would somehow be "outed." I could accept that members of the community may not want to share their experiences with me out of the concern of reliving the past or because I was working with HET. However, I was less willing to accept that I may miss the opportunity to talk to them because of my sexuality.[13]

As I contemplated the risks and benefits of outing myself, I decided against revealing my sexuality. Practicing what Fisher (2003) describes as a "strategy of concealment," I became very conscious of my gender performance when I attended a community event or conducted an interview. Instead of dressing in jeans and a weathered baseball hat, I found myself styling my hair more carefully and feminizing the way that I dressed to "soften" my appearance in a way that would allow me to blend into my understanding of Northern Irish, working-class femininity. During this period, these impression management techniques became as integral to conducting my fieldwork and it became clear to me that negotiating how I performed my sexuality in the field had become a central and practical issue in the execution of the project.

Reflecting on my experience conducting fieldwork as a queer researcher illustrates several ways in which LGBT and queer approaches can be instructive for both the theory and practice of security studies. First, the fieldwork reaffirmed the importance of using reflexive practice in the research process. That is, a commitment on behalf of the researcher to be constantly aware of the ways that our own varied identities directly impact the ways we approach our investigations.[14] From the choice of subject matter, to the implementation of the study, to the ways we make meaning from our findings – our identities are never left at the office. Whether our identities are normative or non-normative, we are always already part of the research process. Second, building on these insights from the process of reflexive practice, LGBT and queer approaches urge scholars of security studies to consider that "who we are" as researchers has an effect on the stories that our subjects are willing to tell, the information we are able to apprehend, and the meaning we make from the information we collect. In other words, LGBT and queer approaches remind us that no insight or observation should be considered incapable of having analytical value. Rather, we should consider that even those insights that may have previously been believed to be trivial are, in concert with one another, important components to our process of meaning making.

"Homosexuality" undermining peacetime priorities

A further consideration of the impact of sexuality on the study of postconflict studies is the way that LGBT identities undermine the peacebuilding processes of wartorn communities. Enloe (2004), Niner (2011), Phan and Turner-Gottschang (2003) and O'Rourke (2012–13) affirm the need for postwar communities to reinstate the conservative gender roles that existed in the pre-war period and/or even invented exaggerated gender roles that were not as marked in the pre-war era. Similar to what the U.S. observed with Rosie the Riveter's return to suburban homes from her work in aircraft factories during the Second World War, the postwar period marks a process of reinstating and reinventing gender roles to comfort a beleaguered nation turned inside out by war. The U.S. came through the crisis of the war and returned to the bedrock ideals of heteronormative family and home. Suggesting both the importance and power that traditional gender roles play in postwar transition periods, we see this same process occurring in communities that have fallen victim to political violence more sporadically (for example, Israel) or that may have suffered a significant one-time loss of life which greatly diminished its security (for example, the attacks in New York City in 2001).

Insights from LGBT and queer theory identify that this very same process, one that is necessary for the larger population is, at its base, a heteronormative equation.[15] In other words, while the return to traditional gender norms provides comfort and reassurance to many people in postconflict societies, such processes can simultaneously destabilize LGBT-identified people. We could imagine the increased feelings of isolation that LGBT people might feel in a context in which collective community building efforts are predicated on a highly heteronormative script. For example, many Indigenous communities rely on communal rituals and practices that have great healing value. In postwar Zimbabwe, the Ndebele community used a process of exhuming victims of the war whereby the spirits of the dead "guide and nurture" family. This ritual is symbolically powerful for loved ones. "If a spirit is not honoured with a funeral and the *umbuyiso* ritual completed, it can become restless and angry, bringing bad luck to the family and the community" (Bloomfield et al., 2003: 85–86).[16] The Zimbabwean case illustrates the possibility that grieving members of the LGBT community, who may be unable to publically grieve over the death of their partners, could not engage with and benefit from some community-based healing processes.

In Northern Ireland, I was engaging deeply with women members and/or supporters of LPOs and, who by virtue of their work inside militant Loyalism, on many occasions were operating very much outside of traditional Northern Irish gender roles. Although Loyalism is generally considered to be conservative political and cultural tradition (deriving much of this ideology from the Protestant church), the Troubles disrupted this script. For decades, women in Loyalist communities struggled to maintain some sense of normalcy for their children as large numbers of men were incarcerated,[17] or away from home serving or supporting paramilitary activities. Women were responsible not only for all of the domestic duties traditionally left for women but were also tasked with finding some way to financially support their families for extended periods of time. Over time, women became accustomed to this new reality but when the GFA was signed and/or men were released from jail, Loyalist men and women reported to me that they quickly returned to traditionally gendered Protestant and male/female arrangements.

Our understanding of some of the challenges to human security for LGBT people in postconflict environments is further hindered by what appears to be limited interest in exploring the issue by much of mainstream security studies scholars and/or IR more broadly. To date, information regarding LGBT persons in such contexts comes from relief and humanitarian organizations. For example, Colombian paramilitary groups carried out "social cleansing operations" in the country. The operations would often take place in "poor urban neighborhoods, where the victims are often young people accused of being petty criminals, drug addicts or sex workers. Lesbian, gay, bisexual and transgender people are also targeted" (Amnesty International, 2011). The UN Office for the Coordination of Humanitarian Affairs also cites a report from Human Rights Watch in Nepal that documented police attacks on transgender people, calling the violence a "sexual cleansing drive."[18] While not precisely focused on LGBT persons in the postwar period, Wilkinson and Kirey (2010) and Wilkinson (2011) are among the few scholars reflexively exploring the role of scholars in the research process in the field of security studies including some focus to better understand the experiences of LGBT youth in developing states such as Kyrgyzstan.

Heterosexuality, security, and post-conflict

In many encouraging ways, the field of feminist security studies, women's and gender studies, psychology, law, and medicine (to name a few) has exploded with scholarship that examines the complicated period that communities and nations experience when major hostilities come to an end. We have gained insights on the ways in which postconflict aid is distributed (Mazurana et al., 2011), the use of sexual violence in refugee camps (Amowitz et al., 2002), and the complications and benefits of developing transitional justice schemes (O'Rourke, 2012–13). We also know more about the prosecution of war criminals, the gendered processes of disarming of perpetrators of political violence, to name a few. In many ways, the field of postconflict studies is booming.

Yet, each of the aforementioned areas of research assumes that the primary referent of research is not only male but also *heterosexual*. That is to say, the excitement and energy generated in the field is largely devoted to exploring one vector of postwar identities – straight men. Critics of this assertion might suggest that because the number of LGBT men and women in postconflict environments is so small in comparison with their straight counterparts that the criticism I wage here amounts to nothing more than an annoying splitting of hairs. However, most would admit that such a dismissal is not just impulsive but irresponsible. It is irresponsible for several key reasons, but primarily because in actual fact we have no verifiable sense of the number of LGBT-identified people living in any postconflict zone. We can only speculate what the analytical value of examining sexuality, gender, and conflict might be given how understudied the subject is. Simply put, we really do not know what we are missing. The field of security studies – the field most often associated with examining the security-seeking behavior of states and its citizens – still neglects significant lenses of analysis that could enhance its understanding of the world.

Yet, we might still ask, what could such an inquiry reveal? Attempts to answer that question immediately elicit more questions that themselves illuminate our knowledge gaps. For example: In what ways has sexuality been deployed, manipulated or ignored in conflict and postconflict environments? By whom and for what gain or benefit? How is state security policy threatened or advanced with a more sophisticated understanding of sexuality in the postwar period? How can transitional justice processes better accommodate and protect and allow for variation within LGBT populations? Who will oversee such a process and ensure that restorative justice programs include the LGBT population? How will the rights of LGBT populations be codified in any postconflict constitutional reimagining? How are the wartime experiences of LGBT people (as perpetrators and victims) similar to and/or different than their heterosexual brothers and sisters?

Again, feminist scholars of IR appear to be best prepared to confront this big knowledge gap. As a discipline they have already conducted wide-scale research projects in war-affected countries to track the gendered effected of aid distribution and the forced marriage of girls (Mazurana et al., 2011), traced women's participation in the systematic use of wartime sexual violence (Sjoberg, 2014), measured the impacts of truth and reconciliation commissions (Hirsch et al., 2012), examined the relationship between sex, security, and United Nations (UN) Security Council Resolutions peace processes (Shepherd, 2011), and women perpetrators of state-supported political violence (McEvoy, 2009).

Perhaps one of the most compelling examples of how LGBT and queer perspectives can contribute to security studies can be seen through a reexamination of the hugely popular topic of disarming, demobilizing and reintegrating (DDR) processes and former combatants in the postconflict period. The UN defines DDR as:

> a process that contributes to security and stability in a post-conflict recovery context by removing weapons from the hands of combatants, taking the combatants out of military structures and helping them to integrate socially and economically into society by finding civilian livelihoods. (UN in Jennings, 2008: 328–29)

The short definition belies a remarkably complex process that is fraught with pitfalls that are too numerous to review here. But, to be clear, it is precisely because of the multilayered and multifaceted nature of the individual and community rehabilitation that IR scholars have been so devoted to the topic. Of principle concern to scholars of security studies had been disarming former combatants, especially men and boys. At the most basic level, the removal of an armament is intended to add stability and safety to the surrounding community. To facilitate the process, the UN and its member states fund programs to pay former combatants to turn in weapons. While the financial compensation is not enormous it is also intended to recognize that the arm has been a valuable resource for the combatant. The literature accurately identifies some of the many negative and very dangerous side-effects created by removing an automatic rifle from a former member of a militia or insurgent group. Most difficult to manage is the effect that the removal of a gun has on the former fighter's sense of masculinity. One of the earliest scholars to take militarized masculinities seriously, Cynthia Enloe (1990), stressed that carefully cultivated over the course of the conflict, performances of militarized masculinity and hypermasculinity serve multiple forms of protection for the fighter (also see Connell & Connell, 2005). In the absence of the weapon, fighters have been known to return to combat, and/or become violent in other ways in the community. These important insights have helped aid organizations better shape DDR processes in a way that prepares communities when cases of volatility emerge.[19]

Scholars of security studies also fail to engage the heteronormative and hyper-heteronormative performances of masculinity. Facilitated by insights from LGBT and queer theory, we see that the DDR process is fundamentally a heteronormative one that recognizes the destructive potential of a former combatant, assesses the risks of that potential and shapes postwar policy to reward violent masculinity. Given that part of my own research also attempts to understand violent femininity, it is reasonable to query how the removal of weapons from former female combatants plays out and/or whether this same dynamic may negatively affect either the combatant or the community in which she resides. At this time, no data have been presented that suggest a similar pattern of postconflict violence has emerged. However, violence *against* women combatants (including domestic violence and rape) has been recorded when women's weapons are surrendered (Ward & Marsh, 2006).

Outside of postconflict environments, LGBT approaches can help us identify other contexts in which hypermasculinity and hyperheteronormativity are constantly at play. Somewhat unsurprisingly, the armed forces are fruitful areas for examination. In these contexts, heterosexual masculinity is vigilantly cultivated in order to create the virulent human beings we send off to war. Within boot camps, obstacle courses, and battlefields, coaches, instructors, and drill sergeants groom a special type of militarized, heteronormative masculinity. The idea is to create what military commanders often refer to as "unit cohesion," a process that could also be described as an intense relationship (typically) of dependence on other men. It is in these highly militarized, extremely intimate relationships where heterosexual men actually mimic homoeroti-cism. For example, we often see men cling to one another, cry with one another, endure physical and psychological pain and joy with one another, and know that they also live and die with (and for) one another. Whereas military men are hyper-masculinized and hyperauthoritarian, in real terms, they are performing homosexuality in many, many ways.[20] Without an LGBT and queer curiosity, the field of security studies is far less able to understand these highly gendered and sexed dynamics of heterosexual militarized masculinity. Without such an understanding, I argue that we are not only less likely to identify the kinds of threat that hypermasculinized and hyperheterosexual bodies may pose but we critically misunderstand effective policy responses to it.

Conclusion

This chapter illustrated some of the ways in which traditional security studies has failed to keep pace with a rapidly evolving global cultural and political landscape that has experienced change and challenge at an alarming rate. More specifically, the chapter asserted the subfield's inability to compensate and accommodate LGBT and queer perspectives, especially in the postconflict period. At a practical level, the chapter highlighted how such perspectives were helpful in making additional meaning of my own fieldwork experiences with politically violent women in Northern Ireland. In this way, a unique amalgamation of security studies, sexuality studies, political violence, and conflict studies was made, and one that in itself creates more challenges, questions, and uncertainties.

I am under no illusion that the arguments that I have made here related to the benefits of incorporating LGBT and queer approaches in mainstream security studies thinking will shift the field – now or even in the next decade. As I reflect on the work of some of the earliest scholars of feminist IR, many of whom I have had the privilege of getting to know, these battles (and they are!) will be hard fought and take time. The top 10 most cited and well-tenured members of the academic-based security studies community will likely retire from the discipline before LGBT and queer perspectives find a place on the required reading lists at top IR programs. Convincing these scholars of the analytical and practical benefits of such perspectives has not been (and should not be) the ambition. Instead, we might be more satisfied in these somewhat early days if we can commit ourselves to maintaining an intellectual dialogue that avoids the disciplinary battles we have all witnessed and work toward ways in which the richness of multiple approaches can together yield both the practical and methodological benefits we seek.

Finally, I am reminded of an account by Dolan (1998) (in Renn, 2010) of the 1997 decision by Yale University to reject a multimillion dollar offer by playwright and civil rights activist, Larry Kramer, to establish a gay studies program at the university. Reportedly, Yale was concerned that it would develop a reputation for creating "another identity-based area studies track" (140), despite the fact that Yale, since the 1980s, had already established itself as a powerhouse for queer theorizing. Renn recalls that Boswell, Butler, and Chauncey flourished at the school and that they did so in truly interdisciplinary ways, honing their skills in departments across the institution. Noting the strange curiosity, Renn states: "Queering theory was acceptable, but queering the organization was not" (138). I am hopeful that the queering of the *discipline* of security studies will not be met with the same angst.

Notes

1 For an examination of the use of telling in Northern Ireland, see Burton,1978.
2 The term "Loyalist" is a contested term. It is most often used to describe the portion of the Protestant population in Northern Ireland that wants to maintain the political union

between Northern Ireland and the United Kingdom. Underpinning Loyalism is an affirmation of a Protestant cultural identity. While not all self-identified Loyalists endorse the use of violence to defend this union, some do. See Taylor (2000).

3 With thanks to Andrea Dottolo who provided invaluable insight during my fieldwork and to this current project.

4 Northern Ireland endured a deeply sectarian conflict from 1968–98. The conflict ended in 1998 with the signing of the Good Friday Agreement (GFA). The GFA allowed most paramilitaries from both sides of the conflict early release from prison. In the 16 years since the GFA, increasing numbers of Protestants have begun to retract their support for the agreement.

5 While there are many variations to the definition of queer theory, Abes and Kasch (2007) offer a clear and concise definition: "Queer theory refers not to identity per se but to a body of theories that critically analyzes the meaning of identity, focusing on intersections of identities and resisting oppressive social constructions of sexual orientation and gender."

6 For an examination of the theoretical and practical tensions between queer theorizing and LGBT studies, see Lovaas et al. (2006).

7 For example, at the time of this writing, fighters from the Sunni militant group the Islamic State of Iraq and Syria (ISIS) have violently taken control of nearly one-third of Iraq, including much of the country's Western territory, several key towns and three western borders with Jordan and Syria. Concern continues that additional territory will be captured. In the former Russian Caucuses region, Russia, with remarkably little military force, has taken control of the area of Crimea from Ukraine. While the international community expressed outrage with Russia's audacious action, Crimea was officially annexed with support from a strong pro-Russian constituency in the country and remains under Russian control. In the Gaza Strip, Israel is leading a (disproportionately) large military offensive against Hamas for the killing of three Israeli teenagers, leaving over 2,000 Palestinians dead.

8 Arguably, the dominance of U.S. foreign and domestic policy has played a significant role in this process. Following the terror attacks in New York City in 2001, the U.S. has convincingly branded almost anything and everything as a threat to "the homeland." In so doing, many scholars of political violence, security, and foreign policy would agree that the U.S. has remarkably made even security fashionable. There are inherent dangers in this behavior. For more information on the ways in which radical securitization of public spaces, see the Institute for the Study of Conflict Transformation and Social Justice at Queen's University, Belfast.

9 Also see Enloe (1990, 1993, 2000, 2004), Sjoberg (2009, 2010), Tickner (1992), Wibben (2010) and Zalewski (2007).

10 To date, scholars have concentrated on Republican men and women's participation in political violence. Comparatively little attention has been paid to Loyalist women's participation, motivation or attitudes toward political violence in the region (see Alison, 2004; Stapleton, 2013; Potter, 2014).

11 Coincidentally, the timing of my fieldwork coincided with the formal launch of the Historical Enquires Team (HET). HET is an effort by the British government to investigate unsolved high priority crimes committed during the conflict, focusing largely on crimes committed by paramilitary organizations. For more information on the HET team inquiries, see Lundy (2009, 2011).

12 For more information on methodological approaches to conducting critical Security Studies fieldwork, see Wilkinson (2008, 2011).

13 While sexuality and gender are the focus here, race, class, nationality, able-bodiness among others are also important identity vectors.

14 For additional information on the relationship between modernity and homophobia, see Bosia, this volume.

15 For additional information on community healing programs in post-conflict environments see Jones et al. (2014).

16 Men and women from Republican and Loyalist communities were jailed without trial. This "remand" system meant that a husband, wife, or partner could be imprisoned for years without a trial and/or sentence. One of my interviewees, "Chloe," reported that her husband was on remand for 16 years and was released only under the terms of the GFA.

17 For more information on the experiences of LGBTI people in emergencies, see Integrated Regional Information Networks (2014).

18 Of course, many different kinds of gay masculinity exist but we have not yet been required to manage this form in the post-war/DDR process.

19 The process described here is also reminiscent of American and European football. Both sports are highly visible forms of hypermasculinity but ones that mirror the relationship that male soldiers have with one another. In no other context that I can think of do self-identified heterosexual men behave in such blatantly homoerotic and/or gender queer ways. From the slapping of buttocks, hugging, the jumping and wrapping of legs around one another following a goal, to hysterical public weeping following a humiliating World Cup loss.

Suggested further reading

Eliatamby M (2011) *Women Waging War and Peace: International Perspectives of Women's Roles in Conflict and Post-Conflict Reconstruction*. London: Bloomsbury Academic.

Lovaas K, Elia J, and Yep G (2006) *LGBT Studies and Queer Theory: New Conflicts, Collaborations, and Contested Terrain*. Binghamton, NY: Harrington Park Press.

Sjoberg L and Gentry C (2011) *Women, Gender, and Terrorism*. Athens: University of Georgia Press.

Taylor P (2000) *Loyalists*. London: Bloomsbury Publishing.

Wibben A (2011) *Feminist Security Studies: A Narrative Approach*. PRIO New Security Studies. Abingdon: Routledge.

Bibliography

Abes E S and Kasch D (2007) Using queer theory to explore lesbian college students' multiple dimensions of identity. *Journal of College Student Development* 48: 619–36.

Alison M (2004) Women as agents of political violence: gendering security. *Security Dialogue* 35(4): 447–63.

Amnesty International (2011) Colombia: impunity for conflict-related sexual violence against women. http://www.amnesty.org

Amowitz L, Reis C, Lyons K H, Vann B, Mansaray B, Akinsulure-Smith A M, et al. (2002) Prevalence of war-related sexual violence and other human rights abuses among internally displaced persons in Sierra Leone. *Jama* 287: 513–21.

Bloomfield D, Barnes T, and Huyse L (2003) *Reconciliation After Violent Conflict: A Handbook*. Stockholm: International Institute for Democracy and Electoral Assistance.

Burton F (1978) *The Politics of Legitimacy: Struggles in a Belfast Community*. London: Routledge.

Brettschneider M (2011) Heterosexual political science. *Political Science* 44(1): 23–26.

Connell R and Connell R (2005) *Masculinities*. Fullerton, CA: University of California Press.

Detraz N (2012) *International Security and Gender*. Cambridge: Polity Press.

Dwyer S and Buckle J (2009) The space between: on being an insider-outsider in qualitative research. *International Journal of Qualitative Methods* 8(1): 54–63.

Enloe C H (1990) *Bananas, Beaches, and Bases: Making Feminist Sense of International Politics*. Berkeley: University of California Press.

——(1993) *The Morning After: Sexual Politics at the End of the Cold War*. Berkeley: University of California Press.

——(2000) *Maneuvers: The International Politics of Militarizing Women's Lives*. Berkeley: University of California Press.

——(2004) *The Curious Feminist: Searching for Women in a New Age of Empire*. Berkeley: University of California Press.

Eriksson M (2012) *Beyond "Gender and Stir": Reflections on Gender and SSR in the Aftermath of African Conflicts*. Uppsala, Sweden: Nordiska Afrikainstitutet.

Evans G and Newnham J (1998) *Dictionary of International Relations*. London: Penguin Books.

Fisher D (2003) Immigrant closets: tactical-micro-practices-in-the-hyphen. In: Yep G, Lovaas K, & Elia J (eds.) *Queer Theory and Communication: From Disciplining Queers to Queering the Discipline(s)*. Binghamton, NY: Harrington Park Press.

Gamson J (2000) Sexualities, queer theory, and qualitative research. In: Denzin N K & Lincoln Y S (eds.) *Introduction the Discipline and Practice of Qualitative Research*, 2nd edn. Thousand Oaks, CA: Sage Publications.

Hirsch M, MacKenzie M, and Sesay M (2012) Measuring the impacts of truth and reconciliation commissions: placing the global "success" of TRCs in local perspective. *Cooperation and Conflict* 47(3): 386–403.

Honeychurch K (1996) Researching dissident subjectivities: queering the grounds of theory and practice. *Harvard Educational Review* 66: 33–55.

Integrated Regional Information Networks (2014) Lost in the chaos – LGBTI people in emergencies. http://www.irinnews.org/report/100489/lost-in-the-chaos-lgbti-people-in-emer gencies

Jennings K (2008) Unclear ends, unclear means: reintegration in postwar societies – the case of Liberia. *Global Governance: A Review of Multilateralism and International Organizations* 14(3): 327–45.

Jones A (1998) Engendering debate. *Review of International Studies* 24(1): 299–303.

Jones N, Cooper J, Presler-Marshall E, and Walker D (2014) The fallout of rape as a weapon of war: the lifelong and intergenerational impacts of sexual violence in conflict. ODI. http://www.odi.org/sites/odi.org.uk/files/odi-assets/publications-opinion-files/8990.pdf

Kanuha V K (2000) "Being" native versus "going native": conducting social work research as an insider. *Social Work* 45(5): 439–47.

Khorrami N (2011) Arab Spring: Syrian episode. *Foreign Policy Journal*. http://www.foreign policyjournal.com/2011/04/08/arab-spring-syrian-episode/

Kollman K and Waites M (2009) The global politics of lesbian, gay, bisexual and transgender human rights: an introduction. *Contemporary Politics* 15 (1): 1–17.

Lovaas K, Elia J, and Yep G (2006a) *LGBT Studies and Queer Theory: New Conflicts, Collabora-tions, and Contested Terrain*. Binghamton, NY: Harrington Park Press.

——(2006b) Shifting ground(s). *Journal of Homosexuality* 52(1–2): 1–18.

Lundy P (2009) Can the past be policed? Lessons from the Historical Enquiries Team Northern Ireland. *Journal of Law and Social Challenges* 11(2): 109–56.

——(2011) Paradoxes and challenges of transitional justice at the "local" level: historical enquiries in Northern Ireland. *Contemporary Social Science* 6(1): 89–105.

McEvoy S (2009) Loyalist women paramilitaries in Northern Ireland: beginning a feminist conversation about conflict resolution. *Security Studies* 18: 262–86.

MacKenzie M (2009) Empowerment boom or bust? Assessing women's post-conflict empowerment initiatives. *Cambridge Review of International Affairs* 22(2): 199–215.

Mazurana D, Benelli P, Gupta H, and Walker P (2011) *Sex and Age Matter: Improving Humanitarian Response in Emergencies*. Medford, MA: Feinstein International Center, Tufts University.

——(2014) Recovery in Northern Uganda: how are people surviving post-conflict? Secure Livelihoods Research Consortium briefing paper. http://www.securelivelihoods.org

Nickeson M M (2012) *Mothers of Conservatism: Women and the Postwar Right*. Princeton, NJ: Princeton University Press.

Niner S (2011) Hakat klot, narrow steps. *International Feminist Journal of Politics* 13(3): 413–35.

O'Rourke C (2012–13) Dealing with the past in a post-conflict society: does the participation of women matter? Insights from Northern Ireland. *William & Mary Journal of Women and the Law* 19: 35–68.

Phan T H and Turner-Gottschang K (2003) *Hidden Warriors Women on the Ho Chi Minh Trail.* Worcester, MA: Hen Hao Productions.

Potter M (2014) Loyalism, women and standpoint theory. *Irish Political Studies* 29(2): 258–74.

Rao R (2010) *Third World Protest: Between Home and the World.* Oxford: Oxford University Press.

——(2014) Queer questions. *International Feminist Journal of Politics* 16(2): 199–217.

Renn K (2010) LGBT and queer research in higher education: the state and status of the field. *Educational Researcher* 39(2): 132–41.

Shepherd L J (2011) Sex, security and superhero(in)es: from 1325 to 1820 and beyond. *International Feminist Journal of Politics* 13(4): 504–21.

Shultz R, Godson R, and Greenwood T (eds.) (1993) *Security Studies for the 1990s.* New York: Brassey's Press.

Sjoberg L (2009) Introduction to security studies: feminist contributions. *Security Studies* 18(2): 183–213.

——(ed.) (2010) *Gender and International Security: Feminist Perspectives.* London: Routledge.

——(2014) *Gender, War and Conflict.* Cambridge: Polity Press.

Spivak G C (1998) Can the subaltern speak? In: Nelson C & Grossberg L (eds.) *Marxism and the Interpretation of Culture.* Basingstoke: Macmillan.

Stapleton K (2013) Conflicting categories? Women, conflict and identity in Northern Ireland. *Ethnic and Racial Studies*: 1–21.

Steans J (2013) *Gender and International Relations.* Hoboken, NJ: John Wiley & Sons.

Taylor P (2000) *Loyalists.* London: Bloomsbury Publishing.

Tickner J A (1992) *Gender in International Relations: Feminist Perspectives on Achieving Global Security.* New York: Columbia University Press.

——(2004) Feminist Responses to International Security Studies. *Peace Review* 16(1): 43–48.

——(2010) Feminist security studies: celebrating an emerging field. *Politics and Gender* 7(4): 576–80.

Tickner, J A and Sjoberg, L (eds.) (2011) *Feminism and International Relations: Conversations about the Past, Present and Future.* London/New York: Routledge.

Ward J and Marsh M (2006) Sexual violence against women and girls in war and its aftermath: realities, responses, and required resources. A paper presented at the Symposium on Sexual Violence in Conflict and Beyond, Brussels, Belgium.

Weaver O (1995) Securitization and desecuritization. In: Lipschutz R (ed.) *On Security.* New York: Columbia University Press.

Wibben A (2010) *Feminist Security Studies: A Narrative Approach.* PRIO New Security Studies. Abingdon: Routledge.

Wilkinson C (2008) Positioning "security" and securing one's position: the researcher's role in investigating "security" in Kyrgyzstan. In: Wall C & Mollinga P (eds.) *Field Work in Difficult Environments: Discussing the Divergence between Theory and Practice.* Berlin: Lit Verlag.

——(2011) Letting realities interfere with theory: towards a "how" of fieldwork-based securitization studies. A paper presented at the International Studies Association Annual Convention. Montreal, Canada.

Wilkinson C and Kirey A (2010) What's in a name? The personal and political meanings of "LGBT" for non-heterosexual and transgender youth in Kyrgyzstan. *Central Asian Survey* 29(4): 485–99.

Zalewski M (2007) Do we understand each other yet? Troubling feminist encounters with(in) international relations. *British Journal of Politics and International Relations* 9(3): 302–12.

CONCLUSION

LGBTQ politics/global politics/international relations

Laura Sjoberg

In September of 2014, Ty McCormick of *Foreign Policy* reported that U.S. President Barack Obama would be meeting with Sam Kutesa, describing Kutesa as "the controversial Ugandan diplomat serving as president of the United Nations General Assembly," such that the move to meet with him "is sure to frustrate rights activists who say Kutesa's support for virulently anti-gay legislation makes him unfit to lead the world's parliament." McCormick (2014) quotes Maria Burnett from Human Rights Watch as explaining that "his human-rights credentials are fundamentally undermined by his defense of Uganda's discriminatory Anti-Homosexuality Law as well as other concerns." The Anti-Homosexuality law to which Burnett refers permits the sentence of life in prison for "aggravated homosexuality" – or, being gay and having sex more than once (McCormick, 2014). McCormick (2014) suggested that Obama was unlikely to spend his meeting with Kutesa criticizing his positions on gay rights, instead choosing to focus on other issues of importance to the United States in the United Nations, including but not limited to the Islamic State and Ebola.

While there is no evidence that the issue of gay rights came up at the meeting between the two leaders, Obama did reference it in his speech to the General Assembly that preceded the leaders' meeting. Ned Price, speaking for the United States National Security Council, explained that "More broadly, the Obama Administration has long spoken out – including with the Ugandans – in support of universal human rights and fundamental freedoms for all, including lesbian, gay, bisexual, and transgender individuals" such that Kutesa 'is well aware of our concerns" (Lavers, 2014). Obama, then, addressing the General Assembly, argued that "the people of the world look to us, here, to be as decent, as dignified, and as courageous as they are in their daily lives" (Lavers, 2014). Obama was arguing, as he has before (e.g., Myers & Cooper, 2011) that it is a quality of good states to grant rights to their LGBTQ citizens, and emblematic of problems wider than queer rights when states treat LGBTQ citizens poorly. How a state treats "its"

LGBT population, then, comes to be a signifier of state modernization and normative value.

Yet, although condemned by LGBTQ activists and subject to sidelong comments by Obama, Sam Kutesa remains both a supporter of Ugandan anti-gay legislation and the president of the United Nations General Assembly. Like the example that Manuela Lavinas Picq and Markus Thiel use to open this book about Russia during the 2014 Olympics, this tension around gay rights shows both that gay rights issues are on the international agenda, and that there is a high salience of sexual discrimination in domestic conflicts. It demonstrates a homologization between Western, liberal politics and gay rights. The debate around the Obama–Kutesa meeting suggested the simultaneous "securitization" of LGBTQ politics and the wide variety in responsiveness to issues of gay/gendered/sexual rights across a wide variety of states in global politics. As in the case of discussions of Kutesa's position, and as many of the chapters in this book show, LGBT politics have never been more visible in global politics than they are now, and that trend seems to be continuing on an upswing. The increased *visibility*, however, has not (yet) translated directly to increased *empathy* or *openness*, or consistent material gains for LGBTQ populations. In fact, sometimes visibility has been related to increased conservativism about sexual politics (see, e.g., discussions in Gamson, 1998; Stryker & Whittle, 2006).

The chapters in this book explore the implications of the rising salience of LGBT politics in a global context, dialoguing with, utilizing, and looking to extend the disciplinary knowledge in international relations (IR). As the editors explain in the Introduction, the contributions in this book are interested in LGBTQ perspectives, rather than in (related but separable) queer theorizing, feminist/gender theorizing, or LGBT rights discourses. Looking to move scholarship from and on LGBT perspectives outside of its traditional situation within post-structuralist research in IR to complement that work with empirical studies of where, what, and how LGBT people (and their social movements) *live in, experience,* and *impact* global politics.[1] The editors then have an interest in asking "what contribution LGBTQ politics can provide for theorizing the political subject," as well as the international political arena in which that political subject lives.

With their eye on the question of finding and understanding LGBT perspectives and LGBT politics in a global context, the editors of and contributors to this book look to perform nuanced analyses of subjects as diverse as Muslim homophobia (Rahman) and European Union antidiscrimination policies (Thiel), keeping in mind feminist and queer theorists' emphasis on complicating gender and sexuality constructions, and working without slipping into a naïve, neoliberal interpretation of sex and gender (e.g., Weber, 2014). To this end, the book consists of diverse case studies from different regional and policy situations that demonstrate both the diversity of LGBTQ perspectives and the ability to dialog across them. It deploys those case studies both to learn about LGBTQ politics, and to learn about the ways that understanding LGBTQ politics might contribute to rereading and reinterpreting IR theories.

After reading these diverse chapters and becoming familiar with the impressive number of examples and theoretical frameworks offered by the editors and contributors, then, it becomes appropriate to evaluate what we, as readers, have learned and can learn from this endeavor to rethink the theory and practice of global politics, reliant on LGBTQ perspectives. This chapter, to conclude the volume, will consider different ways to take stock of, and different ways to look forward for and within, a research program on the theory and practice of LGBTQ politics in IR. It does so primarily through the exploration of three questions. First, it explores the utility of and information provided in the use of case studies, particularly in terms of the way that they can be used to build, critique, and rethink IR theory – understood through the lens of the LGBTQ politics cases included in this book. Second, it explores the ways in which the authors' and editors' utilization of LGBTQ perspectives can be seen as unique, or distinct from the deployments of feminist theorizing and queer theorizing in disciplinary IR to date, asking particularly if there is a value-added to the inclusion and analysis of LGBTQ perspectives above and beyond current approaches to gender and sexuality in the discipline. Third, this conclusion draws inferences from the contributions to the book to suggest the ways in which its material might dialog with, and function as a critique of, IR theorizing as traditionally understood. The chapter ends by suggesting some future directions for the recognition and study of LGBTQ politics in IR.

Case studies for theory-building

One of the contributions that this volume angles to make is related to the claim that the employment of case studies for the purpose of theory-building in IR is underutilized. Having invited their contributors to reflect on a wide variety of case study materials for the purpose of thinking about how LGBTQ perspectives can help scholars and students to understand more not only about the experiences of LGBTQ people and the successes and struggles of LGBTQ movements, but also about the functioning of global politics more broadly, the editors are interested in bringing case studies to the theory-building core of IR because, as they argue, case studies can be useful in the core enterprise of theory-building. The cases in this book, individually and collectively, do support the argument that theory-building enterprises can be aided significantly by looking at the nuances of case studies. Preliminary evidence in support of this point can be found in the nuances and complexities that the case studies in this book draw attention to, especially inasmuch as those nuances and complexities contradict inherited expectations of how rights are awarded and/or defended, how identities are formed, how progress is made, and how social movements function.

We learn from Sandra McEvoy's chapter that one of the axes of inclusion that efforts to broadly represent the population in peace processes needs to be LGBTQ rights, and the failure to pay attention to LGBTQ identities in constructing post-conflict orders can be problematic for peace. In Northern Ireland, as McEvoy explains, the exclusion of LGBTQ concerns and LGBTQ peoples from the peacebuilding processes resulted in a return to values associated with hetero-normativity in the organization of familial, community, social, and political life, which were both directly (in terms of freedom of lifestyle) and indirectly (in terms of non-belonging) detrimental both to the lives of LGBTQ people and to the construction of the postconflict peace. While it might be initially theoretically difficult to see the ways that the exclusion of LGBTQ people and the marginalization of LGBTQ rights intervene in the making of peace, the case evidence that McEvoy supplies that addresses the lack of access for LGBTQ people to the common tools of grieving and the lack of availability to LGBTQ people of the tools and goods that would constitute human security shows the causal path between the reimposition of homonormativity and the vulnerability of postconflict equilibrium. McEvoy's case study, then, serves to add a dimension to existing theorizing about the implications of inclusivity and exclusivity in the building of peace agreements.

Another area to theorizing to which the chapters in this book make contributions is the question of the effectiveness of policies for the provision of human rights and basic needs for LGBTQ persons in states, regional organizations, and international organizations. Markus Thiel tells readers about the fact that "in the 28-member bloc of the European Union (EU), gender and sexuality rights are highly regarded as part of the catalog of fundamental rights available to EU citizens, and the EU is viewed as a vanguard in promoting LGBTQ rights internationally." Thiel, however, suggests that the self-proclamation of policy success is not as straightforward as it seems, since the legal basis for EU antidiscrimination policies is in single market legislation. In other words, EU antidiscrimination policies are limited in scope to policies that can be justified by the impact that discrimination might have on markets – a limit which impacts the shape and impacts of the policies differently than other limits, or the lack of limits, might. When it comes to LGBTQ rights policies, differences in organization structure and legal fabric tend to produce different results. In the context of the EU, Thiel suggests that it is important to challenge the market orientation of the EU legal structure providing for non-discrimination for LGBTQ people.

Along somewhat similar lines, Francine D'Amico inquires into the adequacy of United Nations and other global legal structures to provide human rights to persons identified as LGBTQ, or provide recourse when those rights are violated. D'Amico points out that, while very few international human rights law frameworks actually explicitly mention protecting the rights of LGBTQ people, many provisions in those (in theory) sexuality-neutral frameworks might be usefully applied to look out for the specific needs of LGBTQ people and block discrimination against LGBTQ populations. After exploring both the texts of the legal frameworks and the mechanisms for enforcement thereof, D'Amico suggests that there are some potential pathways for the enforcement or redress of violation of the rights of LGBTQ people, but that those pathways can sometimes be indirect, difficult, or insufficiently specific. D'Amico argues that these universal human rights laws are a necessary but insufficient condition for the provision of LGBTQ rights. In the context of international law, D'Amico notes that universal human rights laws are helpful, but limited in LGBTQ-specific ways, for the provision of LGBTQ rights.

A fourth theoretical contribution that the case studies in this book make is engaging the question of where and how the wellbeing of LGBTQ people becomes the subject of contestation within and among states, nations, and ethnic groups. Within a state, Mehmet Sinan Birdal's study of the evolution of the position of LGBTQ people in Turkey in the Gezi and post-Gezi era demonstrates the way in which a globalized notion of LGBTQ rights with a local flavor was a source of domestic political contention. A number of the other chapters in the book highlight the tensions between governance, personal lives, and international tension – from Momin Rahman's discussion of the links between the framing of modernity in Muslim states and readings of "Muslim homophobia" to Michael Bosia's discussion of the ways in which states identify themselves, absolutely and in terms of relative position, as relates to the ways in which their policies police (or embrace) homosexualities. These case study contributions in this book show that LGBTQ politics can be a source of, and wrapped up in, political contentions both within and between states.

A fifth theoretical strand of analysis that weaves through the chapters in this book is the exploration of the relationship(s) between transnational and local social movements; between transnationally promoted values and locally espoused values. Looking at LGBTQ positionalities in Turkey, Birdal suggests that the international LGBT movement and the local LGBT politics *interact* but are not *identical* – "though the recognition of international LGBT rights remains an important resource for local LGBT movements across the globe, the main challenge for them lies in building political alliances with local actors." In other words, the contestation about LGBT rights is not only on the queer/non-queer axis, but also on the axes of domestic/international and particular/universal dichotomies. Instead of international movements shaping Turkish movements, or Turkish movements shaping international agendas, there is an uneasy hybridity to the shape of the movement. This uneasy hybridity reflects the combination of imported understandings of LGBTQ positionalities and locally arising interpretations – as Birdal phrases it, the "universality in its particularity."

A different sort of hybridity can be seen in Manuela Picq's case study discussion of Amazonia. Picq finds, simultaneously, the presence of a number of international concepts and vocabularies of recognition of LGBTQ lifestyles *with* a longstanding, localized diversity of sexual roles, sexual identities, and sexual practices. As Picq explains, "the adoption of LGBT discourses indicates the influence of international frameworks in Amazonia. It also implies that such sexual practices preexisted the arrival of Western codification." From Picq's case study, then, it is possible to learn that it is essential to understand both the global transmission of norms and local, preexisting normative complexities in order to fully grasp local identity matrices.

The book's editors and authors are interested in offering "comparative case studies from regional, cultural, and theoretical peripheries to identify ways of rethinking IR," and "to argue that LGBTQ perspectives can impact theory-making in IR" (editors, Introduction). In my view, the chapters do just that, by the very existence of their deep case study analysis that does in fact contribute to how one might theorize IR/global politics. We learn from McEvoy that the failure to include LGBTQ perspectives in peace processes makes them less likely to succeed – an insight important for theorizing both peace processes and LGBTQ politics. We learn from Thiel that the effectiveness of human rights policies varies with certain interpretations of LGBTQ identities, and with certain motivations for rights-endorsing policymaking – something that adds value to analyses both of human rights policymaking and of LGBTQ status. From D'Amico, we learn that the insufficiencies in international jurisprudence when it comes to protecting LGBTQ rights possibly betray wider structural insufficiencies – which could constitute important lessons for scholars of the meaning, purpose, and function of international law and international organizations, as well as those interested in transnational justice for LGBTQ persons. From Birdal, we learn that LGBTQ issues can be issues of domestic and international contention, and that, in times of protest, unlikely expressions of queer solidarity and queer repression can coexist. These insights can be useful when theorizing political upheaval and political coalitions in domestic and transnational context. From both Birdal and Picq, we learn that the local and the international interact in hybrid, multidirectional ways in the formation and performance of LGBTQ identities – insights that are not only useful for theorizing LGBTQ identities, but for theorizing the workings of social movements, global norm building, globalization, and even glocalization.

The notion of theory-oriented case study research for research in political science and IR is not new – even traditional, positivist scholars have suggested that there is utility both to cross-case comparisons and within-case analysis, by congruence testing and process tracing (e.g., George & Bennett, 2005). A growing tradition of case study research in political science (e.g., Kittel & Kuehn, 2013; Yin, 2013; Daigneault & Beland, 2014) suggests *analytic* induction, rather than raw empirics – where there is specific attention paid to context, to social cues, and to situational politics – to produce "contingent generalizations" (George & Bennett, 2005: xi). Another school of thought on case studies in IR looks not for generalizations, but for contextualizations and complexities. For example, coming out of feminist roots in IR, J. Ann Tickner (2006: 30) suggests that feminist work tends to "research from the lives of some of the most marginalized, disempowered women and demonstrate how their lives and work impact on, and are impacted by, national security and global economy" in ways that "use ethnographic methods and participant observation to conduct in-depth case studies, methods not typical of IR." Tickner is distinguishing the deployment of case studies in most feminist research in *quality* from the positivist deployment of case studies – suggesting that feminist research asks different questions of different people from different perspectives. If this is, roughly, a spectrum of the use of case study methods for theory development in the discipline, the chapters in this book fall at different points on the spectrum. For example, Picq uses information from the margins of global politics to theorize about the nature of identity, using ethnographic research and participant observation to draw out *what is different* about experiences at the margins of global politics than is assumed by theorists whose worlds are subsumed in the core. D'Amico's case study, by the same token, can be read as process tracing for the purpose of theory development. While both are interested in similar issues, they use different sorts of case study method towards different epistemological ends.

In my view, this diversity is both impressive and welcome – where various case studies of various LGBTQ issues and perspectives around the world contribute to a wide variety of theorizing about international relations and global politics. This shows the breadth of the potential contributions not only of case studies generally, but of case studies with a focus on locating and analyzing the LGBTQ in global politics. At the same time, the utility of these case studies for many of the theory-building purposes and with many of the theory-building mechanisms used by both traditional and critical IR to contribute to many of the theoretical research programs that already exist begs another question – is there anything unique *about* the LGBTQ perspectives that the authors and editors of this book utilize that make those case studies different from, or a special contribution to, existing disciplinary debates? I take up that question in the next section.

Are LGBTQ perspectives unique?

In the introduction to this book, the editors asked the audience to think about to what extent LGBT perspectives "go beyond" feminist and queer theories – is there such thing as LGBTQ politics, and, if so, can it constitute a unique contribution to the theorizing of IR/global politics? This section takes up both issues – the framing and the substance of the question.

First, I do think it is important to recognize, as has been recognized before, a number of substantive and political tensions that have existed between feminist movements and LGBTQ movements, as well as between feminist research agendas and LGBTQ research agendas, in political science and more broadly (see, e.g., discussions in Shotwell & Sangray, 2009 and Sjoberg, 2012b explicitly addressing trans-positionality). Those tensions, while real, I have argued, are constituted by theorizations of both feminisms and LGBTQ positionalities that are fundamentally limited. With Cressida Heyes (2003: 1094), I argue that "feminists of all stripes share the political goal of weakening the grip of oppressive sex and gender dimorphisms ... with their concomitant devaluing of the lesser terms *female* and *feminine*." In my view, feminisms (plural) at their best are interested in LGBTQ perspectives and queer theorizing, such that one can speak from LGBTQ and feminist perspectives at once (e.g., Scott-Dixon, 2006: 45). Not only *can* one do so, one ought to, as Heyes (2003: 1093) points out, "it is not clear that feminist politics need to speak of (and be spoken by) many more subjects than women and men, heterosexual women and lesbians" – to "engage bisexuality, intersexuality, transexuality, transgender, and other emergent identities." In this view, what feminist politics gets from queer politics is a further delineation, deconstruction, and understanding of sexed and gendered categorizations, in order to create a scholarly agenda that "disrupts, denaturalizes ... and makes visible the normative linkages we generally assume to exist between the biological specificity of the sexually differentiated body [and] the social roles and statuses that a particular form of body is expected to occupy" (Stryker, 2006: 3, cited in Sjoberg, 2012b: 341). What queer politics gets from feminist politics is a contextualized understanding of the relationality, power-laden organization, and performativity of sex and gender politics, from the home to the international arena (see discussion in Sjoberg, 2012b). In other words, it is important to think about feminist theoretical perspectives, queer theoretical perspectives, and even (possibly) a third category of LGBTQ perspectives on theory – and even the tensions between them in practice – but doing so does not require *being* or *doing* one to the exclusion of others.

In the past, I have suggested that the theoretical insights to be gained from transtheorizing might successfully be leveraged to make transfeminist approaches to IR which are stronger, more comprehensive, and more effective than either transapproaches or feminist approaches might be without being informed of each other (Sjoberg, 2012b, 2014). In making this argument, I proposed that "(feminist) IR should come to value trans-gender theorizing, not only toward the end of 'making the world safe and just for people of all genders and sexualities' (Serano, 2007: 358), but also [toward the end] of better explaining and understanding global politics generally" (Sjoberg, 2012b: 351). I was (and am still) suggesting *both* that there is something unique about transtheorizing for theorizing both gender and global politics, *and* that the uniqueness of that theorizing is not incompatible with, and in fact can improve and be improved by, a long and rich tradition of theorizing about both gender and sexualities in global politics. I see *dialog*, rather than further categorization, distinction, and difference, as a way to build and honor diversity in scholarship about global politics (e.g., Sjoberg, 2011, 2013).

In these terms, I do not see it as necessary to judge the effectiveness of queer theorizing (although I find it vibrant and useful in IR, see, e.g, Sjoberg, 2014; Sjoberg & Weber, 2014), or the limits of existing feminist work in IR (which I find open to, and frequently in the position to utilize, LGBTQ perspectives, e.g., Belkin, 2012; Zalewski, 2013) in order to ask the question of the uniqueness and utility of LGBTQ perspectives in the analysis of (and practice of) global politics. I am, despite the different paths that we used to arrive at the question, in agreement with the editors both that it is important to think about the uniqueness of LGBTQ perspectives in global politics and that there is an important and affirmative answer to the question to be found, both within the material in this book and beyond it.

Before exploring the substance of the uniqueness of LGBTQ perspectives, however, it is important to take a moment to think about the (in)validities of that phrase that have to be kept in mind when deploying it for the purposes of the scholarly analysis of LGBTQ/global politics. In feminist thought, standpoint theory – the idea that there is a standpoint that *women as women* might have that would differ significantly enough to be theoretically important from the standpoint produced by *men as men* – has a long and controversial history (see, e.g., Gilligan, 1982; Harding, 2004). These debates are both too long and too nuanced to discuss in great detail here – but they revolve around the utility of evaluating a "feminist standpoint" compared with the harms of gender essentialism (reifying the notion that there are essential traits associated with female sex and feminine personality) (e.g., Bordo, 1990). Many feminist theorists have come to talk more about gender expectations, gender hierarchies, and gender performativity than *feminist standpoints* (e.g., Butler,

2000; Sylvester, 2013), even recognizing that those gendered elements of social and political life have a *positioning effect* (e.g., Sjoberg, 2012a, 2013) and gendered positioning in turn structures politics (e.g., Cockburn, 2010; Sjoberg, 2013).

Such a balance seems to me to be crucially important to thinking about LGBTQ perspectives and LGBTQ politics. I am wary to talk about "a" or "the" LGBTQ perspective, both on general theoretical grounds and in light of the diversity of scholarship about LGBTQ people, their positionality, and their influence on politics in the global arena both inside and outside of the pages of this book (see also, e.g., Agathangelou et al., 2008; Kollman & Waites, 2009; Lind, 2010). To me, the appropriate way to frame the question is how and what we learn about global politics, about gender identities, and about gender identities in global politics from paying attention to the location and *lived experience* of LGBTQ people that we would not learn, or could not learn as well, without paying attention to those people.[2] To me, this mission is part of, and commensurate with, but never subsumed by, feminist and queer work in the discipline.

One does not have to spend long with the chapters in this book to be convinced that there are indeed insights to be gained from looking for, and at, the lives of LGBTQ people in global politics. Part of these insights can be gained from looking generally at a politics of marginality (e.g., Brown, 1988; Darby & Paolini, 1994; Tickner, 2006), or from looking generally at a politics of gender (Tickner, 2001; Sjoberg, 2013; Peterson & Runyan, 2014) in the global arena. For example, feminist analysis can see the fluidity of gender roles within gender hierarchies in global politics (e.g., Belkin, 2012; Kronsell, 2012). Still, there is something to be added when thinking directly about the place and lives of LGBTQ people. For example, the fluidity of gender roles is shown in qualitatively and quantitatively different ways by transexperience and analysis of "crossing" (e.g., McCloskey, 2000; Roen, 2002) than it is by analysis that does not explicitly focus on those forms of gender fluidity and those lived experiences of gender roles. This value-added, and uniqueness of analysis, is evident throughout the chapters of this book.

For example, it is difficult to imagine Sandra McEvoy's nuanced understanding of disarmament, demobilization, and reintegration (DDR) processes having been produced without a queer curiosity both about the research process and about the subject of the research. Particularly, interested in where LGBTQ people are, what their life experiences are, and how they matter in the construction of postconflict dynamics, McEvoy is able to recognize the ways in which what she calls hyper-heteronormative understandings of masculinities became complicit if not causal in the construction of postconflict orders less effective at establishing and keeping stability than would have been possible if there had been space for pluralities of both gender roles and sexualities. Looking for LGBTQ perspectives, broadly speaking, McEvoy comes to a realization about the ineffectiveness of the postconflict order in Northern Ireland unique to looking for, and looking to understand, the lives of LGBTQ people.

If the unique contribution of the utilization of LGBTQ perspectives in McEvoy's chapter comes from the integration of gender analysis, queer theorizing, and

LGBTQ perspectives, Markus Thiel is looking to understand the differences among those things, suggesting that he hopes "to uncover if transnational LGBT advocacy is different from gender-related politics." Among the potential unique questions for the queer in global politics, according to Thiel, are visibility, assimilation, and normalization. Thiel, looking at these questions through an exploration of "how the construction of sexual differences conditions the work of LGBTQ advocates in regional markets in the context of the EU's rights policy discourse," finds that sexual orientation plays a volatile role in human rights discourses, and that human rights are a volatile issue for LGTBQ communities and LGBTQ identities. The unique contribution of LGBTQ perspectives in Thiel's chapter is in the differences in the dynamics of LGBTQ advocacy (and the reception of that advocacy) in global political forums.

The theme of queer thinking about visibility extends into Anthony J. Langlois' chapter. Citing extensively from Cynthia Weber's (2014) argument that queer theory in IR exists but appears not to, Langlois is interested in the ways that a similar dynamic plays out in international law and jurisprudence about human rights. Particularly, Langlois sets out ground for the uniqueness of a queer claim that human rights matter, when there is a tendency to ignore them. This "ignoring" is dimensional, where, often, the failure to acknowledge the right *to be* LGBTQ is compounded by the failure to recognize the ways that LGBTQ persons experience "universal" rights from a different position than (and often with less "success" than as traditionally defined) persons who fit the assumed norm of heterosexuality. These divergences can be understood as even broader when complicating them with Rahman's understanding of a "historical diversity of sexual behaviors" both within and among different cultural groups. One of the unique contributions of thinking about LGBTQ lives in this work, then, is understanding the ways in which LGBTQ people are differently situated, often both explicitly and implicitly, in politics of human rights, as well as politics of security, political economy, and law in the international arena – both because they are LGBTQ and within the wide spectrum of people classified as LGBTQ. Francine D'Amico's analysis of the different practical problems that LGBTQ people often have with international human rights jurisprudence serves to supplement this point about the diversity and salience of the (LGBTQ) situation. This contribution can shed light both on the dimensions of positionality (and axes of subordination) in global politics, and on the substantive constitution of these areas of global politics – information which might not be obtained without the specific focus on LGBTQ lives.

This contribution paves the way for Mehmet Sinan Birdal's analysis of the hybridity of social movements – both in terms of their inclusion of LGBTQ people and in the expectations that LGBTQ people can have in particular political situations. Looking between the universal and the particular in the Gezi protests in Turkey, Birdal analyzes a movement that unified unlikely bedfellows against what he characterizes as the AKP's "neoliberal populism," and the impacts of that diverse movement on Turkish politics. LGBTQ politics are both a mobilizer and a subject of controversy in the situation Birdal is evaluating, which means that there is neither a clear 'happy ending' for LGBTQ people in Turkish politics nor a clear cause for despair. Instead, post-Gezi, Birdal explains, there are both opportunities and risks for LGBT people. Birdal makes a convincing case that these opportunities are unique but not singular. In other words, he argues that there are things that make the post-Gezi situation of LGBT people in Turkey *contextualized* and *particular* to Turkey, to Turkey post-Gezi, to the Gezi protest movement, to LGBT people, and to the current time and political structure. At the same time, "between the universal and the particular," Birdal suggests that the specific context is important, but not fully dispositive, in understanding what happens to LGBT people, and how LGBT politics is structured, locally. The sexual politics of the particular/universal dichotomy can often be invisible without reference to where and how LGBTQ people experience global (and local) politics.

Manuela Lavinas Picq takes making the sexual politics of the particular/universal dichotomy a step further, by suggesting that paying attention to LGBT lives at the margins of global politics shows that an LGBT perspective reveals "a vibrant cosmopolitanism at the peripheries of world politics." Picq's argument is that LGBT gazes can shed light on other invisibilities in global politics, particularly the invisibility of complex and sophisticated (originally local) roles of gender and sexuality that defy heteronormative assumptions about how families "traditionally" work. The empirical work in Picq's chapter makes the point of the potential uniqueness of this sort of analysis *in spades* – where, looking at Amazonia, Picq finds communities' very "traditional" organizations of social and political life containing a wide variety of sexual roles and structures which appear to have existed prior to Western engagement with those towns, *alongside* events like drag shows and LGBT pride parades. Looking for LGBT practices, Picq finds unexpected dynamics of cosmopolitanism that impact how cosmopolitanism might be theorized in ways that could only have come from looking for the positionality and perspectives of LGBTQ people in global/local politics.

LGBTQ politics/global politics/IR

If thinking about where LGBTQ people are in global politics, and how their lives are lived and experienced, provides unique insights about the ways that global politics, and gender politics, works – as the chapters in this book show – then how does that impact the ways that IR has traditionally been theorized, both inside and outside of a (perceived) American mainstream (e.g., Waever, 1998)? As McEvoy's chapter in this book argues, "LGBT perspectives and examinations of sexuality and gender identity are finding a place in international law, policy, and human rights agendas" – and those perspectives are often finding their way into those places of *practice* in global politics more quickly than they are finding their ways into the scholarship of disciplinary IR. McEvoy explains that this can be a double-bind, where "the sexual identity of LGBT communities is an identity vector that is frequently overlooked by security studies, however, attention paid to LGBT communities by North American scholars is not unproblematic." Rahman's chapter suggests that the primary source of the problematic nature of attention paid to LGBT communities by North American scholars is a misunderstanding – an association between the existence and recognition of LGBTIQ identities and modernity that is "based on a number of conceits about Western societies that generalize the Western experience of modernity to all societies." Rahman's chapter, in addressing the diversity of sexualities across a variety of Muslim cultures across time, shows the inaccuracy of the assumption that, globally, LGBTIQ identities are all mirrored off, and less advanced versions of, Western LGBTIQ identities. This point is echoed in a different context by Picq, who offers a powerful critique of the idea that creative sexual identities are associated with (a Western) modernity.

According to McEvoy, this mistaken assumption can be easily translated into insidious appropriation that is harmful not only generally but to LGBTQ people specifically. In other words, while LGBTQ politics and perspectives are frequently overlooked by scholars in IR as traditionally defined, they are perhaps as frequently appropriated as parts of narratives of American or even broader Western superiority.

That is why Rao (2013, cited in McEvoy, this volume) "cautions that LGBT rights have become a Western foreign policy priority such that Western governments use the mistreatment of LGBT individuals as an indication of how 'uncivilized' portions of the Third World can be and how dangerous the Third World is." In a world where, as McEvoy explains, the straight (white, Western) male is the primary referent of research, complex hyper- and invisibility of LGBTQ people in IR/global politics sheds not only new light but new dimensionality and relationality on the importance of being reflexive, considering identities, and considering identities' complexities when doing research (as a researcher), when evaluating the results of empirical research (in terms of the dynamics among the researched), and when navigating disciplinary politics (in terms of research positionality). While other research agendas have suggested understanding contingency, complexity, and the instrumentalization of oppression, looking at the positionality and practice of LGBTQ scholars and LGBTQ scholarship in IR brings both new layers of complexity and a sharp focus to these issues.

This is especially true when it comes to Thiel's understandings of the depoliticization of LGBT inclusion. As McEvoy and Bosia (especially) note, the politics of LGBTQ inclusion is anything but simple. Bosia explains that, in addition to the Western appropriation of the cause of queer rights for imperial purposes of demonstrating superiority, there are various other forms of the regulation of homosexuality of the state, both in terms of its partial/strategic recognition and its prohibition. As Bosia observes, "State homophobia has been the helpmate of the Western modernist project since the British spread sodomy laws throughout their empire in the nineteenth century." In this matrix, "modernist assumptions enabled and compelled the transformation of sexual identities in order to cultivate reproductive social relations that the state can apprehend and regulate." Given, then, how *political* is the *inclusion* of LGTBQ people and perspectives in the rights and protection politics of states, the depoliticization of inclusion (as Haritaworn et al., 2013, call it, "murderous inclusion") is itself a *politics of queer subordination*. This is how, as Langlois reminds us, statism plays the "good gays" against the "bad gays" in a politics of queer liberalism which is (in my words, not Langlois') neither particularly queer nor particularly liberal. These readings, of course, have implications for an IR liberal politics of inclusivity, suggesting that inclusivity is not always a positive politics – it can be both instrumental in service of normatively negative forces and itself a normatively negative force. Among other things, as D'Amico suggests, homonationalist state policies allow state leaders to hijack the political agenda of LGBTIQ rights, with impacts like fueling backlash and they muzzling domestic movements. Theorizing these impacts has potentially transformative implications not only for liberal politics of inclusion but also for traditional theorizing of the relationships between domestic and international politics in the construction of state identity.

Along these lines, Bosia suggests that looking at how states come to regulate, appropriate, and violently enforce particular roles for both LGBTQ people and LGBTQ-related values and ideas. Looking at the impacts of state homophobia on people's lives paired with the production of state homophobia, Bosia presents a radical theorizing of the state as a psychopath – by definition emotionally insensitive to the needs of the people inside it. This twist on the theorization of the nature of the state (particularly of the United States *as a state*) has transformative potential for the theorization of structure and sovereignty in global politics. Suggesting that there is a sense in which, in Uganda where his fieldwork was done, the "Western gay menace" constitutes "a preferred trope in statecraft," Bosia argues that "the LGBT rights agenda, then, is now tethered to the global interests of the U.S." While this account is important for its empirical content, I suggest that it is as important if not more important for its potentially transformative theoretical contribution: it shows the ways that statecraft is queer politics and queer politics is statecraft (see, for more discussion, e.g., Peterson, 2014).

These are just a few of the potentially transformative contributions that the chapters in this book specifically and queer theorizing more generally can make to rethinking the traditional subjects, processes, and objects considered in IR theorizing. They suggest rethinking well-settled notions of rights progress, postcolonial relations, state sovereignty, and statecraft, and those interventions are only the tip of the iceberg. As Manuela Lavinas Picq suggests, looking for LGBTQ people and LGBTQ politics in global politics has the potential, empirically, to tell us about previously undiscovered dynamics in that arena, and theoretically, to "contest IR's disciplinary straightjacket," by suggesting new ways to think about, and, relatedly, new ways to live, global politics.

Looking forward to LGBTQ IR

Thinking about queer perspectives and queer theorizing as transformative, then, provides both reason to think that there is a bright future for work like that contained on the pages of this book and reason to think seriously about the ways that that future is shaped. I agree with Langlois' argument that sexuality and gender politics shapes our readings of international politics – but want to push that further to suggest sexuality/gender politics *is* international politics, which *is* sexuality and gender politics. This is true, and important to recognize, both at the level of "empirics" as IR traditionally conceives of them (the observed world "out there") and at the level of "research epistemology" as IR traditionally conceives of it (the relationship between the knower and the known).

That is why, to me, the future of LGBTQ/queer IR needs to pay attention, in McEvoy's terms, not only to queer dynamics in global politics and queer dynamics in disciplinary politics – that is – not only to queer scholar*ship* – but also to queer scholars. The positionality of the LGBTQ is not just "out there" in the world that scholars study, or even in the world of disciplinary politics (e.g., Weber, 2014), but also in the world of *the scholar*, where, as McEvoy explains, "as a queer scholar, I too was trying to make sense of the social and political environment of the city." As I discussed briefly earlier, the LGBTQ is not often an area of reflexivity, reflection, emotion, and security/ insecurity considered when scholars think about the vulnerability of researchers in the field and the relationship between the knower and the known – until those scholars are LGBTQ scholars in the field. In this way, then, the first important direction for LGBTQ/queer IR in the future that the chapters in this book reveal is using what we have learned about LGBTQ positions, practices, lives, and experiences "out there" to revisit the structure and function of disciplinary research processes.

The second important direction for LGBTQ/queer IR that the chapters in this book suggest is an LGBTQ/queer suspicion of the structure and function of the state in contemporary global politics. This suspicion brings with it not only solidarity with postcolonial and feminist suspicions of the sexisms and racisms of particular states as well as of the state system, but additional complexities that might amplify those preexisting suspicions. For example, Picq suggests (and I agree) that an important way forward for scholars looking for LGBTQ persons and experiences in global politics is to "foment dialogues between LGBT perspectives and postcolonial thought." According to Picq, such an approach can have the transformative effect of beginning to "destabilize conventional ideas of where the international is to be found, question what political modernity is made of, and why neither can be taken to signify a Western political core." Birdal's chapter suggests a mechanism for doing this in Butler's (2000: 35) idea of cultural translation, which he suggests creates space for the possibility of antisystemic LGBT identities.

Still, Rahman's analysis complicates these dynamics further. While Rahman has some interest in the intersections of LGBT and postcolonial analysis, he also sees danger in conflating postcolonial and queer issues. Instead, he contends, "we need to acknowledge both the global intersecting sociological and political formations of sexuality across cultures of East and West, and the legitimacy that certain post-colonial states derive from deploying homophobia as a nationalist tool, exemplified by, but not limited to, Muslim cultures." This deployment of homophobia as a nationalist tool, recognized in several other chapters across this volume, leads Rahman to the conclusion that the appropriate direction is not a politics of inclusion in the notion of modernity/ies. Instead, as Rahman argues, there is a "need to reject both modernization arguments and those that imply multiple modernities, whereby non-Western cultures are framed as fundamentally distinct from the West but both following and/or resisting Western formations," thinking instead about "connected histories" of race, gender, sex, and sexuality in global politics.

This notion of connected histories links to a third important direction for the future of LGBTQ/queer IR contained within the pages of this book – the notion of the construction of the categories of L, G, B, T, Q, I, and even 'homosexual' – constructions that are often ignored in rights politics and just as often insidious to those included in them. From Thiel's suspicion of the depoliticization of inclusion to Picq's and Rahman's recognition of localized and Indigenous sexual identities not tied to (Western) globalized category constructions, it is clear that there is no global "gay" or "homosexual" or "LGBTQ" who is a stable referent from whom generalizable deductions can be gained. In fact, the attempt to impose these categories on the wide variety of people in the case studies in this book shows the very (empirical) absurdity of the categories themselves. Bosia's recognition that even the homophobic state "gives life to the very notion of homosexuality it seeks to abort" can function as instructive about the harms of trying to delineate, categorize, and indeed straightjacket the LGBTQ/queer in IR/global politics.

This brings me to the fourth, and last, important direction for LGBTQ/queer IR that I see in the pages of this book – last, because I am not sure that many of the authors whose work lines these pages would agree with it, even if they would agree with the analysis that leads up to it. I am interested in an integrative approach to looking for LGBTQ lives/experiences, and to queer theory, in IR, despite the radical critique of the foundations of most (even critical) scholarship in IR that LGBTQ/queer IR has to offer. I suggest an integrative approach both because we learn more from dialog than we do from alienation, and because only with integrative approaches do we see the multiple layers of complexity, and therefore the multiple possibilities for critique, that lie within the possibilities of not only LGBTQ perspectives, but in LGBTQ/queer IR and LGBTQ/queer/feminist/critical/ postcolonial/mainstream IR. It is those dialogs that the work in this book, by definition, both makes possible and makes impossible, that excite me so much for the future of LGBTQ/queer IR.

Notes

1 When I think about this question, I take dual inspiration from Cynthia Enloe's (e.g., 1983) relentless exploration of where *women* are in global politics and Christine Sylvester's (e.g., 2013) interest in war as sensed, experienced, and lived (see also discussion in Sjoberg, 2013).
2 By *lived experience*, I am thinking about the ways that the idea of experience has been used lately in war theorizing (e.g., Sjoberg, 2013).

Bibliography

Agathangelou A M, Bassichis D, and Spira T L (2008) Intimate investments: homo-normativity, global lockdown, and the seductions of empire. *Radical History Review* 100: 120–43.
Belkin A (2012) *Bring Me Men: Military Masculinity and the Benign Façade of American Empire, 1898–2001.* New York: Columbia University Press.

Bordo S (1990) Feminism, postmodernism, and gender-scepticism. In: Nicholson L (ed.) *Feminism/Postmodernism*. New York: Routledge.

Brown S (1988) Feminism, international theory, and the international relations of gender inequality. *Millennium: Journal of International Studies* 17(3): 461–75.

Butler J (1990) *Gender Trouble*. New York: Routledge.

——(2000) *Antigone's Claim: Kinship between Life and Death*. New York: Columbia University Press.

Cockburn C (2010) Gender relations as causal in militarization and war: a feminist standpoint. *International Feminist Journal of Politics* 12(2): 139–57.

Daigneault P and Beland D (2014) Taking explanation seriously in political science. *Political Studies Review*, May 9.

Darby P and Paolini A J (1994) Bridging international relations and postcolonialism. *Alternatives*: 371–97.

Enloe C (1983) *Does Khaki Become You? The Militarization of Women's Lives*. Boston, MA: Pluto Press.

Gamson J (1998) Publicity traps: television talk shows and Lesbian, gay, bisexual, transgender visibility. *Sexualities* 1(1): 11–41.

George A and Bennett A (2005) *Case Studies and Theory Development in the Social Sciences*. Cambridge, MA: MIT Press.

Gilligan C (1982) *In a Different Voice*. Cambridge, MA: Harvard University Press.

Harding S G (ed.) (2004) *The Feminist Standpoint Theory Reader: Intellectual and Political Controversies*. New York: Psychology Press.

Haritaworn J, Kuntsman A, and Posocco S (eds.) (2013) Murderous inclusions. *International Feminist Journal of Politics* Special Issue 15(4): 445–578.

Heyes C (2003) Feminist solidarity after queer theory: the case of transgender. *Signs: Journal of Women in Culture and Society* 28(4): 1093–1120.

Kittel B and Kuehn D (2013) Introduction: reassessing the methodology of process tracing. *European Political Science* 12(1): 1–9.

Kollman K and Waites M (2009) The global politics of Lesbian, gay, bisexual, and transgender human rights: an introduction. *Contemporary Politics* 15(1): 1–17.

Kronsell, A (2012) *Gender, Sex and the Postnational Defence: Militarism and Peacekeeping*. Oxford: Oxford University Press.

Lavers M K (2014) Obama broadly references gay rights in United Nations address. *Washington Blade*. http://www.washingtonblade.com/2014/09/24/obama-references-gay-rights-u-n-address/

Lind A (2010) *Development, Sexual Rights, and Global Governance*. New York: Routledge.

McCloskey D (2000) *Crossing: A Memoir*. Chicago, IL: University of Chicago Press.

McCormick T (2014) Obama to meet with Ugandan defender of anti-gay law at United Nations. *Foreign Policy*, September 23. http://thecable.foreignpolicy.com/posts/ 2014/09/ 23/obama_to_meet_with_ugandan_defender_of_anti_gay_law_united_nations_unga

Myers S L and Cooper H (2011) U.S. to aid gay rights abroad, Obama and Clinton say. *New York Times*. http://www.nytimes.com/2011/12/07/world/united-states-to-use-aid-to-promote-gay-rights-abroad.html?pagewanted=all&_r=0

Peterson V S (2014) Sex matters: a queer history of hierarchies. *International Feminist Journal of Politics* 16(3): 389–409.

Peterson V S and Runyan A S (2014) *Global Gender Issues*. Boulder, CO: Westview Press.

Roen K (2002) "Either/or" or "both/neither": discursive tensions in transgender politics. *Signs: Journal of Women in Culture and Society* 27(2): 501–22.

Scott-Dixon K (2006) Transforming politics: transgendered activists break down gender boundaries and reconfigure feminist parameters. *Herizons* January 19(3): 21–45.

Serano, J (2007) *Whipping Girl: A Transsexual Woman on Sexism and the Scapegoating of Femininity*. Emeryville, CA: Seal Press.

Shotwell A and Sangray T (2009) Resisting definition: gendering through interaction and relational selfhood. *Hypatia* 24(3): 56–76.

Sjoberg L (2011) Arguing gender and international relations. In: Marlin-Bennett R (ed.) *Alker and IR: Global Studies in an Interconnected World*. New York: Routledge, 55–68.

——(2012a) Gender, structure, and war: what Waltz couldn't see. *International Theory* 4(1): 1–38.

——(2012b) Towards trans-gendering international relations? *International Political Sociology* 6(3): 337–54.

——(2013) *Gendering Global Conflict: Toward a Feminist Theory of War*. New York: Columbia University Press.

——(2014) *Gender, War, and Conflict*. London: Polity Press.

Sjoberg L and Weber C (eds.) (2014) Queer international relations. *International Studies Review* 16(3).

Stryker S and Whittle S (eds.) (2006) *The Transgender Studies Reader*. New York: Taylor & Francis.

Sylvester C (1994) *Feminist Theory and International Relations in a Postmodern Era*. Cambridge: Cambridge University Press.

——(2013) *War as Experience: Contributions from International Relations and Feminist Analysis*. London: Routledge.

Tickner J A (2001) *Gendering World Politics*. New York: Columbia University Press.

——(2006) *Gendering Global Conflict: Toward a Feminist Theory of War*. New York: Columbia University Press.

Waever O (1998) The sociology of a not so international discipline: American and European developments in international relations. *International Organization* 52(4): 687–727.

Weber C (2014) Why is there no queer international theory? *European Journal of International Relations* OnlineFirst: 1–25.

Yin R K (2013) *Case Study Research: Design and Methods*. London: Sage.

Zalewski M (2013) *Feminist International Relations: "Exquisite Corpse"*. London: Routledge.

GLOSSARY

Bisexual: a person who is emotionally and/or sexually interested in someone of the same gender and someone of the opposite gender in roughly equal proportions (Newton, 2014). These individuals often experience bi-erasure, a process by which their particular sexual expression is being negated or ignored.

Gender identity: refers to each person's deeply felt internal and individual experience of gender, which may or may not correspond with the sex assigned at birth, including the personal sense of the body (which may involve, if freely chosen, modification of bodily appearance or function by medical, surgical, or other means) and other expressions of gender, including dress, speech, and mannerisms (Yogyakarta Principles).

Genderqueer: a gender identity that is not constructed in relation to the man/woman binary, or oscillates between both genders and combines sexual minority status with gender critique.

Heteronormativity: what makes heterosexuality seem coherent, natural, and privileged. It involves the assumption that everyone is "naturally" heterosexual, and that heterosexuality is an ideal, superior to homosexuality or bisexuality (EU Agency for Fundamental Rights, 2009).

Homocolonialism: the deployment of LGBTIQ rights and visibility to stigmatize non-Western cultures and conversely reassert the supremacy of the Western nations and civilization. Momin Rahman (2014) understands homocolonialism as reassurance of Western civilizational superiority through the presence of increasingly homonormative versions of homosexuality (such as gay marriage) in contrast with their absence in Eastern multicultural communities worldwide. These characterizations rely on a monolithic version of culture, purporting a uniform, static culture that delineates East and West. Homocolonialism can be understood as a key component of how the process of triangulation of Western exceptionalism operates (Rahman, 2014).

Homonationalism: has been described as national homonormativity, in the framework of which domesticated homosexuals provide ammunition to nationalism.

Homonormativity: has been described as a neoliberal sexual politics, which does not contest the dominant heteronormative institutions but upholds them and is anchored in domesticity and consumption (Gross, 2013).

Homophobia: the irrational fear of, and aversion to, homosexuality and to lesbian, gay, and bisexual people based on prejudice (EU Agency for Fundamental Rights, 2009). It can exist on both state and societal level, and improvements on one level do not automatically transfer to the other.

Homopositivity: the positive portrayal of LGBTQ individuals/relationships in the public.

Intersectional(ity): the theory of how different types of discrimination interact in multidimensional ways involving structural and political oppression. Kimberley Crenshaw (1991) considered how the experiences of women of color are the product of intersecting patterns of racism and sexism. Intersectionality revolves around the notion that subjectivity is constituted by mutually reinforcing vectors such as race, gender, class, and sexuality (Nash, 2008). It holds that sexism, homophobia, and transphobia do not act independently of one another but interrelate to forge a system of oppression that reflects the "intersection" of multiple forms of discrimination.

Intersex: a general term used for a variety of conditions in which a person is born with a reproductive or sexual anatomy that does not seem to fit in the typical definitions of female or male (Newton, 2014).

MSM: men who have sex with men. In contrast to self-asserted LGBT identities, the term emphasizes the behavior, rather than the identities, of the individuals involved.

Pinkwashing: to present something, or to rebrand a state, as LGBT friendly so as to downplay aspects of its reputation that may be considered negative.

Queer: an individual or process whose mode of functioning is both interactive and resistant or transgressive, participatory yet distinct, claiming simultaneously equality and difference and demanding political representation (De Lauretis, 1991)

Sex: a categorization based on the appearance of genitalia at birth. Refers to the biological characteristics chosen to assign humans as male, female, or intersex.

Sexual minority: a subset of the population that experiences prejudice, social oppression, and discrimination based on sexual orientation or gender expression (Chung, 2001).

Sexual orientation: each person's capacity for profound emotional, affectional, and sexual attraction to, and intimate and sexual relations with, individuals of a different gender or the same gender or more than one gender (Yogyakarta Principles).

State homophobia: a distinct configuration of repressive state-sponsored policies and practices with their own causes, explanations, and effects on how sexualities are understood and experienced in a variety of national contexts (Weiss & Bosia, 2013). In other words, "homophobia" is defined and created by politics and varies between nations.

Trans*/transgender: a broad term used to encompass all manifestations of crossing gender barriers. It describes a wide range of identities and experiences of people whose gender identity and/or expression differs from conventional expectations based on their assigned biological birth sex. It includes all who cross-dress or otherwise transgress gender norms. Some commonly held definitions include: someone whose behavior or expression does not "match" their assigned sex according to society; a gender outside the man/woman binary; having no gender or multiple genders. Some definitions also include people who perform gender or play with it. Historically, the term was coined to designate a transperson who was not undergoing medical transition (surgery or hormones) (FIU).

Transgression: to step outside the gender binary. For instance, if a woman shaves her head or dresses butch, or a man lives as a man but dresses somewhat femininely.

Transphobia: a reaction of fear, loathing, and discriminatory treatment of people whose identity or gender presentation (or perceived gender or gender identity) does not "match," in the societally accepted way, the sex they were assigned at birth. Transgendered people, intersex people, lesbians, gay men, bisexuals, and other non-monosexuals are typically the target of transphobia (FIU).

Transvestite: person who regularly, although part-time, "dresses up" in clothes that are mainly associated with the opposite gender than their birth gender (EU Agency for Fundamental Rights, 2009).

WSM: women who have sex with women. In contrast to self-asserted LGBT identities, the term emphasizes the behavior, rather than the identities, of the individuals involved.

Sources

(If none is mentioned, they are the editors' own definitions.)

Chung B (2001) Work discrimination and coping strategies: conceptual frameworks for counseling lesbian, gay, and bisexual clients. *Career Development Quarterly* 50: 33–44.

Crenshaw K (1991) Mapping the margins: intersectionality, identity politics, and violence against women of color. *Stanford Law Review* 43(6): 1241–99.

De Lauretis (1991) Queer theory: Lesbian and gay sexualities: an introduction. *Differences: A Journal of Feminist Cultural Studies* 3(2): 1–10.

EU Agency for Fundamental Rights (2009) Homophobia and Discrimination on Grounds of Sexual Orientation and Gender Identity in the EU Member States. Part II. Wien: European Agency for Fundamental Rights.

Florida International University (FIU) *LGBTQA Glossary of Terms*. http://mpas.fiu.edu/ LGBTQA_glossary.html

Gross A (2013) Post-/colonial queer globalisation and international human rights. *Jindal Global Law Review* 4(2): 98–130.

Nash J (2008) Rethinking intersectionality. *Feminist Review* 89: 1–15.

Newton D (2014) *LGBT Youth Issues Today: A Reference Handbook*. Santa Barbara, CA: ABC CLIO.

Rahman M (2014) *Homosexualities, Muslim Cultures and Modernity*. Basingstoke: Palgrave Macmillan.

Weiss M and Bosia M (2013) *Global Homophobia: States, Movements, and the Politics of Oppression*. Illinois: University of Illinois Press.

INDEX

Lightning Source UK Ltd.
Milton Keynes UK
UKHW02f2328270718
326426UK00003B/86/P